NO FEAR

Management

Rebuilding Trust, Performance, and Commitment in the New American Workplace

NO FEAR
Management

Rebuilding Trust, Performance, and Commitment in the New American Workplace

Harry E. Chambers
Robert Craft

S^t_L

St. Lucie Press

Boca Raton   Boston   London   New York   Washington, D.C.

Library of Congress Cataloging-in-Publication Data

Catalog information may be obtained from the Library of Congress.

© 1998 by CRC Press LLC
St. Lucie Press is an imprint of CRC Press LLC

No claim to original U.S. Government works
International Standard Book Number 1-5-7444-119-1
Printed in the United States of America 1 2 3 4 5 6 7 8 9 0
Printed on acid-free paper

TABLE OF CONTENTS

PREFACE

Things have changed in the American workplace. We wrote this book to help today's leaders, at all organizational levels, clearly identify the behaviors necessary to succeed in meeting today's challenges.

This is not just a *what* to do book; it is a guide for *how* to do it!

The original title for this book was *The Rise and Fall of Third Reich Management.* Our publisher was concerned that some readers might be offended by this allusion. Yet, we remain convinced that it is a fairly accurate description of a management style that is all too prevalent in many contemporary organizations. We intend it to refer to management that is dictatorial, insensitive, uncaring, abusive of others, and, ultimately, self-destructive. Managers who employ this style care only about themselves and their personal destiny. They are perfectly willing to destroy the organization and its members for personal aggrandizement. They view themselves and their personal glory as superordinate goals to which any and all may be sacrificed.

We fervently believe that this approach to management is as inappropriate to the governance of organizations as the Third Reich was to the rule of Germany (and, by extension, the world). We hold the further view that this harsh and unfeeling management style is not one that can bring success to organizations in the interdependent, global economy of the 21st century.

The rules have changed in the American workplace. We want to help you play today's game by today's rules.

In this book, we describe fear-based, or Third Reich, management and make our case for why it is not appropriate for today's managers. We offer an alternative, *performance-driven leadership,* an approach that we believe is more likely to result in the success and survivability of organizations.

Performance-driven leadership is explicated and a case is made for its preferability for making organizations work better and for making them better places in which to work.

We wrote this book for all managers, supervisors, department heads, administrators — anyone who is responsible for leading others, especially those who have not been trained to do so.

LEADERSHIP IS
THE LEAST TRAINED SKILL IN AMERICA TODAY.

We don't train people for leadership — we push them in the pool to see if they can swim. If they can't, we pull them out and throw someone else in until we find a "bobber." We hope if we leave them in the water long enough and shout enough encouragement to them, they will teach themselves how to "stroke around the pool." Unfortunately, the strokes they teach themselves are at best adequate or mediocre, and not the skills to drive trust, commitment, and performance.

We can no longer afford to call every manager "Bob." The stakes are too high.

As we begin the next century, we confront a paradox: There will be a shortage of highly skilled workers *and* there will be a chronically unemployable segment of the population lacking the requisite skills for success in the workplace. We suggest that performance-driven leadership can help address both these problems. Performance-driven leadership will offer a higher probability that highly skilled people can be attracted and retained and that their skills do not erode over time. It can also identify, communicate, and provide much of the necessary training for those who enter the organization without the requisite skills.

After identifying both fear-based management and performance-driven leadership, we make our case for the latter and offer a practical guide to how an organization can accomplish the transformation. Continuing, we provide the aspiring performance-driven leader with the necessary tools for success:

- ◆ The skills for managing change
- ◆ Participative management techniques
- ◆ Communication guidelines

- Training outlines
- Recognition and rewards

We believe that managers who can transform themselves by mastering these essential processes can transform their organizations into ones poised for success in the 21st century. We also believe that organizations under such leadership will attract, retain, challenge, and obtain commitment from satisfied and productive organizational members. This relationship will be symbiotic, increasing the value of both the organization and its people.

In this book we will introduce you to real-life leaders, men and women who are effectively utilizing these tenets to drive their organizations successfully in today's workplace. This book is not a history lesson — it is current events.

If you think that you have "The Right Stuff" to be a performance-driven leader, read on!

ABOUT THE AUTHORS

The authors, Harry E. Chambers and Dr. Robert Craft, bring a healthy blend of scholarship, academia, and real-world experience to this book.

Harry E. Chambers is an internationally known public speaker and organizational trainer specializing in leadership-development topics. He brings his 25+ years of workplace experience at the staff, supervisor, middle management and executive levels to anchor his writings and presentations with content rich in realism and "double pragmatism." His experience ranges from Fortune 500 giants to small, privately held service organizations.

Dr. Robert Craft blends an exceptional academic background with extensive real-world experience, including serving as CEO of cable TV companies, founder and part-owner of a radio station, and experience in industrial quality control. His academic background includes positions as director, department head, and dean. Dr. Craft is also a veteran of Desert Storm and retired in 1994 as Airforce Lieutenant Colonel, Special Forces.

DEDICATION

This book is dedicated to Christine, the world's greatest wife, mother and my best friend, and to our children, Patrick, Shari, and Michael, who give life its greatest meaning.

To Papa and the loving memory of Grandma June.

To Matthew Nousak, the most courageous young man on the planet.

Harry E. Chambers

No attempt will be made to individually identify those persons who have done so much for me. They are too numerous and some of them are gone forever from our presence. They include family, teachers, colleagues, employees, employers, acquaintances and friends. I owe them much and they know that I know. My fondest hope for the future is that everyone will someday be afforded the same measure of opportunity that I have enjoyed.

Bob Craft

A Special Tribute

To Susan Goode Douglass, whose extraordinary love and commitment brought no small measure of joy to my final days.

Bob Craft

TRIBUTE

As this book was going to print, co-author Dr. Robert Craft was diagnosed with inoperable terminal lung cancer, an exceptional teacher with an excellent mind is being silenced by a ravaged body. Dr. Craft was a veteran of Desert Storm, having served with The XVIII Airborne Corps. He was notified that he was exposed to contamination in the destruction of Iraqi chemical and biological weapons. Something happened over there ... and many brave men and women like Dr. Bob Craft are paying a horrible price.

Harry E. Chambers

ACKNOWLEDGMENTS

A sincere thank you is owed to a lot of people for their help and inspiration. Mickey Beatty was a tremendous help, and without her patience, perseverance, and flexibility, this book may have never gone to print. She has the ability to interpret illegible writing with disjointed thoughts and pull it all together to create a manuscript that somehow makes sense.

Our gratitude goes out to Dennis McClellan and Drew Gierman of St. Lucie Press, who were willing to take a risk and provide an opportunity for two first-time authors. The editorial guidance from Gerry Jaffe and Donna Cogshall was extremely helpful and their insights were invaluable. A special thank you to all of the St. Lucie people who expedited the publication of this book in response to the diagnosis of Dr. Craft.

Thanks again to Lani Arredondo, Michele Atkins, Kathy Foltner, George Mosher, and Ron Stewart for sharing their thoughts and time in the interview process; and to Jack Canfield, B. Eugene Griessman, Gregory P. Smith, Mark Howard, and Robert M. Radigan for their generous recommendations and endorsements.

CHAPTER 1

PERFORMANCE-DRIVEN LEADERSHIP

Leadership has been analyzed and postmortemed "ad nauseam" in the last 5 to 10 years. Some of the compelling reasons for this focus are

- Our realization of the absence of true leadership in today's organizations
- The damage that is being inflicted by poor leadership
- The ongoing horrible price that is being paid by workers and organizations for consistent uncorrected poor leadership

Perhaps no other topic in the field of management has been as continuously and actively investigated. More than 8000 studies have attempted to assess this powerful organizational force. That effective leaders can wield great power has been widely chronicled. However, the power and influence exercised by leaders can be directed toward "good" objectives (e.g., John F. Kennedy, Martin Luther King) or toward "bad" ends (e.g., Hitler, Saddam Hussein). What we propose here is acknowledging the value and contributions of effective leadership when they are directed successfully toward the objectives of the organization; hence, the term *performance-driven leadership*. Some leaders have aimed toward personal objectives, such as accumulating personal power, while others have focused on some "greater vision" (peace, civil rights, winning wars). Some have been willing to sacrifice organizations (and their members) for their own personal gain. We seek to identify and develop leaders throughout the organization, who are willing to commit their arsenal of leadership qualities and skills to the successful accomplishment of the objectives of the organization, leaders with focus and commitment.

1

The definition of leadership is illusory, not easy to formulate, and is an ever fluctuating shade of gray. We offer the following.

Management vs. Leadership

Management has been described as guiding people in the policies and boundaries of today, ensuring that they perform their specific tasks. Leadership has been described as preparing people for and guiding them into the challenges of tomorrow. Leadership means using one's personal influence to get people to act.

Managers and supervisors are appointed. Leaders are not. Leadership is an evolutionary process. No one can make you a leader. No one can appoint you as a leader. No one can anoint you as a leader.

LEADERSHIP IS EARNED AND THEN GIVEN.

One of the painful truths of American organizations is we have an epidemic of managers and supervisors who are not leaders. They struggle at best to get the job done "today" and are falling woefully short of leading us into "tomorrow." We believe there are four critical components of leadership and the performance-driven leader toils unceasingly to further perfect these areas.

Aspects of Performance-Driven Leadership

1. Performance-driven leaders have a clear vision of tomorrow and where they and the organization are going. Coupled with this vision is the ability to articulate clearly their message. It is not enough for performance-driven leaders to just have the vision. They have to be able to share it with others in a way that is clear, concise, and readily understood. Vision is extremely important to those of us in Western culture. We know where we have been. We know where we are now. We want to know where we are going. We all want to know the next move on the chessboard, what is in store for us, what is next. (Some plan for that next move, some are just waiting for it to happen, but all are focused on tomorrow.)

Critical are

♦ The leader's ability to "future think"
♦ The leader's ability to articulate change successfully
♦ The leader's commitment to self-educability and awareness of current and future trends
♦ The leader's ability to communicate — not just "talking good" but ensuring complete understanding and comprehension

2. Performance-driven leaders enhance the value of the people around them. They enhance their value to themselves, to the organization, and, in this era of mobility and flexibility, perhaps to their next employer.

The mantra of politicians seeking reelection has become "Are you better off now than you were before I was elected (2 years ago, 4 years ago, 6 years ago, etc.)?" The performance-driven leader's mantra is "Are employees better off than when they first came here? Do we make them more employable? Have we raised their value?"

Critical are

♦ The leader's ability to train successfully
♦ The leader's effective use of recognition and rewards

3. The performance-driven leader collaborates for mutual success. A true leader is not an exploiter of people. Leadership is not succeeding at the expense of others. It is not sacrificing people for personal gain. True leadership ensures that everyone experiences success and everyone participates in the rewards and payoffs in an appropriate way. True leaders roll up their sleeves and work with their people, side by side, each carrying out his or her role to ensure the success of the greater good. Leadership is *we* vs. *me.*

Critical are

♦ The leader's willingness to practice participative management
♦ The leader's ability to listen

4. The quality of character consistency. The performance-driven leader leads by consistent example. Instead of conveying, "Do as I say, not as I do," the performance-driven leader projects, "Follow me, I will show you how it is done." Performance-driven leaders consistently model appropriate behaviors, including

- ◆ Trusting before being trusted
- ◆ Being unwilling to take shortcuts
- ◆ Communicating the truth at all times as they know it
- ◆ Being willing to admit mistakes when they are made
- ◆ Demonstrating integrity consistently, not just when it looks good

We believe the essential challenge for performance-driven leaders will be influencing human behavior in environments with high levels of uncertainty. In this book, we will offer various means of influencing human behavior in these circumstances.

In the book *The New Leader: Bringing Creativity and Innovation to the Workplace,* author Gregory P. Smith states: "A leader is a person who inspires you to take a journey to a destination you wouldn't go to by yourself. The new leader is a person who creates an innovative environment that unleashes the natural creativity and the potential of the workforce. The new leader removes barriers and obstacles built up over years of bureaucratic management."

This new leader provides direction and looks out for the needs of people, while creating an environment of pride and loyalty, not fear and intimidation.

Manager	Leader
Carries out planning and budgeting	Charts a course providing direction
Oversees organizing and staffing	Provides guidance and counsel
Follows orders	Encourages people to follow his or her example
Controls and solves problems	Motivates and inspires
Maintains control and order	Creates an environment for change
Protects status quo	Builds relationships and trust
Writes memorandums	Trains and teaches
Follows rules and regulations	Questions rules and regulations

Smith identifies nine traits that leaders share:

1. They have a mission.
2. They create a vision.

3. They trust their employees.
4. They keep their heads in a crisis.
5. They encourage risk taking.
6. They are experts.
7. They know what is essential.
8. They listen.
9. They are teachers and mentors.

IS MANAGEMENT DEAD?
NO, NOT YET, BUT IT IS ON LIFE SUPPORT!

'We are now witnessing the death of management." Management's death knell was thus sounded by Robert J. Samuels in a 1993 *Newsweek* article. He goes on to chronicle the massive failures of the managers of once-prominent (and successful) American companies. To paraphrase Mark Twain, we believe that "reports of the death of management are premature." In fact, it may be the tenacious survival of outdated management practices that is proving fatal to so many American firms. In this book, we will argue that management practices of the past should be taken off "life support" (from their continued practice and from business school curricula) and turned over to the "Jack Kevorkians" of the organizational world. Rather than keeping anachronistic management practices alive, we should actively assist in their demise. Ancient management practices are no more suited to survival in the 21st century than Cro-Magnon man would be. If managers will follow the example of our species, they will find that providing a climate where things (their organizations) can grow and flourish will be a more effective survival technique than hunting (for fault) and killing (drastic layoffs). Management may not be dead, but it certainly ails, and we believe that this malady is causing unnecessary pain and suffering throughout our economy.

CORPORATE KILLERS.

This invective screams from the cover of the February 26, 1996 issue of *Newsweek*. Early evidence is accumulating that the drastic surgery of massive layoffs is not improving the health of the patient. Although top executives and shareholders may reap enormous short-term gains, the longer-term profitability of these firms does not seem to be showing significant improvement. We must shift our vision from the techniques of the past to the challenges of the future.

The challenges facing American organizational leadership are changing. The management styles, strategies, and tactics of the past are no longer "paying off" with high levels of worker performance. Management behaviors that have brought us to this point in our economic development will not continue to keep us competitive through the next phases of this economic cycle.

AMERICAN MANAGEMENT MUST CHANGE.

Command-and-Control Management

The old command-and-control style of management was successful in America for many years. Our intention is not to criticize the events of the past but to proclaim loudly that today and tomorrow are different. The old command-and-control model had three primary tenets:

1. *We told people what to do.* Managers would give blind orders to their people without explaining what the task was about or preparing them to do the task well. Enlightened managers were polite, using please and thank you (not all were enlightened!). But the bottom line was all managers were issuing orders and telling people what to do.

2. *We demanded obedience.* People were told what to do and were expected to obey. "Do it because I told you to" and "Do it because I'm the boss." Employees did not have the "right" to ask questions, seek clarification, or to have a better idea.

3. *We motivated by fear.* The ever present fear of job loss, interruption of earnings and livelihood, and disruption of future security was an oppressive cloud that hung over the American workplace. The message (stated or implied) was clearly "Do what I tell you to do or I will fire you."

Fear was a compelling motivator. It played upon the lack of real options. Workers may not have had other options. Their skills were not transferable. The loss of a job carried a significant negative social stigma that does not exist today. While certainly not all past managers were abusive and inhumane, the excesses of the command-and-control style management led to many workplace upheavals, including the emergence of a successful labor movement.

Fear was such a successful motivator in the past that workers came to work every day driven by the goal of making their boss happy. The best way to avoid incurring the wrath of the boss and the full force and punishment of fear-based management was to make sure that the boss liked you and was always happy with what you had done.

Compelling question: How many of your employees/staff come to work every day driven to make you happy?

Another significant result of the old command-and-control model was to keep everyone in the organization focused on pleasing the person they reported to daily. This upward-only focus resulted in customers playing second fiddle. If the boss and the customer needed something at the exact same moment, the worker with any brains was responsive to the boss at the expense of the customer. Serving the customer first meant not being responsive to the boss and that carried severe negative consequences!

- ◆ "Keep the boss happy; don't get the material to the next department quicker."
- ◆ "Keep the doctor happy; let the patient wait."
- ◆ "Keep the owner happy; overcharge the customer when you can."
- ◆ "Keep the manager happy; don't worry about safety."

Alignment of Authority and Responsibility

Probably the most unproductive aspect of the command-and-control model was the distortion of the alignment of authority and responsibility. The command-and-control model is best exemplified by the timeworn figure of the pyramid or triangular organization:

Employee/staff — Generally speaking, when people join the triangular organization, they are employed at entry-level positions, usually at the bottom of the pyramid. At this level, employees have

---

LOW AUTHORITY, LOW RESPONSIBILITY.

Their role is to come into work, do their job, and go home — low authority, low responsibility. People are basically told what to do. Obedience is demanded, and the threat of termination is ever present.

Many people stay at this level of the organization throughout their careers. We can hope that they are compensated well enough to provide for the basic needs of life while peforming at this level.

Middle management — Some employees will evolve to the next level and be promoted into supervision and/or middle management roles. This is where the major distortion takes place; authority and responsibility are misaligned.

HIGH RESPONSIBILITY, LOW AUTHORITY.

Many middle managers in America are given responsibility but not delegated the authority necessary to accomplish those responsibilities successfully. The results have been very harmful and expensive.

◆ Middle managers cannot make long-term corrective decisions. Their decisions tend to be short-term, "stop-the-bleeding" type of emergency reactions, while the long-term, truly impacting decisions must be made by upper management.

◆ Middle managers make commitments they cannot always keep. They will make a decision to correct a problem and then be told by upper management that they have overstepped their boundaries or should not have done what they did. They then must go back to their people and embarrassingly rescind or clarify the previous decision. Upper management often overrides middle management decisions merely to continue to exercise managerial influence over the middle manager. Even if the middle manager makes a good decision, on principle it can't be allowed to stand and must bear the influence, signature, or imprint of the upper-level manager.

◆ Middle managers do not always tell the truth. It's not because they are intentionally lying; it's because they do not always have the complete package of information. They will make decisions and find out later they did not have all the facts and data necessary to make the correct decision. The result is that middle managers are continually going back to their people, explaining and clarifying what they really meant to say or why what they told everyone yesterday wasn't accurate.

The result of this is pretty obvious. Employees and staff have learned that if you really want to know what's going on around here, or you really need a firm decision, go around the middle managers to the management level above them. Why are we surprised that middle management has been judged to be an inefficient layer in organizations and subjected to so much exposure in restructuring (downsizing, upsizing, rightsizing, etc.) movements? If middle management has truly been inefficient, it is not due to the incompetence of the managers but to the refusal of the system to align the authority necessary to be effective.

Authors' note: We believe that a great visual example of a typical American middle manager is the little Dutch boy who stuck his finger in the dike. He had the *responsibility* of preventing the dike from breaking and avoiding the subsequent flooding. He did not have the *authority* to take the appropriate action (perhaps incurring costs by calling in sandbaggers or ordering an evacuation, etc.). So what did he do? He stuck his finger in the dike to solve the immediate problem and yelled for someone with true authority, true power, true influence, and the managerial intellect to solve the problem!

Upper-level management — In this strata of the organization, responsibility and authority are aligned. You have

---

HIGH RESPONSIBILITY AND HIGH AUTHORITY.

Here authority is commensurate with responsibility, and upper-level management is an effective decision-making layer. However, in reality, this is where another distortion has taken place. Why?

UPPER-LEVEL MANAGEMENT PUSHES RESPONSIBILITY
DOWNWARD IN THE ORGANIZATION
AND KEEPS AUTHORITY AT ITS OWN LEVEL.

Others in the organization have been made responsible, but authority has been hoarded at the upper levels. The result has been inefficiency. The necessity of obtaining layers and layers of management approval inflicts great stress upon the lower levels of the organization.

The Role of Fear

The most critical challenge facing American leadership is the need to change the overall organization culture and environment. We must seek, as Dr. W. Edwards Deming suggested, to reduce the existence of "fear" in our organizations. An emerging fact of life is

---

FEAR IS NO LONGER A SUCCESSFUL MOTIVATOR.

There are two primary reasons why fear is no longer a successful motivator:

1. *The law.* Laws and protections exist today to ensure that employees are insulated from and not subjected to abusive management practices. Never before in our history have employees and staff had the

umbrella of legal protections that exists today. The law weighs heavily against fear-based motivation and management.

2. *Lack of job security.* In the past, fear-based management has been successful because it was anchored by the threat of interrupting job and economic security: "If you don't do what I tell you to do, I will fire you and take away your earnings, your economic well-being, your benefits, and your long-term security." Well, guess what? In today's economic environment, we cannot guarantee long-term job security — so how can we threaten to take it away? Fear has been rendered a useless tool! You can't threaten to take away something that you can't guarantee. We all realize that job security today can be disrupted at the drop of a hat. People are losing their jobs based on decisions of strategy, economic considerations, and the impact of unsuccessful management actions, not just because of poor performance or for aggravating the boss. When we cannot guarantee job security, the threat of taking it away has a hollow ring.

A result of these current conditions is employees are not as hesitant to change jobs today as they were in the past. We are a much more mobile and flexible people. Just as organizations cannot guarantee that jobs will be secure in the long term, employees and staff (and managers as well) cannot realistically guarantee they want to be there long term. Most employees cannot truthfully say they want to be with the same organization, doing the same job long term. People are constantly reevaluating their positions and two-year commitments may be seen as long term. If employees are not happy with the culture and environment or if they sense fear-based motivation, they are quick to leave to find a healthier environment.

There is no doubt that fear-based management styles have been successful in the past. However, the American worker has changed to such a degree that fear-based management now demotivates and results in high turnover rates of creative, top-performing employees, driving productivity downward dramatically.

The American worker has changed significantly during the last 8 to 10 years of this economic cycle. Two of the most visible changes are

1. *The American worker is demanding that management listen.* One of the greatest advantages of the "team concept" that is gaining popularity and paying off with big productivity increases is that it provides workers and staff

with an appropriate format for making their intellectual contribution to the organization and for influencing "how things are being done around here."

The drive to be heard is not confined to the workplace. We see it in all aspects of our daily lives. Many of us have been raised by parents with the parental philosophy of "Children should be seen and not heard." Is that a successful parenting style in today's world? Obviously not! Children must be seen, *heard*, and responded to if we are to prepare them to compete *effectively* in this world as highly productive adults.

Further proof of this demand to be heard is the explosion in popularity of talk radio, talk TV (call-in shows), and the Internet. Do you really think that people are staying up until 4:00 A.M. and coming to work blurry eyed the next day because of the wealth of information that they are gathering on the "net"? I don't think so. What are they doing? They are "chatting," and it's a further demonstration of this demand to be heard. "If I can't get someone in the house to listen to me, I'll get somebody on the machine to listen to me. I am going to be heard!"

2. *American workers are demanding to be told "why."* We are no longer willing to be told what to do or to accept "blind orders" without understanding why. If we aren't told why, we tend to reason it out — relatively. There will always be a way. Management, however, gets to choose whether it's accurate or a negative fabrication.

The American worker is also much more mature, highly educated, flexible, mobile, and, in many cases, feels much less "bonded" to the employer. We will address all of these significant changes in subsequent chapters.

High-Fear, Low-Trust Management

A seminar participant once coined the phrase "Third Reich management" to describe the authoritarian, nonresponsive, fear-generating, trust-obliterating management style of his organization. We have adopted this phrase throughout this book to identify high-fear, low-trust management. Our intent is not to demean or trivialize any memory or emotion that may be attached to a painfully oppressive and inhuman time in the history of humankind. We use it to describe the essence of mismanagement:

♦ Using fear as a motivator
♦ Obliterating trust
♦ Demeaning people

- ◆ "Telling" people what to do
- ◆ "Not listening" or giving anyone input
- ◆ Valuing your organizational growth and survival above the well-being of all others in your environment

In Chapter 2, we list, in detail, 16 specific identifying traits of a Third Reich manager.

THIRD REICH MANAGEMENT.

In essence, Third Reich management is a management style whose hour has passed because it produces outcomes that are counterproductive to organizational success and survivability. Third Reich management has evolved throughout the years and is best exemplified by the "my way or the highway" management mentality. It has been taught in formal management training sessions and has been passed on from generation to generation by example. What was once perceived to be a decisive management style, maintaining strict control through the exercise of raw authority and power, is seen today as a style of insecurity and weakness. Third Reich managers confirm their self-perceived lack of management skills with their aggressive, authoritarian behavior. Their implied message is "I have no other abilities with which to influence you so I will attempt to control you by bullying, threats, and intimidation."

This is not unlike the dictator who maintains power through a strong internal police force whose function is the control of the masses, hence, the name Third Reich management.

Performance-Driven Leaders in Action

Throughout this book, we focus on *how* to develop further your performance leadership style in the real world. We do not want to limit ourselves to just identifying *what* you should do or to discussing theoretical management ideas. You are leading people in the real world, and we want this book to be grounded in real-world application. Throughout the book you will meet a series of performance-driven leaders, men and women who are successfully using these techniques to lead and "grow" their organizations. These are not the high-profile leaders that we may read about in *The Wall*

Street Journal, Fortune, Forbes, Business Week, Time, or *Newsweek.* They are effective, performance-driven leaders, men and women who are winning the daily battles not by an antiquated fear-based management style but by implementing leadership strategies that elicit top performance from the people they influence. They are "fire-tested professionals" and we will all learn from their insights. They are as follows (in alphabetical order):

Lani Arredondo

Lani Arredondo is a specialist in relational skills. After an award-winning career with IBM in customer education and management, she formed her own professional development firm. She has served a diversity of clientele: Fortune 500 companies, government and educational groups, industry and trade associations, and business and women's conferences.

Lani is the author of *How to Present Like a Pro* and *The McGraw-Hill 36-Hour Course in Business Presentations.* She is featured in video training presentations on *How to Overcome Negativity in the Workplace* and *The Essentials of Credibility, Composure & Confidence.* Her work has been featured in *Success* and *Executive Female* magazines.

An honors graduate of the University of California, Lani is a member of the adjunct faculty of National University School of Business and Management and holds a lifetime credential as a community college instructor.

Michele Atkins

Since 1986, Michele Atkins has been the executive director of the Make-A-Wish Foundation of Western Pennsylvania, a position she accepted after serving 3 years as a member of the foundation's founding board of directors. The mission of the foundation is to fulfill the wishes of children under 18 diagnosed with life-threatening illnesses. As executive director, Michele oversees all of the foundation's wish-granting, fund-raising, and administrative activities.

Michele has been an administrative and fund-raising professional since 1982. As the director of the Child Care Center (1982 to 1986), she was responsible for building a facility which encompassed a nursery school, a full-service day-care center, a drop-in care service, and an after-school latch-key program. Michele initiated these programs, created a board of directors, and implemented the growth of the facility.

Michele is a member of the National Society for Fund Raising Executives, the American Society of Association Executives, the Pittsburgh Society of Association Executives, Leadership Pittsburgh, and is a certified national trainer for the Make-A-Wish Foundation of America. In addition, she is on the boards of a number of non-profit agencies and has received numerous awards for public and philanthropic service. She is a graduate of Carlow College and holds CFRE certification from the National Society for Fund Raising Executives.

Kathy Foltner

Kathy Foltner, M.A., CCC-A, currently serves as vice president of operations for HealthCare Capital Corporation. With over 50 offices and 200 employees, HealthCare Capital Corporation is one of the largest providers of hearing health care services and hearing aids in North America.

Kathy founded Audio-Vestibular Testing Center, Inc., in 1980. That company grew to five locations in the greater Lansing, Michigan area and was sold to Hearing Health Services, Inc., of King of Prussia, Pennsylvania in July of 1994. Following that acquisition, the company name was changed to SONUS and Kathy was appointed vice president—midwest region. All 14 SONUS offices located in Michigan, Illinois, and Indiana were subsequently acquired by HealthCare Capital Corporation of Portland, Oregon in November of 1996.

Kathy received her master's degree in audiology from Michigan State University in 1976 and her bachelor of science degree from Ithaca College in New York. She holds the Certificate of Clinical Competence from the American Speech-Language-Hearing Association, is a member of many professional associations, and has earned numerous honors and awards. Her company was ranked among Michigan's fastest growing companies in the 1992 Michigan Private 100. In 1993, Governor John Engler of Michigan appointed Ms. Foltner to the Michigan Board of Hearing Aid Dealers. She served as chairperson of that board during her tenure.

Kathy is a successful businesswoman who demonstrates and practices performance-driven leadership. She founded and "grew" a privately held company, sold that company, and currently serves as an executive officer of a public company.

George Mosher

George Mosher is the president of National Business Furniture, a company he co-founded with his wife, Julie, in 1975. National Business Furniture

sells office, church, and school furniture via catalog throughout the United
States, with sales of approximately $85 million per year. Along with head-
quarters in Milwaukee, they have branch offices in Atlanta, Los Angeles,
and Boston. They have also purchased Alfax in New York City and Dallas
Midwest in Dallas, as well as Factory Direct Furniture.

Prior to founding National Business Furniture, George was president of
Business and Institutional Company, which also dealt in furniture sales via
catalog. Originally from Boston, George worked in New York for *Look*
magazine and is a graduate of the Harvard Business School.

Ron Stewart

Ron Stewart is plant manager for Nakanishi Manufacturing Corporation in
Winterville, Georgia. He has a bachelor's degree from Purdue University
and an M.B.A. from Bowling Green State University in Bowling Green,
Ohio. Ron spent a number of years with the Dana Corporation, the last 3
of which were as the facility manager of the Southeastern Regional Distribution Center in Athens, Georgia, an automotive and light truck parts distribution center. During this time with Dana, Ron participated in the closing
of the facility, and he will share his strategies and insights from that experience. His Dana experience included serving as a senior product engineer,
marketing and sales manager, and product manager. He also has experience
with the General Electric Corporation as a material and process evaluation
specialist. While serving with Dana, Ron was chairman of the Dana Corporation Supplier Diversity Council and a Dana Corporation Certified Supervisor.

Ron has over 23 years of demonstrated success working within world-
class organizations in various disciplines. He blends an entrepreneurial approach with excellent team-building skills to move organizations toward the
future. He has developed innovative, effective, profit-oriented strategies and
initiatives and has successfully demonstrated performance-driven leadership
under challenging circumstances. Ron is also a member of the Society of
Automotive Engineers.

Real-World Challenges

Of the myriad leadership studies, many have attempted to identify the essential qualities and characteristics of successful leaders. Unfortunately,

much of the evidence examined was anecdotal and whatever lists of characteristics were proposed, examples of successful leaders who possessed some of the desired characteristics and not others could be found. In fact, successful leaders could be found who demonstrated any mix of have and have-not qualities from the list. Here, however, we are talking about more than successful leaders. We see leaders who are equipped for success and are willing to commit their efforts to the success of the organization. We believe that these performance-driven leaders will share certain critical qualities and will exemplify crucial leadership behaviors.

A huge challenge facing organizations and leaders today is the method of selecting who will actually assume leadership. Most people are promoted into initial supervisory or management roles because they demonstrate exceptionally competent *technical skills.* They are capable of doing the job well, so they get to be the boss! While these technical skills may earn us our first promotion, subsequent promotions and success are dependent not upon technical skills but upon interactive/people skills. It is no longer the individual's ability to do the job. It is the ability to get the job done "with and through others." Unfortunately, these interactive/people skills are the *least*-trained skills in America today. It has been estimated that 10 to 15% of American managers are formally trained. The other 85 to 90% learn their management style by modeling their past managers (perhaps a Third Reich management style) or by on-the-job training. You perform well, so you are promoted. You get to be the boss. You are told, "Just go get people to do what you did." When you ask, "How do I do that?" You are told, "Listen, we are behind you a thousand percent; just go do it." Is it any wonder we are facing a leadership crisis in America today?

Ron Stewart had this to say:

> I see a lot of people who are in management today who are there for the wrong reasons, and they got there for the wrong reasons. Maybe they were good producers, very good at what they did. But, they didn't get trained or their idea of what management is and what they should be doing in leading people is radically different from successful practices, actions, and behavior. That breeds a lot of fear, mistrust, and incontinuity in the workplace. It's not that people come in and purposely cause those things to happen. They happen because of the environment. I wish I could divide the people who are really committed to moving an organization the right way, through the positive things that need to occur in the workplace, like communication, involvement, participation, measuring the right things

and evaluating processes versus blaming people. I would separate these people from those who are only there for the wrong reasons. Maybe because they feel that management is a way to earn more money, it's a way to play golf occasionally, or do all of the other things that they perceive management is all about. They are not really committed to improving or to the advancement of the organization through developing the people within the organization.

Leadership Qualities

The performance-driven leader will be a person from any level of the organization who is flexible, open-minded, trustworthy, decisive, self-confident, energetic, tenacious, empathetic, caring, enthusiastic, and intelligent. To the extent that these qualities can be assessed in organizational members (or potential members), these individuals can be developed, through experience, mentoring, and both formal and informal learning mechanisms, to be successful performance-driven leaders. Of course, some of these leaders will develop naturally, or without assistance from the organization (indeed, in spite of the organization). However, this is a rather chancy process upon which to depend. The more astute organization will attempt to identify and develop this leadership potential.

Critical Tools

A significant component of this development process will be the honing of the critical tools to be employed by the performance-driven leader. These include change management, communication, and participative management, each addressed in detail in later chapters of this book.

Critical Activities

Successful performance-driven leaders engage in activities designed to inspire organizational members to commit their considerable skills and talents toward the pursuit of a set of objectives resulting in successful outcomes for both the organization and the individual. These critical activities will include

Vision — The leader must possess and communicate a clear, global vision of what the organization can and will become in a rapidly changing world.

Michele Atkins related the following comments on vision:

> In 1988 I wrote a vision statement for our board. I decided the first thing I had to do was to sit down and think where do I want to go. It never makes any sense to me to just go do something without figuring out what does it look like when you get there. Then I went to the board and said here is where I want to go. That was the first step — to figure out what did I want this agency to look like and how soon we were going to get there and to communicate this vision effectively. Not unexpectedly, there was some initial resistance. It was a 5-year vision statement and 5 years later we had exceeded every one of our goals.
>
> We made it and now there is a new vision because we have a lot more work to do in order to ensure that every eligible child that wants a wish can have one. So our vision is under constant reinvention. New challenges surface and therefore the target needs to move based on the realities of today.

Change Management — The leader must understand and direct the change process. Change management is such a significant challenge that an entire chapter (Chapter 3) is dedicated to its discussion.

Communication — Interpersonal communication, especially effective listening, is one of the most significant leadership activities.

George Mosher gave us an example of listening:

> One of the things that we do every 2 months is to have each manager ask his employees a series of six questions that are rated on a 1 to 10 scale. It starts off with how's everything going, on a 1 to 10 scale how are you feeling, what would it take if it was a 7 to bring it up to a 9, what's keeping it from being a 5, how are you feeling about the space, the temperature? Do you have any suggestions for the company? If you were running this company, what would you do differently? You get your base numbers established on the 1 through 10 scale, then over time you can see how happy people are and evaluate all shifts. Once it's done it becomes part of the culture and people welcome the chance to say something and have input.

Empowering or Enabling Others — Successful performance-driven leaders will not attempt to do it all themselves or attempt to drive or coerce others into action. They will provide the vision, the guidance, the training and development, the resources, and delegate the authority to enable others to achieve.

Respecting and Valuing Others — Performance-driven leaders care about others; they always treat others with the respect due any human being (Kant's categorical imperative) and will value, recognize, and encourage the contributions of others.

PERFORMANCE-DRIVEN LEADERS NEVER STRIP ANYONE OF DIGNITY.

Practicing What They Preach — Performance-driven leaders will be more than messengers of vision and commitment. They will, indeed, "walk the talk." They will lead by example.

Ron Stewart said:

> You have to have certain values and you must be unwilling to compromise those values, your leadership, your beliefs, and what you do in the workplace. You just keep doing it and doing it and the results will come. People will examine that and they will measure you. They are going to look at what you say, what you do, and they are going to judge your actions. I think if you do the right things, and if you're really committed to managing the right way with people instead of against people, and have a *we* attitude, you will be much more successful.

Having Strong Personal Values — Performance-driven leaders will possess, will articulate, and will exhibit strong personal values of integrity, honesty, and openness.

Michele Atkins made an interesting statement that may capture the essence of performance-driven leadership:

> Core values should never be sold down the river for expediency. I watch leaders — political leaders, corporate leaders, media leaders — violating their core values, what they believe in fundamentally, for a slightly better stock price or an immediate short-term gain on the bottom line. These have nothing to do with where the organization ought to be 5 years from now. We have core values that are important and stand by them until hell freezes over. We don't compromise core values.

George Mosher has compiled his vision and values into a clear, concise communication he calls "Mosher Maxims":

Leadership

1. *Know what is going on* — walk around.
2. *Verify numbers.*
3. *We do not do things on the come,* such as hiring (trail a little).
4. *We hire carefully* and we try very hard not to lay off; however, we will prune people who are not producing.
5. *Do not blame people;* focus on establishing an environment where employees are *excited* about their jobs.
6. We try hard to *hire highly skilled people* and pay above-average wages for above-average work.
7. *We expect people to do their jobs.* Train, but do not do it for them.
8. *Employees must take full responsibility for their jobs* — be open to all possible ways to solve a problem. Challenge them to find better ways to service our customers.
9. We must conduct our business with the highest code of *ethics and honesty.*
10. *Think through tasks,* sorting them by importance and relevance.
11. *Agonize* over only one thing — *hiring.*
12. For the most part, we expect people to supervise their own desks on a day-to-day basis (we do not hand-hold).

Tolerant and Supportive — Performance-driven leaders will encourage initiative, creativity, and innovation by tolerating the mistakes of others who dare risk mistakes. Further support will be provided to ensure that people can learn and grow from their mistakes.

Rewarding Recognizing, and Celebrating — The performance-driven leader makes certain that the successful behaviors of others are consistently and fairly recognized, rewarded, and celebrated. This leader is a team player, a "we" not "me" person.

**CONTINUOUS IMPROVEMENT PROGRAMS, WITHOUT
REWARD, RECOGNITION, AND CELEBRATION,
BECOME CONTINUOUS CRITICISM PROGRAMS.**

Gregory Smith, in *The New Leader: Bringing Creativity and Innovation to the Workplace*, identifies seven leadership beatitudes:

1. Be Bold and Challenge Status Quo.
2. Be a Risk Taker.
3. Be Authentic and Approachable.
4. Be a Role Model.
5. Be Out and About.
6. Be Courageous.
7. Be Inspirational.

In Chapter 2, we provide a more-detailed discussion of Third Reich management.

CHAPTER 2

WHAT LEADERSHIP ISN'T: THE ESSENCE OF THIRD REICH MANAGEMENT

The identifiable traits of Third Reich management are

1. *Telling workers what to do* (issuing orders)
2. *Demanding obedience* and one-sided loyalty
3. *Failing to listen* to workers and staff
4. *Encouraging internal competition*
5. *Fostering suspicion* of workers and staff
6. *Compartmentalizing* tasks and responsibility
7. *Blaming* workers and staff for mistakes and failure
8. *Using corporate execution* to achieve problem closure
9. *Misaligning* authority and responsibility
10. *Failing to recognize* workers and staff for their contributions
11. *Having low tolerance for mistakes* within the organization
12. *Refusing to share success*
13. *Focusing on the short-term*, failing to assess the long term
14. *Recreating itself* (selecting people in its own image)
15. *Tolerating ethical breaches* — highly visible illegal, unethical, or immoral behaviors
16. *Motivating by fear* — the hallmark of Third Reich management

MOTIVATING BY FEAR — THREATENING THE ECONOMIC SECURITY AND JOB LONGEVITY OF WORKERS AND STAFF.

Telling Workers What to Do

Third Reich managers issue orders to their employees and expect them to be carried out exactly as the manager intended. There is no explanation of why the task is important or identification of the "upside" to doing the task well or the "downside" to poor-quality performance. It is assumed that workers/staff are expecting to be told what to do. These same managers will then lament that their workers/staff do not take any initiative, can't think for themselves, and have low motivation.

This behavior ignores the basic truth that

PEOPLE ARE MOTIVATED BY
DOING WHAT MAKES SENSE TO THEM.

Think of yourself. How motivated are you to carry out blind orders that are issued by someone in authority? Aren't you much more willing to do high-quality work when you understand the reason behind the request?

> Example of the Third Reich management style: "Take care of this."

> The performance-driven alternative: "John, we need you to do this and here is why it's important."

The "telling" style results in at least three negative outcomes.

Resistance to the Task Is Increased

In the absence of explanation, workers/staff assume that the task is of low importance and probably intended to just "keep them busy." They perceive the task is "arbitrary" and not well thought out. Resentment runs high, because the new task is perceived to be an interruption and a barrier to completing their ongoing "important" tasks. Most of us are familiar with the Third Reich manager for whom each new task assumes the highest priority. Third Reich managers fail to distinguish the difference between what appears to be urgent and what is actually important. Urgent means if we don't do it immediately, we may lose the chance to do it at all. Importance addresses the significance of whether or not it is to be done at all.

Have you ever been assigned an urgent task that totally consumed your time and energies only to be told 24 hours later that it no longer had to be done and that another "911" urgent (for the moment) task was assigned in its place?

Worker/staff feelings of disconnectedness unimportance are reinforced, providing additional confirmation that management views workers only as "objects," not appreciating them as individuals and without regard for their intellect.

Mediocre Performance Is Guaranteed

Mediocrity becomes entrenched; without a clear understanding of the task, the importance is diminished and workers/staff see no reason to produce a quality result. It is not uncommon for a "telling" environment to generate a culture of "just getting by," with workers doing only the minimum necessary to keep their jobs.

IN A THIRD REICH ENVIRONMENT, NOT UNDERSTANDING THE IMPORTANCE OF THE TASK LEADS TO EXERTING THE MINIMUM EFFORT NECESSARY TO DISPOSE OF THE ASSIGNMENT AS QUICKLY AS POSSIBLE.

Employee Initiative Is Reduced or Eliminated

Without a clear understanding of the task, or its importance, workers have no basis for generating creative ideas or for taking extraordinary action. In fact, they have probably been punished in the past for not doing the tasks "as directed," for "coloring outside the lines."

IN THE THIRD REICH ENVIRONMENT, WE ARE NOT REWARDED FOR TAKING RISKS; WE ARE PUNISHED FOR FAILURE.

Doing more than the minimum increases employees' exposure and therefore the risk.

ALL CREATIVE BEHAVIOR ENTAILS RISK.

In the tale of *Alice in Wonderland*, Alice is running down the road and is suddenly confronted with several forks or alternative routes and she must make a decision as to which path to take. She looks up at the grinning Cheshire cat in a nearby tree and asks, "Which road should I take?" The cat asks, "Well, where are you going?" Alice replies, "I'm not really sure," to which the cat says, "Then it doesn't matter, any road will get you there." If employees don't understand the task or its importance, how will they know which path to take?

Demanding Obedience

Third Reich managers issue orders and demand obedience. Workers are expected to "do what they are told," and flexing of power is ever present. *"Me manager, you worker"* is the dominant theme, much like the parent who tells a child, "You will do it because I'm the mom/dad and I told you to do it." Demanding obedience depersonalizes the work environment and embeds in employees the reality that they are an interchangeable part whose only value to the organization is their willingness to follow commands mindlessly.

One of the results of demanding obedience is that workers will do only exactly what they are told. Incomplete instructions are left undone, much to the chagrin of management. But such behavior is one of the ways employees can passively act out their distaste for and resistance to Third Reich management. A tactic frequently used by disgruntled employees is "working to book" — doing exactly and only what the directions prescribe. Demanding obedience makes a significant contribution to employees' lack of initiative, low motivation, and reluctance to take risks.

When Third Reich managers demand obedience, what they are really demanding is unswerving loyalty to themselves. Not obeying is seen not only as unacceptable performance but as a personal affront to the manager (a disloyal act). Even loyal employees quickly learn that this relationship is not reciprocal. The Third Reich manager will not show loyalty in return.

LOYALTY CANNOT BE COMMANDED!
IT MUST BE EARNED.

Failing to Listen to Workers and Staff

The American worker is demanding that managers listen. They are saying and saying very loudly: "I have a brain." "I may have an idea to take us out of this current problem." "I may have the next multimillion dollar idea." "It is worth hearing what I have to say."

Nothing builds trust and respect like taking the time to listen. If you think of people for whom you have a high level of personal trust and respect, it is probable that your perceptions are based on their willingness to take the time and put forth the effort to listen to you. They value your intellect. Third Reich managers do not exercise listening skills for many reasons, including

1. They don't value their employees. Underlings are simply not worth the attention.
2. They don't perceive that a mere worker/staff person could possibly have worthwhile ideas. Not listening to people sends the message that they are not worthwhile, they couldn't possibly have a significant thought process, and managers are infinitely brighter and have more value.
3. They are threatened by the possibility that someone else's idea might be better than theirs, and they don't know how to deal with that possibility. To avoid such risk, it is prudent not to allow anyone else's idea to see the light of day!

When listening activity among authority figures is high, organizational negativity, rumor, gossip, and grapevine activity tend to be low (never totally nonexistent). When listening activity by authority figures is low or not evident, negativity, rumor, gossip, and grapevine activity rise rapidly and stay at high levels.

Encouraging Internal Competition

One of the strategies of the practicing Third Reich manager is "Divide and conquer." Keep workers and staff internally competitive and at each other's throats. Effort becomes focused on achieving at the *expense* of co-workers. This encourages workers to establish barriers in co-workers' paths to inhibit their success. This is evident in worker sabotage, withholding information, workers/staff informing on each other, and many other passive/aggressive organizational behaviors that Americans have elevated to an art form.

Third Reich managers may spread rumors about an employee and, when confronted strongly, deny their actions, hinting that they suspect it was done by someone else. High-profile assignments are manipulated to incite jealousy and resentment among those not chosen, and "spy resources" are established when employees are encouraged to, and rewarded for, informing on others.

The primary payoffs of this Third Reich management behavior are

1. The manager benefits from individual conspiratorial alliances with some employees based upon an "us-against-them" mentality. Employees each perceive they are the only one who has this "special relationship" with the boss and can be easily manipulated to spread rumors, inform on others, and pursue the manager's personal agenda. Third Reich managers focus on having employees curry favor with them as opposed to providing quality work.
2. Employees who are embroiled in competition with each other tend not to unify in their resistance to their manager. Their complaints are horizontal, directed toward each other, as opposed to vertical, directed at the manager or the organization.

In an internally competitive environment, employees unifying against their manager is highly unlikely because they are so suspicious of each other. The Third Reich manager typically lacks the skills necessary to deal with employee challenges and uses whatever tactics and strategies are necessary to avoid them, including keeping employees pitted against each other.

A common tactic of Third Reich managers is to assign, surreptitiously, two employees the same task. Gradually, each learns of the other's activity, emotions escalate because each feels that the manager has a low level of confidence in them and that the other has been sent to "check up" or "spy" on their work.

Third Reich managers send the overall message to their people that they do not trust them and that they are determined to catch them doing something that could cost them their job. A significant amount of time is spent in observing employees' behavior and, in extreme circumstances, listening to their phone conversations.

Other examples of this behavior are routinely challenging the accuracy of production reports, questioning of minute incidental claims on expense reports, and punishing every employee when one is found to be dishonest or in violation of policy (suspecting all of the sins of the few).

Third Reich managers actually distort the total management function within an organization. Rather than being positively focused on the present and future through activities of planning, prioritizing, establishing goals, evaluating existing processes, and experimenting with alternatives; they become investigatory and are negatively focused on the recent past. They sift through the results searching to expose the mistakes, failures, and omissions necessary in maintaining a high-fear environment. They are more cop than manager.

Fostering Suspicion of Workers and Staff

Probably the greatest example of this tenet is Captain Queeg in Herman Wouk's novel *The Caine Mutiny*. The captain trusted no one and ordered a shipwide investigation, with imposed sanctions to determine who had his missing strawberries. A nonfictional example is the catwalks and "peepholes" used by some organizations, including the U.S. Postal Service, for supervisors to spy on workers.

The "suspicion base" of Third Reich managers is very evident in much of the reporting they require of employees. The bottom line to much of the reporting is "Prove to me that you have been busy." The reporting doesn't address productivity, but only the illusion of activity. Tremendous amounts of time are invested inefficiently in writing reports that do nothing but allege activity. Ironically, creating activity that can be reported is relatively easy to do and while it satisfies the demands of the Third Reich manager, it does not contribute to productivity. We are much more effective when our reporting requirements are based on productive accomplishments and outcomes than on the "mirage" of flurries of activity. This reporting is inefficient but it keeps the boss happy!

Another example of the Third Reich manager's suspicion is the explosion of surveillance in the workplace today. Technological developments provide avenues for electronic observation as well as visual and auditory surveillance. In today's workplace the following protocols are prevalent: keystroke counting and time logs (on and off) for computer operators; measuring of phone activity, such as number of calls made, number dialed, length of calls; and listening to monitor content. Alarms are available to "sound" when computer games are being played, or inappropriate programs are entered. Sophisticated video monitoring joins personal observations such as the Postal Service catwalk platforms.

Monitoring, in and of itself, is a valuable tool in driving productivity and evaluating the efficiency of current methods and procedures. They help to discover opportunities for improvements. However, monitoring to "keep employees in line" or "catch them in the act" uses fear as a control device to ensure conformity. This destroys morale and results in an us-against-them, antagonistic workplace. Trust and respect are not built with peepholes and listening devices.

TRUST, LIKE LOYALTY, MUST BE EARNED.
TRUST DESTROYED IS DIFFICULT TO RECREATE.

Compartmentalizing of Tasks and Functions

This trait establishes each department as an island unto itself. It places individual managers in exalted positions, exercising great influence and power over their domain. Each department functions as its own autonomous entity rather than being a "link in the overall organizational chain." It is the antithesis of teamwork or collaboration.

Individual managers make decisions based upon what's best for their department, regardless of the impact it may have on other groups, individuals, or even the ultimate customer. Deming referred to this as suboptimizing — stressing specific individual or departmental performance to the detriment of others. It promotes the us-against-them mentality, creating adversarial relationships between departments.

In one manufacturing company, the manager of the quality assurance laboratory ended her department's workday at 3:00 P.M. This avoided overtime costs and allowed her staff the convenience of a 7:00 to 3:00 workday. The problem was the production department worked until 5:00; any work completed after 3:00 could not be released until the next morning, causing delays and increased cost. The production department was paying overtime each day to four employees to come in an additional 2 hours early to finish processing completed work awaiting the next morning's release by the quality assurance laboratory. What worked well for one department was terribly expensive to another.

Third Reich managers are often threatened by the alignment or linkage of their functional area with the rest of the organization, perceiving it to be an erosion of their power and influence. Results of increased efficiency, cost containment, and better quality of service to the ultimate customer are of little concern.

Blaming Workers and Staff for Mistakes and Failure

Third Reich managers make great effort to distance themselves from any responsibility for mistakes or failures. They will always have someone or something to blame. A common refrain is "Okay, who screwed up?" The assumption is that everything that goes wrong must be someone's fault, and mistakes are to be punished. A typical response is "You didn't do this correctly and I'm going to make sure you to do it right next time." Some form of punishment is then inflicted: a letter in the personnel file, removal from a key project or task, days off without pay, or the ultimate sanction — firing the offender to set an example for the rest of the employees.

Third Reich managers make C.Y.A. (cover your anatomy) an art form, and their employees learn to take extreme measures to protect themselves from the predictable managerial blame. Creativity and productivity suffer when so much time and effort is spent inoculating oneself from negative responsibility.

Picture the typical "problem-solving" meeting. The first hour is spent by going around the table and having everyone distance themselves from the problem. Does this sound familiar? "My department and I are very eager to help correct this problem, but before we go on, I want to make it perfectly clear that we were not the cause of it happening. We did our jobs, no one else did theirs" or "I guess my department was at fault. John, the new guy, really messed up, and although I personally had nothing to do with the problem, steps have been taken to ensure that John will never do that again."

**THIRD REICH MANAGERS HAVE NO QUALMS ABOUT
HANGING A SUBORDINATE OUT TO DRY.**

Which leads us to our next tenet.

Using Corporate Execution to Achieve Problem Closure

**IF WE FIND SOMEONE TO BLAME,
WE DON'T HAVE TO DEAL WITH THE PROBLEM.**

Not only must someone be blamed, someone must be punished visibly so that everyone can see the price to be paid for "screwing" up.

What are the ways we publicly "execute" in the organization? Obviously, termination for a visible failure is the ultimate sanction. Often these terminations are brutally carried out; offices locked, sentries posted, security witnessing the ritualized "cleaning out of the desk," being prominently escorted off the property with threats of lawsuits and innuendos to the surviving staff of "other acts that cannot be discussed publicly."

In many organizations, when someone is dismissed character assassination is taken to new heights. Past achievements are denigrated and minimized, contributions previously celebrated are now ridiculed, and everything negative that happens for the next year is somehow retroactively blamed on the dismissed person. "Global warming is probably the fault of the people we just fired!" This is a process psychologists refer to as denigrating the victim. It helps us "justify" executing someone — after all, they deserved it.

Other forms of execution or sentencing are demotion; removal of key valued tasks; reassignment (banishment) to another, less-attractive department, location, or assignment; parking spaces taken away; valued overtime denied; and permanent ineligibility for promotion.

All of these are designed to punish and to serve as visible warnings to others not to make the same mistake. In medieval times, people were executed by public hanging or beheading. After execution, the body was publicly mutilated, often dragged behind a galloping horse throughout the village streets, with the severed head jammed onto a pike and displayed at the city gates for all to see.

Have we really matured far from that in many organizations?

The primary negative result of closure by execution is that workers and staff learn not to take risks or to demonstrate initiative. It's better to have your manager disappointed in you than punishing you for making mistakes. C.Y.A. activity explodes; trust and creativity erode.

Frequently, when management indicts workers for low motivation, creativity, and initiative, the root cause is management's knee-jerk reaction of punishing people who demonstrate these qualities, but make mistakes along the way.

While Third Reich managers elevate themselves above any negative responsibility (in their own minds), those of us who are mere mortals realize that we don't always make the correct decisions. We make mistakes, and so do our workers/staff. What's the reaction in your organization when mistakes are made?

Misaligning Authority and Responsibility

One of the top stressors in organizations today is having responsibility without the appropriate authority to support it. A trait of Third Reich managers has been to hold authority to themselves and push responsibility downward to others. Empowerment to a Third Reich manager is making other people more responsible without relinquishing any authority to them.

One of the reasons that the number of middle management positions blossomed and is now being reduced by recent waves of downsizing is that upper-level management was very willing to create new layers of subordinates to assume responsibility and, thereby, distancing themselves from accountability. However, when authority wasn't delegated along with the responsibility, these middle managers became ineffective, not because of any personal incompetence, but because failure was predetermined by the reluctance or refusal to part with authority and control.

For example, a vice president of sales for an insurance firm gave total sales responsibility to his regional sales managers. However, any sales-impacting decisions must have his approval, i.e., hiring, firing, training, bonuses, territory reassignment, etc. In typical Third Reich management style, he delayed in approving initiatives until he "felt good about them" and refused to implement any for which he could not take credit. When sales results didn't meet his expectations, heads rolled, and when new managers were appointed, they weren't given the appropriate authority either, perpetrating the same cycle of frustration and failure.

Increasing worker/staff responsibility is a big part of empowerment and is an integral aspect of participative management. However, if the appropriate authority is not extended as well, we predetermine failure. Success in a situation where responsibility is not supported by authority is strictly based on luck.

Failing to Recognize Workers and Staff for Their Contributions

Third Reich managers hold recognition for themselves, fail to extend it to their workers and staff, and often take credit for the accomplishments of others.

Silence is perceived by the Third Reich manager to be positive recognition. The overall message conveyed to workers and staff is "If I'm not criticizing you, you are doing an acceptable job." Words and phrases such as good job, exceptional work, thank you, and we appreciate your contributions don't exist in their vocabulary.

Many Third Reich managers are actually threatened by high performance in others and are not comfortable with praising those efforts. They feel it reflects negatively on their own personal achievements to allow others to be recognized. An extreme example is the treatment of war heroes in Iraq. They are demoted or executed so as not to pose a competitive threat to the supreme leader. It is not uncommon for Third Reich managers to manipulate situations so that recognition is focused on them. They may pull a partially completed task away from an employee and finish it themselves, or they may assign tasks to employees in their areas of weakness rather than their areas of strength, ensuring the employee will ask for their assistance.

Employees who do achieve often find that their goals or performance appraisal targets are increased to unrealistic levels. Third Reich managers frequently punish good performance instead of encouraging a pattern of success (you only get to look good once!). After all, overachieving employees could become a challenge, threat, or a competitor for upcoming promotions. In fact, in a Third Reich organization anonymity is safer than recognition: "The buck with the big rack gets shot first."

It is very difficult for high achievers to maintain top production in an environment of little or no recognition. They will frequently reduce their performance, often in an attempt to punish their manager and/or the organization for failing to recognize their contributions. When they pull back or reduce their performance, they take less and less pride in the job they are doing, resulting in reduced job satisfaction and lower self-esteem, which often engenders "attitude" problems.

When the Third Reich manager takes personal credit for the results of others, it causes tremendous resentment and a dissolution of trust and respect. Workers and staff refuse to take initiative or overachieve because they don't want to make their boss "look good."

In an environment of low or no recognition, talented, high performers will leave to seek employment elsewhere. The costs of such turnover are high. People who remain in this environment are those who are either satisfied with mediocre performance or who have little or no option to relocate (perceived or real).

Having Low Tolerance for Mistakes within the Organization

We addressed some of the aspects of this trait in previous sections; however, some additional points should be made. In Third Reich organizations, the higher you are on the organizational ladder, the greater the tolerance for making mistakes. The lower you are on the organizational ladder, the greater the intolerance for making mistakes and the greater the chance the mistake will get you punished. Mistakes made at the top, if they are acknowledged at all, are usually accompanied by the statement, "We made a mistake, we are going to learn from it, put it behind us, and move on."

This tolerance for making mistakes at the top is no more clearly demonstrated than the announcement in January of 1995 by AT&T of the elimination of 40,000 jobs in their effort to downsize. The chairman of AT&T, Robert Allen, clearly acknowledged that mistakes were made by himself and other executives that led to the decisions to eliminate jobs (including the expenditure of $7.5 billion to purchase N.C.R.). Yet their jobs remain secure as their fortunes are enhanced when the stock market reacts positively to their corrective actions.

One current formula for success: Assume leadership of an organization and make grandiose bad decisions, depressing the value of the organization; then act decisively to correct your own mistakes by downsizing deep and hard, and cash in on the results.

WHO MAKES THE MISTAKES?
WHO PAYS THE PRICE?

Consider this paradox, as recounted in the book *Collision*, by Maryann Keller. In the depressed postwar economy of Japan, Kiichiro Toyoda, the founder of Toyota Motor Company, announced his intention to lay off approximately one fourth of his workforce (1600 employees — a paltry number by today's standards). In the resulting backlash, Toyoda was himself forced to resign to acknowledge *his* responsibility in disgracing and disrupting the lives of 1600 of his employees. In this case, the price paid for the mistakes was shared in a more appropriate manner.

Mistakes made at the lower levels within the organization are punished in an attempt to teach people not to err by inflicting some form of pain or censure. Punishing to teach is not an effective technique in organizations desiring to stimulate initiative, commitment, and performance.

Mistakes should be seen as steps in the process of elimination, not as an end result. They are not necessarily proof that someone is incompetent or incapable. Mistakes are a teaching opportunity and workers who aren't making mistakes aren't extending themselves. Failure to learn from mistakes may indicate a training problem or a worker's inability to do the job. If training or ability is the real issue, does punishment play a role?

**A WISE MANAGER ONCE SAID,
"IT'S NOT THE ERRORS OF COMMISSION THAT KILL US,
IT'S THE ERRORS OF OMISSION."**

Low tolerance of mistakes increases the likelihood of errors of omission. It seems safer to do nothing than to risk making a mistake.

Refusing to Share Success

Third Reich managers attempt to succeed at the expense of their workers/staff. They are exploitive rather than developmental. Employees are expected to produce so their boss can get a raise or a promotion. Little or no concern is given to their share any of the success. Profits for increased productivity are not shared, savings incurred through cost reduction are not dispersed, the payoff for success is "You get to keep your job."

Should leaders be rewarded for the success of their people? Of course, and so should *everyone* enjoy the fruits of positive results. If the victorious general dines luxuriously while the successful army continues on low rations, the army soon refuses to fight!

Focusing on the Short Term

Third Reich managers have a difficult time planning, prioritizing, or evaluating results on a long-term basis. They tend to view everything from the short term. Employees are only as good as their current performance. Seasonal fluctuations, no matter how predictable and consistent, are greeted with surprise and are reacted to with intense negativity instead of proactively anticipated. Short-term downturns are treated as "ominous indicators" of impending disasters inviting overreaction.

We learned of a retail manager whose outlet was maintaining a 22% growth rate through the first 8 months of the fiscal year. The goal for the year was projected at 12% growth, and they were obviously well ahead of their plan. In the 9th month of the fiscal year (June), the growth rate dipped to only 8% (still maintaining a 20% growth rate year-to-date). This short-term "blip" was treated as cataclysmic, and in a knee-jerk reaction, management canceled all vacations until "We get back on track." Family plans were disrupted, trip prepayments forfeited, and morale dropped dramatically. The result was the employees were severely punished for being 8% above their projected goal through three quarters of the fiscal year.

Third Reich managers make short-term decisions on investment, staffing, resource allocation, etc. Preventive maintenance is delayed because "We don't have time right now." Equipment repair is done haphazardly because "We can't afford it right now." Training is often delayed because it doesn't fit into the demands of the moment. All of these examples have short-term gain and potentially disastrous long-term downside consequences.

The short-term focus of Third Reich managers also ensures that everything will always be a crisis. Lack of long-term vision dictates that problems readily avoided by successful planning will continually explode as the intense crises of the moment. Interestingly, Third Reich managers pride themselves on their ability to perform under stress or in the heat of battle. Crisis is a circumstance where autocratic/authoritarian management is appropriate and the Third Reich manager is well served by prolonging these situations. Lack of vision and ability to plan, prioritize, or evaluate is well disguised by keeping all demands at a crisis level.

Recreating Itself

Third Reich managers tend to hire/select employees in their own image. They hire people who think like them, act like them, look like them, and talk like them. While this tendency to surround ourselves with people with whom we are most comfortable is understandable, it is also dangerous to the organization. Some primary areas for concern:

1. ***Lack of creative input.*** Nobody colors outside the lines because everyone sees the same lines. There is no diversity of opinion as everybody tends to be in agreement because of their "sameness." In truth, anyone who disagrees or offers creative alternatives is snubbed or viewed suspiciously because "He is not one of us." Ideas, decisions, and patterns are consistently recycled over and over, reminiscent of old wine in new bottles. An anthem of Third Reich managers is "If you want to get along around here, go along." They select people who will do just that.

2. ***Third Reich management behaviors become institutionalized.*** As Third Reich managers move on through promotion, demotion, termination, or attrition, they leave behind a mirror image of their style, strategies, and practices. One of the reasons organizations don't break the cycle of Third Reich managers is because they have never been exposed to another alternative. New generations of managers model the behaviors perceived to have been successful in the past.

"IT'S THE WAY WE HAVE ALWAYS DONE IT AROUND HERE."

---

3. ***Diversity is ignored.*** Because of the rejection of anything different, the organization fails to benefit from the wealth of contributions from the diversity of its members. Tremendous talent goes unnoticed (or is encouraged to go elsewhere to achieve fulfillment). Opportunities are lost and chronic problems are not solved because of the Third Reich manager's tendency toward homogeneity. Frequently their refusal to assimilate diversity violates the law.

Tolerating Ethical Breaches

Managers are very potent influences on the ethical climate of an organization and subordinates will often model their behavior on what they observe in their successful boss. The manager's behavior is considered a blueprint for success and if the boss "talks" one standard of behavior and "walks" another, the "walk" usually has more impact. If the manager is observed resorting to questionable shortcuts or outright ethical breaches, this sends a powerful message to subordinates and may be considered standard operating procedure.

The president of a small manufacturing company was attempting to build his export business and establish contacts with various agents of importers in the Republic of South Korea. Appointments for three agents were set for three successive weeks to determine which of the three would best meet his and the company's needs. At the end of the first meeting, the president was so convinced by what he heard he offered the agent an exclusive contract to represent their products in South Korea. However, in the next 2 weeks, as other agents came to call, he offered each of them exclusive contracts also. The net result, three competitors, all with signed contracts granting them exclusive rights. The president then turned to his people and said, "We have a problem and you had better come up with a way to solve it."

Frequently, employees are asked to do something for the benefit of the organization which is actually counterproductive to their performance or career (e.g., a special project interferes with their completion of traditional tasks or forces them to step out of a fast-track promotional pattern). The employee is appeased by the promise of "Don't worry — you will be taken care of." However, when the time comes, these vague commitments are not honored or acknowledged and are conveniently forgotten.

Managers also influence the ethical climate through the selection of which behaviors they reward and which they punish. There is a clear message sent when the boss says: "I want this project completed on schedule no matter what it takes and I don't want to know how you did it!" The translation is — stretch ethical or legal boundaries if necessary, but keep me out out it. Protect me at all costs, but expose yourself. The results are rewarded with praise or informal payoffs, and the cycle of behavior continues until it is exposed and the employee pays the price. Employees who refuse to violate ethics or expose unacceptable behaviors may be cruelly ostracized or targeted for dismissal. Look at the history of "whistle-blowers" in today's organizations.

MOTIVATING BY FEAR — THREATENING THE ECONOMIC SECURITY AND JOB LONGEVITY OF WORKERS AND STAFF.

Today, fear as a management style is a style of weakness. Workers who find themselves in a fear-driven environment quickly move to relocate to

alternative jobs/organizations/departments with less fear and a more-partici-
pative environment. Workers who remain in a fear-based environment tend
to be the people who are not highly productive, creative, or committed.
They also react against the fear-based management style by lowering output
and developing various patterns of fear-based resistance, including sabotage, work slowdowns, efforts to have the manager ousted by going around
them to upper management, and/or unionization.

Is fear ever a legitimate management/motivational style? In fairness, yes
— however, in only a very small percentage of our management opportunities. It is effective when you are dealing with (1) resistant individual
employees (and only as a last resort) and (2) situations of extreme crisis.
However, when utilized as a regular style, it has disastrous effects.

Fear, like other negative reinforcements and punishments, can never
produce the level of performance that committed employees will give,
willingly. The real purpose of our efforts in writing this book is to help
create the type of organization that will attract, challenge, and retain committed members.

In subsequent chapters, we will discuss how we see the telltale signs of
fear in the organization and how we contribute to the overall culture with
our management styles. The move from fear-based management to performance-driven leadership will demand significant change. In the following
chapter, we address how to manage this change successfully and shift the
managerial culture.

CHAPTER 3

MANAGING CHANGE

Successful implementation of a promising new approach to the management of organizations, one that encourages performance-driven leadership, will require a completely new way of thinking about management, on the part of management and on the part of organizational members. This is the essence of the advice given at the beginning of *this* century by Frederick W. Taylor to a congressional committee investigating the then revolutionary approach known as scientific management. Although it took much longer than Taylor must have expected (or hoped!), organizations did eventually accomplish this fundamental shift in the way of thinking about the roles and responsibilities of managers and workers. Eventually combining scientific management, administrative management, the human relations movement, contingency theory, and a succession of additional perspectives and elaborations, especially Weber's theory of bureaucracy and of authority, modern organizations achieved phenomenal levels of effectiveness and efficiency. Considerable contributions made by these powerful organizations to the economic and material quality of life have accrued to benefit society. Today, ordinary citizens can enjoy a level of material comfort not even imaginable in the 19th century or before. Yet, as in all historical social change, these benefits have not come without costs. In Chapter 2, we make the case that, having secured material and financial success, these same hierarchical, fear-driven organizations now extract a terrible price on the physical and mental health of their members and that the costs of fear-driven organizations have undergone a fundamental shift. For example, one of the fastest-growing categories of workmen's compensation claims is workplace stress, and a leading cause of this stress is a "bad boss." (Described as Third Reich management in Chapter 2.) The costs are experienced in many other ways including lower production, high absenteeism and turnover, and the high incidence of sabotage and resistance to change.

Not only have the human and social costs risen to what we believe to be unacceptable levels, but gains in effectiveness and efficiency have dramatically diminished and, in many cases, disappeared. The disruption, displacement, discarding, and disillusionment of increasing numbers of organizational members alert us to the need to resurrect Taylor's advice. Nothing less is required than a completely new way of thinking about organizations, about the roles and responsibilities of their members, and especially about how these organizations ought to be managed and governed.

In many ways, the forces that exist as the 20th century closes are more turbulent and threatening than those faced as the century began. Change, both positive and negative, has for the most part been cumulative. Further, the world in which our organizations must perform and compete is infinitely larger and more interactive. Although the U.S. is arguably still the most powerful economic entity as the world prepares to enter the 21st century, we have many powerful and potentially powerful rivals, e.g., the European Common Market and the emerging Pacific Rim economic alliances. If we are not able to adapt successfully to the new realities, others surely will be. We cannot successfully compete in the 21st century with methods and models of the 20th! The behaviors that brought us *here*, to this level of economic competitiveness, will not take us *there,* to the next levels of competitiveness during the next 10 to 20 years of this economic cycle. Yet, change is never easy, especially the degree of change we are espousing. It is the process of change that is the focus of this chapter.

The Focus of Change

Organizations err when they focus only on bottom-line issues. This has been a trend in America for the last 10 to 20 years and is a common focus of Third Reich managers. As we will discuss, bottom-line issues are crucial to the survivability of the organization: if the organization is not profitable, or "funding justified," and cannot continue to exist long term, then even excellent working conditions are meaningless.

However, bottom-line issues must share billing with

- Employee-centered issues
- Customer-centered issues

We offer the analogy of a camera mounted on a tripod; if the tripod is balanced on three equal legs, a competent photographer is able to take quality photographs. However, if any leg of the tripod is the wrong length (too long because of overemphasis or too short because of lack of priority), even the most highly trained professional photographer would find it difficult, at best, to achieve quality results.

Employee-Centered Issues

One of the great truths of today's marketplace is

PEOPLE ARE AN ORGANIZATION'S GREATEST ASSET.

It's not necessarily what you do, but how you do it! Your long-term success will be determined by employees' competency and speed in discharging their duties, how they interact with each other and the people they serve, and their willingness to meet organizational goals and objectives. To disregard issues considered to be crucial by the bulk of individuals within the organization is to restrict the flow of support to and from your greatest asset, your people. Some of these issues include

- Good internal communication
- Fair and equitable compensation
- Treating people with dignity and respect
- Reasonable support systems (from benefit packages to the cafeteria food quality to traffic flow in the parking lots)
- Appropriate input into the decision-making process
- Training
- Safety and security
- And many other key issues concerning the workplace environment

Customer-Centered Issues

Over the past few years volumes have been written concerning the importance of the customer to the organization. Most people today understand that we have external customers (the person or group that receives our product or services and usually offers a monetary exchange as compensation) and internal customers (the next person, department, or team in the process within our organization). Evidence is accumulating that employee satisfaction is a leading indicator of customer satisfaction. In other words, satisfied employees today lead to satisfied customers in the future.

A compelling truth is that today everyone serves someone. If we do not focus on the needs of our customers, we quickly become obsolete or unnecessary. Third Reich managers perceive that their people (department or team) exist to serve and respond to them! Nothing could be farther from the truth.

**MANAGEMENT EXISTS TO SERVE
THE PEOPLE IT INFLUENCES.**

Consider the "replacability factor." Managers can be, and are, replaced without the organization skipping a beat, but try to replace an entire department or team and witness the chaos that is created!

What are typical customer issues? In general, customers want

- Their specific needs met
- A reasonable price (monetary or otherwise)
- An easy process — no hassles

Meeting customers' expectations will leave them satisfied. Exceeding their expectations will bring them back. Do not take our word for it.

**FIND OUT WHAT YOUR CUSTOMERS, INTERNAL AND
EXTERNAL, WANT FROM YOU AND THEN PROVIDE IT.**

Bottom-Line Issues

Organizations must be financially sound. To stress employee issues and customer issues to the detriment of financial stability is foolishness. All three must be addressed in concert. The key is finding the appropriate balance over the long haul. However, bottom-line issues must be addressed in the long and intermediate terms, not just the short-term. Third Reich managers narrow their vision by using the financial situation of the moment as their only barometer. If every decision is addressed on this basis, we buy tape and bailing wire instead of nuts and bolts; we don't train; we don't do preventative maintenance; we wait until something breaks and deal with the major repair, lost production, and other costs associated with downtime, etc.

Organizations faced with financial extinction obviously must make all decisions based on today's finances (or lack thereof). However, healthy organizations and Third Reich managers who consistently plead financial scarcity (especially if it is only intended to inflate already acceptable profits) create the illusion of instability. Key people alter their performance downward and look elsewhere for employment because they fear that the organization is not well.

Do we really want to create the image of financial instability when it's not accurate? The long-term downside of such a tactic is far steeper than the upside payoff of short-term increased profits.

Change and Stability

Managers are confronted with a somewhat paradoxical situation. On the one hand, they must be responsive to the *demands for change* in today's work environment. At the same time, they must respond to the *demands for stability* in the work environment, especially in the core activities from which the organization adds value and derives legitimacy. (Example: while your goal is to completely remodel the restaurant, you want to stay in business and keep serving meals in the process. You can't afford to completely shut down. Some form of the productive status quo must be maintained.)

It is the ability to anticipate change that permits us to be *proactive,* rather than *reactive.* The need for change must be anticipated through vision, not just responded to in reaction (often knee-jerk). Performance-driven leaders who view their accountability broadly realize that they must exercise leadership in bringing change to their organization.

**SUCCESSFUL CHANGE WILL NOT JUST HAPPEN;
IT MUST BE MANAGED.**

The key is to maintain a balance, to focus on the present and the future simultaneously.

EYES TO THE FUTURE;
FEET PLANTED SQUARELY IN TODAY.

Third Reich managers typically view their accountability in narrow terms and focus on exploiting current short-term success. After all, this is the well-spring of their rewards, and so they are willing to risk tomorrow to pay for today. The biggest trap of being focused only on the present is that it robs you of your future. Paradoxically, a manager who is focused on the future fails to maintain today's competitiveness and often threatens the organization's very existence because it is today's successes that provide the foundation for future achievements. Today's managers cannot afford to be one dimensional in their thinking.

Leaders want order, they want work to flow, they want to respond only to exceptions to plans, and they want to minimize the frequency of disruptions. The more fluid and changing a situation is, the more difficult it is to manage efficiently and effectively. Thus, managers must be stability seekers and stability agents.

STABILITY AND CHANGE!

The paradox is that managers must create and maintain work environments that balance the demands of *both* stability and change. Both these demands affect the manager's accountability for performance. At the present time, when the demands for change are so obvious and pervasive, there may be a tendency to minimize the importance of stability to an organization's effectiveness. Everything is not changing; everything does not need changing. The key is identifying and communicating and changing what does need to be changed. Change is expensive. Not only must the new process be more effective than the process it is replacing, but it must also compensate for the costs of change.

The Change Process

Organizational change requires a change in the behavior of people (the crux of moving from Third Reich management), and changing people is a three-phase process. The three phases, unfreezing, moving, and refreezing; recognize that behavioral change is a process that takes time, that people usually do not make significant behavioral changes overnight. Storming the Bastille was not the French Revolution. It was an event in a process and even revolutionary changes take time.

Unfreezing

Unfreezing refers to the idea that before a person will be willing to change present behavior that person has to recognize the present behavior as inappropriate, irrelevant, or in some way inadequate to the demands of a particular situation. Unfreezing is the process of separation from the norm, from past behaviors, from what has been comfortable and is now obsolete. The spark for this process should come from the CEO. The degree of change we are proposing requires that the CEO be a champion of change. During the unfreezing stage, the CEO and other champions of change must communicate an *understanding* of what the nature of the change will be and why it is necessary. This "selling" of change is the first critical step in the unfreezing process, as change is never embraced unless the need for change is acknowledged.

Third Reich managers usually present the need for change as an indictment of the past. When the need for change is presented largely as a criticism of the past, organizational members will resist the change and quickly move to defend their past and present behavior. After all, it is their performance that is being criticized. The Third Reich manager often conveys the message "Everything you have been doing is wrong, and *I* am here to set you straight," but change should be focused on the future. The need for change is an acknowledgment that the present and the future are different from the past. It is much more positive, and we believe effective, to celebrate the achievements of the past while acknowledging that the behaviors that brought us where we are will *not* take us where we must go. "Continuous Improvement Programs" that have turned into "Continuous Criticism Programs" have not been successful. At this stage the organizational leadership (both formal and informal) must communicate to other organizational members a clear understanding of why change is necessary and of what can be gained from a successful change. The entire change process can be off to a much more positive start if unfreezing is achieved by the warm glow of promise for future success rather than the more typical Third

Reich chill of criticism.

CHANGE IS NOT AN INDICTMENT OF THE PAST.

Moving: The Phase of Learning New Behaviors

Unfreezing current behavior creates a vacuum unless alternative, new behavior is available. If enough pressure is brought to bear (a typical Third Reich change technique) without clear communication of what the appropriate new behaviors are, people will turn to new responses in desperation and these "new responses" are often at cross-purposes to management's goals. It is unlikely that new behaviors frantically grasped as an escape from fear and pressure will be those most supportive to the type of positive, committed involvement that we seek in the purging of Third Reich management. However, organizational members must receive guidance toward the new, desired behaviors. It stands to reason that behaviors and activities discarded during the unfreezing stage must be replaced, or this deadly vacuum occurs. Organizational members must also appreciate that understanding both the need for change and the specific change desired is not in and of itself sufficient to achieve a successful change. Like all other organizational activities, change requires performance.

A crucial element in the moving phase, which is often overlooked by Third Reich managers, is training. Change, without the appropriate training to support the new behaviors, makes the terrible assumption that "we were capable of doing it all along!" It assumes that the behaviors and abilities were already in place and that people were "choosing" not to perform.

CHANGE MUST ALWAYS BE SUPPORTED BY TRAINING.

When training is not implemented to support change, some very negative messages are communicated to the entire organization:

1. You are not worth the time and resources necessary to train you.
2. The task is not significant enough to require training, and it doesn't matter if the task is done well or not.
3. The change is so insignificant that you already have the skills nec-

essary for implementation.

CHANGE;
ANYTHING LIGHTLY GIVEN IS LIGHTLY ACCEPTED.

A six-point training model is critical to implementing successful change:

1. *Awareness training* — Establishing the reasons supporting the necessity of change.
2. *Technical skills training* — Introducing the hard technical skills necessary to "do" the change successfully.
3. *Support skills training* — Introducing the soft skills necessary.
   a. Training on the skills of organization (how to set up a file, how to manage a desk to avoid "desk stress," how to set up a work process flow, i.e., the ability to be organized).
   b. People skills training (communication, problem solving, conflict resolution, team behaviors, etc.).
4. *Remedial skills training* — Establishing math skills, reading comprehension, writing skills, etc.
5. *Skills and training evaluation* — Asking: Are we teaching the proper skills? Is our training effective? Are we achieving the desired performance levels?
6. *Fundamental review* — Reviewing *all* of the previously taught skills. This is a favorite area for Third Reich managers to ignore. They assume that once you have learned it, you don't need to be exposed to it again.

FACT: WE HAVE ALL FORGOTTEN MORE ABOUT OUR JOBS
THAN WE WILL EVER REMEMBER — FUNDAMENTAL
REVIEW PAYS HIGH DIVIDENDS IN
INCREASED PERFORMANCE.

An additional point on the time lines of training: training should never exceed the opportunity to reinforce the new skills and knowledge with actual practical application. What good does it do to train people on skills that they will not use for 6 months or more? Organizations tend to err in one of two areas:

♦ Not training enough, or

♦ Training too much too soon.

Consider the scenario of new employees who attend an extended orientation training session (from 2 weeks to 30 days or more). They are exposed to skills that will not be implemented until their 6th or 9th month on the job. While the skills are initially learned, they become "rusty" at best or perhaps "extinct" because of lack of quick reinforcement or practical application.

Third Reich managers embrace only point 2 (technical skills training) in this model. Why? Because they can see the technical skills necessary to do the job and they lack the depth to appreciate how crucial the contribution of organizational and people skills really is. Another truth is that Third Reich managers may be deficient in some of these additional necessary skills themselves and obviously can't teach what they don't know!

Much of the focus of this book will be on the actual behaviors necessary to move from Third Reich to performance-driven leadership. In successful change, understanding must be accompanied by effective performance.

Refreezing

Refreezing of new, learned behavior means that people accept the new behavior as a permanent part of their behavioral repertoire. The new behaviors become habit, and the change is now the status quo. This is where the achievement of a revolutionary new way of thinking about the management of organizations is absolutely critical. People have to experiment with the behavior, see that it is effective, and assimilate it with other behavior and attitudes. The leadership of the change effort must see that the new, desired behaviors are recognized and rewarded. Often, under Third Reich managers, the new behaviors are met with punishment, negative reinforcement, or neglect (leading to extinction). Through positive reinforcement of the new, desired behaviors, leadership can achieve closure over this stage of the change process. By achieving closure as new patterns of behavior are attained, organizational members can then focus on successful performance in the core activities of the organization and on readiness for the next cycle of change (there will be ongoing cycles of change).

If training has been employed in the change process, and it is almost always essential to this process, then an important activity in the refreezing process will be an assessment of the effectiveness of the training. Have the desired skills and behavior been attained? Are the new behaviors regularly exhibited? Have new ideas and attitudes been adopted? As always when training is involved, it is important to assess whether or not the training has produced the desired results.

EVALUATE TRAINING.

Another critical aspect of the refreezing phase involves necessary re-alignment of reward systems, including compensation. In a change of this magnitude, we will find that the old reward system does not adequately address the new behaviors. We *must* modify the reward system to make certain that we do not continue to reward old behaviors that are no longer appropriate, *and* we must redirect compensation and other rewards to reinforce the new, desired behaviors. Appropriate realignment of the reward system will greatly enhance the success of the refreezing process.

ARE WE ASKING FOR CHANGE
BUT REINFORCING OLD BEHAVIOR PATTERNS?

Positive responses to change must be consistently and appropriately reinforced. This will give essential credibility to the change process. As we all know, reward the behavior that you want repeated.

RECOGNIZE, CELEBRATE, REWARD.

When we have successfully accomplished the refreezing phase, we can begin anew the process of determining what behaviors will need to be unfrozen in the next cycle of change. Enlightened management recognizes change as an ongoing, perpetual component of organizational life.

Kathy Foltner describes her challenge: "My superiors told me I had 24 months to institute change and turn the company around. There were 22 people who had never met me."

She describes her initial strategy. "After introducing myself to the staff I made no significant change for a 6-week period. I evaluated their procedures and developed a ten-page 'State of the Company Assessment'." One of the observations she made was that the 17 highly trained audiologists who provided hearing health care services to their customers were using 17 different hearing aid manufacturers. There appeared to be no standardization, and, understandably, this created havoc. Accounting had to deal with 17 different vendors, writing checks, etc.; buying power was diminished as the company was basically a small customer to a lot of vendors, and it was difficult to maintain "expertise" when it was necessary to be current on a bloated product line. Kathy determined that reducing the number of vendors for hearing aids was critical to profitability and efficiency. Her strategy for driving this change follows the three-step model of unfreezing, moving, and refreezing.

Kathy focused her efforts on training and the flow of information realizing that they are crucial to the **unfreezing phase**. "It was important to identify with the staff the reasons why a reduction in vendors was crucial. Aside from the administrative and customer service concerns, we educated the staff on issues of profitability, reduction of cost of goods, and the advantages of consolidating our buying power."

Once the need for and the reasoning behind the change was established, Kathy completed the unfreezing phase by setting the goal. "We will reduce our number of vendors from 17 to 4 within the next 6 months." She informed the staff: "At some point in the near future, I will be asking each of you for your input about manufacturers. Please be prepared to answer those questions."

When memos went out, she received the typical 50% response. She notes that now when the staff are asked to participate in such matters the response approaches 100%. Why the difference between the initial response and now?

We educated them on two key points:

1. They know if I ask them for input, I do want to know. They had never experienced that before. They learned that their input does make a difference.
2. If you don't respond it creates work for others. Someone has to make follow-up phone calls. They interrupt you when you are with your patients which affects our customer service, etc.

After the responses were received, she tallied the data and moved on to the next phase — **moving**. A staff meeting was held and charts were prepared (check sheets) showing how many audiologists favored each of the 17 vendors as their top four. Predictably, the top three were very obvious. However, picking the fourth was open for discussion. An extensive discussion addressed the pros and cons of the remaining 13 vendors. They were evaluated on

- Product quality
- Cosmetic appearance
- Sound quality
- Customer service
- Invoicing policy
- Other factors

The process leading to the consensus decision on the fourth preferred manufacturer was interesting. Kathy's comments:

> Not everyone had an equal voice. I don't believe in democracy in a situation like this. Just because the majority wants to do it does not mean that it is the right thing to do. I believe in consensus. Even if you can't voice it as your choice, you acknowledge that you can live with it, that you can support it. Agreements were adhered to.

Critical to this moving process was that Kathy made a pledge to the staff. "If this change is not successful after a 6-month period, we will consider changing it again." Stressing the experimental nature of the change makes the process much less threatening. One of the keys to experimentation is timely evaluation. And in reviewing the results, the vendor reduction was a change that did accomplish its objectives.

Kathy was then ready to move into the **refreezing** phase. To ensure that the new agreements were adhered to, Kathy emphasized the importance of evaluation, accountability, and feedback. Evaluating the results of and compliance with the change was accomplished by reviewing monthly printouts of each office's product purchases. The staff knew that they were accountable for carrying out the change. Feedback was given on a timely basis to each individual: recognition and encouragement were given to those who embraced the change, and reminders were given to those who resisted.

The result, according to Kathy, was that

> Within 2 months we were 95% down to the four preferred manufacturers. With the exception of one individual, everyone complied. They just went with it. There was enough flexibility with what we agreed to that it didn't threaten anybody's zone of comfort. Originally, I thought it would take 6 months. However, the change was embraced in 60 days, much quicker than I thought. It was the best example of positive change in our company.

Kathy also stressed one other point in this successful change process. In the course of discussions, the staff identified some of their issues and concerns, one of which was the need for updated and organized pricing and product-information manuals. She acknowledged their legitimate request, while emphasizing that with 17 vendors, accurate updated manuals were a near impossibility. She committed to taking personal responsibility for the manuals based on the four approved vendors, which demonstrated to the staff that change is a two-way street.

Introducing Change

Unilateral approaches to introducing change rely on formal-position power and one-way communication. These are usually top down mandates where compliance is demanded and reinforced by the use of internal power. It is the organizational food chain in action! Examples include orders issued unilaterally from managers at one level of the organization to members at a lower level, upper managements decisions to replace key personnel dictates changing organizational design or market strategy or perhaps altering product/service offerings. This approach mirrors a military style of issuing orders applied to the everyday occurrence of organizational challenges.

UNILATERAL APPROACHES ARE TYPICAL OF THIRD REICH MANAGERS.

These approaches fit Third Reich managers' philosophy, their management training, and their experiences. In the past these approaches have often been successful, thereby reinforcing the style of Third Reich management. Make no mistake, this autocratic style is effective in times of crisis and with resistant individual employees who refuse to perform. However, as a consistent style, uniformly applied to every employee, it is counterproductive. A central theme of this book is that past successes are not precursors of future success.

Shared power approaches utilize varying degrees of participation by subordinates in the change process. The emphasis is on sharing, not abdicating. For example, the top leaders of the organization might identify (and communicate) the need for change and articulate the parameters within which the change must occur. Subordinates can then be brought into the process of developing alternatives to meet the need and, eventually, in choosing the specific new approaches. This was obviously the approach successfully used by Kathy Foltner to reduce the number of vendors. Even in an overall environment typified by the prevalence of Third Reich management, shared power approaches have been successful.

In other words, change may be inflicted from above and driven by fear, or change may be elected through active participation in the change process. Inflicted change focuses on the negative aspects of change, while elected change, in tandem with performance-driven leaders, is more likely to focus on the positives of change (the benefits to be derived).

CHANGE SHOULD BE ELECTED, NOT INFLICTED.

A critical aspect of any change is that there is both loss and gain. You are moving toward something and away from something; something is to be achieved and something to be avoided.

DRAMATIC AND SYSTEMIC CHANGE IS REQUIRED.

If you change jobs, you perceive that there is much to be gained — career growth, higher earnings, greater challenges — and you also experience loss — the security of familiarity, friendships, etc. When we elect change we tend to focus on the good to be achieved: "The pain is worth the gain." The change is then embraced, implemented, and there is a committment to succeed. When change is inflicted upon us (we have no choice), we tend to focus on what we are losing. The pain is perceived to be greater than the gain. As a result, resistance sets in, negative emotion runs high, and there is little or no commitment to succeed.

Typically, in organizations the top echelon of management elects the change. It sees the benefit of change, understands the danger of the downside of the status quo, and develops enthusiasm and commitment to successful change. Change is then inflicted on the rest of the organization where the enthusiasm and commitment are not shared because the reaction and focus is on the loss. Third Reich managers attempt to ride roughshod over the resistance and attempt to force the change (unsuccessfully we might add). We have all seen the cartoon of a flogging with the caption "The beatings will continue until morale improves" — a reflection of the Third Reich managers mentality).

Kathy Foltner invited the staff to participate in some of the "decisions of change" and consequently, reduced the perception of inflicted change and increased the perception of elected or collaborative change.

Performance-driven leaders follow this process:

1. *Announce* the change. Emphasize the reasons for the change and what is ultimately to be gained. The timing of this announcement is very important. Announcing the change too far in advance can heighten uncertainty and feelings of insecurity and can give the rumor mill (and early resistors) time to disseminate erroneous and harmful interpretations of what is "really going to happen." Also, the earlier the announcement, the more likely significant modifications will be made before the change is implemented. On the other hand, announcing the change too close to implementation will not give people time to adjust. It may also exacerbate the perception that "this thing is being rammed down our throats." Consider carefully the timing of the announcement of change. Give people time to absorb the essence of the change, but not time to mount sustained misinformation and resistance efforts. The actual timing requires a sensitivity to and understanding of the specific organizational culture.

2. *Acknowledge* the "grieving issues." Create an environment where the perceptions of loss can be identified, discussed, and given a proper burial.

3. *Accentuate* repetitiously the positive outcomes as they are achieved through the successful application of the new change.

**IT IS DIFFICULT TO MOVE AHEAD
IF YOU ARE CLINGING TO ISSUES OF THE PAST.**

Response to Change

Humans are very adaptive. Their capacity for adapting to changing circumstances is limited, but enormous. From the manager's viewpoint of accountability for achieving goals, human response to change can be neutral, positive, or negative. A neutral response may be the most common type of behavioral response to change in organizations. Although changes are taking place constantly in organizations, they do not affect every individual equally, nor is any one individual affected by all changes. In fact, the first reaction of many employees who are unaffected by the change to the claim of widespread and pervasive change could well be "What changes?" As a practical matter, many of the changes swirling around us never directly touch us and our response to them is neutral — from a behavioral viewpoint, we are indifferent to the changes. The degree of change we are espousing for performance-driven leaders cannot afford a neutral response.

A positive response to changes means that, from the perspective of managers, the response contributes to the efficient and effective accomplishment of organizational goals for which the managers are accountable; this is in contrast to the personal agenda of the Third Reich manager. Subordinates who respond positively to change are referred to by enlightened leaders as cooperative, adaptive, progressive, and able to cope with change. Subordinates who respond positively to the Third Reich manager's personal agenda are referred to as "loyal."

A negative response to change by employees is commonly viewed by managers as dysfunctional, as counter to goal achievement. Negative responses to change can be active, overt actions often described as sabotage or they can be covert, benign actions that constitute passive/aggressive behaviors (the acts of "omission," the failure to support or take action). It is often not what we do, but what we do not do that determines the level of support and the success of the change. Managers who respond negatively to change may be viewed as stubborn, uncooperative, set in their ways, and unable to cope. However, from the viewpoint of organizational members, response to change is neither positive nor negative; it is simply behavior that makes sense from their perspective. Their viewpoint may not be the same as that of the organization in which they work (elected vs. inflicted change). Individual members may see the consequences of change, not so much at the level of the organization as at the level of their own social existence as a whole, including their family and community life. We all tend to view events through the prism of how they affect us personally.

We believe that the degree and magnitude of change required to move from Third Reich management will not be possible without the conversion of most organizational members from negative or neutral responses to positive. No amount of fear (or rewards) can generate the level of effort and involvement that committed people will give willingly. Performance-driven leaders can facilitate this development of positive response by the approaches we espouse in this book.

Now we will examine fear in organizations.

CHAPTER 4

FEAR: WHAT CAUSES FEAR
AND HOW WE EXPERIENCE IT

Fear is a basic human emotion. It plays a role in all aspects of life. When individuals enter organizations, they bring with them a set of emotions. Although psychologists have disagreed on how many emotions make up this set, from James B. Watson's three to the eight identified by Ozard, Plutnik, and Tomkins (independently), all agree to include fear as among the most basic.

Fear and *anxiety* are terms that are used by some psychiatrists and psychologists to refer to the same basic emotional state. Others distinguish the two, using *fear* to describe our unpleasant response to specifically identifiable stimuli (or events) and referring to the unpleasant response to vague or ambiguous stimuli as *anxiety*. We prefer the more expansive interpretation of the term and will use fear and anxiety interchangeably, jointly, and separately as referring to components of the same basic emotion. Therefore, we offer this, the following operational definition of fear:

> Fear is an unpleasant emotion caused by awareness or anticipation
> of danger or threat (real or imagined).

Unfounded fear, a reaction to imagined threats, is very powerful. Many people "fear" an unseen, inevitable, impending doom that rarely materializes. Mark Twain is reported to have said, "I have experienced many terrible, horrible, awful things in my lifetime, a couple of which actually happened." We need to address the impact of this fear on the organization.

Fear is *not* the absence of courage. Courage is the ability to act in spite of fear. In fact, it would be incorrect to speak of behavior in the absence of fear as *courage*; this type of behavior might more properly be termed *fear-less*.

FEAR IS PRESENT TO SOME DEGREE IN ALL ORGANIZATIONS.

Since all organizations are made up of human beings, and since all psychologically healthy human beings are capable of experiencing fear, some level of fear will be found in *all* organizations. Some will argue that low levels of fear and anxiety can have positive consequences for the organization by making us more aware and more alert to our circumstances. This is problematic, and we do not intend to enter into that debate in this discussion. Here, we deal with a level of fear that is sufficient to be experienced as unpleasant and to serve as a stimulus to responses of threat or danger, real or imagined.

In their 1991 book, *Driving Fear Out of the Workplace,* Ryan and Oestreich define fear as feeling threatened by possible repercussions as a result of speaking up about work-related concerns. While this is certainly one type of workplace fear, we see the phenomenon of fear as much more broadly manifested in the organizational setting. Certainly not all fear is management driven; some is irrational and may be based on employees' "misperceptions" or may be deeply rooted in an employee's belief system or assumptions. We would include fear of speaking up, fear of change, fear of the unknown, fear of technology, fear of becoming obsolete, fear of failure, fear of discrimination, fear of punishment, fear of harassment, fear of loss, fear of embarrassment, fear of social sanctions, and even fear of success.

Fear of Speaking Up

Fear of speaking up is reflected in behaviors that will restrict the input of organizational members who are willing to contribute to both problem solving and the discovery of opportunity. If people feel more threatened by speaking up than by remaining silent, the probability increases that they will remain silent. This may deprive the organization of valuable information needed to respond to both challenges and opportunities effectively. Here, we use speaking up to mean supplying input or comments verbally, electronically, or in writing. There are many organizational consequences (observed, imagined, or anticipated) that can supply levels of threat significant enough to elicit fear of speaking up. These include an abusive boss who may denigrate, punish, or humiliate subordinates who offer their ideas or expertise. Abusive bosses have been identified as the most prevalent source of work-related stress. These are those bosses who, regardless of the quality of subordinate input, will choose to attack the messenger rather than attend to the message. Why some bosses behave in this fashion is a fascinating topic and may be based on a number of factors, including their own feelings of insecurity or a climate of intense rivalry or corruption. A full exploration of the root causes of abusive interpersonal behavior is beyond the scope of this book.

People may also fear speaking up if they perceive that doing so will evoke censure or ridicule from their colleagues or subordinates. Also, the perceived threat of punitive responses by the organization for saying the wrong thing can easily silence the tongue. How much candid expression exists in a climate of fear where the boss calls everyone together and admonishes us to "say what you really think"? If organizational members have experienced punitive consequences, personally or vicariously, such as someone being fired, demoted, transferred, or ridiculed for expressing unpopular or unwanted ideas, we should not be surprised that they will choose not to speak up. If a "trip to the woodshed" is perceived to be an inevitable consequence of speaking up, why are we surprised that people refrain from doing so? Developing behaviors of pain avoidance is something most of us are quite good at! People may also fear that ideas or information will be used to their personal disadvantage. This is especially likely in climates of intense competition.

Fear of Change

As discussed in Chapter 3, change itself can be very unsettling. In fact, major behavioral change can only take place if it disrupts or unfreezes current behavior. Often, people have experienced major negative consequences associated with change — relocation, loss of power or status, disruption or termination of professional and social relationships, and even loss of employment. A certain level of fear of change may be inevitable;

high performers may fear change because it forces them to give up behaviors and processes with which they are comfortable and adopt new ones that appear to be more problematic. Poor performers may fear change because they believe that they do not possess the skills to be successful.

Michele Atkins stated:

> I think children celebrate change. They go into it gleefully. Somewhere along the line I think it's beaten out of us. By the time we become grown-ups, we become terrified to look at anything which will expand our comfort level even a little bit. So everybody, whether it's in a personal relationship or work relationship, finds that comfort zone and there are parameters to that zone and as long as you are operating within it, it's okay. But don't invade my space or violate those parameters because if you make me stretch, that doesn't feel good.

When asked about the staff reaction to the announcement of pending reengineering and the demonstration of fear of change, Atkins responded:

> What I said to the staff at the beginning was everyone will still have a job at the end of reengineering. It may not be the same job you have now and you may have to change the way you have made decisions along the way, and that may not feel comfortable, but the guarantee is if you still want to be here at the end, your job will be here. That didn't sit well because no one could guarantee what the change would be and what was coming.

The presence of or the threat of high levels of change that portend major negative consequences can generate quite high levels of fear and anxiety, especially if these changes are accompanied by a lack of information or knowledge (as we will discuss in Chapter 8).

Fear of the Unknown

Tolerance for ambiguity and the need to know what one's current circumstances actually are vary greatly from one individual to another. However, no one has an unlimited capacity for "working in the dark"! In fact, our need to know is so strong that we will generate information in the form of rumors or gossip in an attempt to clarify a situation. Organizations in which only those at the very top are permitted to know what is going on and planned are likely to evoke high levels of fear and anxiety. When people don't know why something is happening, they will work it out for themselves, negatively.

Fear of Technology

Much has been written about the fear of computers. This is part of the broader case where the actual or anticipated introduction of major new technology to the work environment precipitates fears of being replaced by the technology or of being unable to master the new technology. Many workers have observed or experienced one or both of those consequences. Because so much attention, even reverence, is given to the fast pace of technological advance and to the need to adopt and master the latest developments, introductions of technology will continue to have significant potential for generating workplace fear. We cannot lose sight of the significance of the individual in our quest to embrace and exploit the explosion of technology.

Fear of Obsolescence

Fear of obsolescence may be closely related to fear of technology. However, it can be much broader in its effect. Even if we do not fear the advent of new technology and are not uncertain about our ability to master it, we may fear that the knowledge and skills that we have developed over the years will no longer be needed. Or, perhaps, the things we do well will simply become less important to the current needs of our organization and, therefore, will become less valued. This may result in economic loss or loss of status, prestige, and social position.

George Mosher stated:

> I think fear in the past tended to be driven by one's personal chemistry or reaction to another person. It was greatest where that other person had all the power and the person needed the job but could lose the job over a single incident at any time. I think fear today is more the marketplace driven by change or skills from the individual point of view. Do I have the skills that are going to be necessary to stay with this company? Am I going to be able to

keep up? We have experienced this in our organization as we have grown rapidly. You have problems where you have elevated people to positions that are not what you would hire for today because the company is maybe five times as big, and so the person is still doing the job. Maybe they are doing an acceptable job, but in their heart, they know that there is someone else out there who has more skills. I also see this happening more in the Peter Principle kind of format, where you've given somebody a little bit too much responsibility, and you have given them a deadline and they don't get it done. The range of their reactions is tremendous. And after that point, they are more fearful than before because they are worried not only about doing the job, but about getting caught for what they have been doing or not doing.

As we will see in Chapter 10, performance-driven leaders' commitment to training and development will overcome this fear of obsolescence in themselves and others.

Fear of Failure

In an organizational climate where mistakes are accompanied by criticism, or even by professional or economic sanctions, risk taking will be avoided, and pervasive risk avoidance is symptomatic of fear of failure. If mistakes are not tolerated, mistakes will be avoided at all costs, or at least not acknowledged. In our discussion on how we see these fears, we will identify how this phenomenon can result in lack of innovation, avoidance or denial of problems, withholding of information, and actual cover-up of mistakes. If fear of failure is great enough, the ethic can develop that it is better to do nothing than to do the wrong thing.

Fear of failure can also be at the root of an employee's deep-seated aversion to measurement. George Mosher stated:

> We basically state up front that we are looking for the above-average performance from above-average people. And if you are only doing an average job, then your future is cloudy. So that also generates fear. Because if you feel you can't really get at least to above-average, then you might be in fear that something will happen to your job.

George Mosher goes on to say:

A book that had a major effect on my life was a book called *Action Management,* which I bought for $2.00 at a rummage sale. I have never seen it on any book list, but it made the point that most people just do not understand the importance of following up and that you need to have systems in place that help to make sure that you follow up effectively. Example, I can generate a lot of ideas. If I have 100 ideas, the 5 most important ones will get done. However, it's almost random as to which of the other 95 will be accomplished. Ultimately, 75 or 80 will be done, and I've developed a note-type system which enables me to keep track of what's been accomplished and what hasn't. Once it's been accomplished, we can move on to something else, but there is a fear on the part of some people because those who aren't really capable of going the extra mile wind up not being able to check off the note as having been done. It gets particularly difficult if they want to go off and do something else which is fine as long as they have done what we have agreed upon, but that certainly doesn't always happen. So that will generate fear on the part of people. I think they see the follow up as overwhelming. For those who are not really capable, the list keeps getting longer. They realize they are not making progress on it; whereas the people who are capable are cutting away at the list and the list stays under control.

Concerning fear of failure, Michele Atkins said, "Generally, as I have watched that, it has come from employees who understand that where we're going is a place they cannot get to. Their competencies are not there or they are fearful they are going to be asked to do more than they are capable of doing. And these employees tend to need to get things stirred up to mask what the real issue is for them."

FEAR TAKES A HORRIBLE TOLL. FEAR IS ALL AROUND, ROBBING PEOPLE OF THEIR PRIDE, HURTING THEM, ROBBING THEM OF A CHANCE TO CONTRIBUTE TO THE COMPANY. IT IS UNBELIEVABLE WHAT HAPPENS WHEN YOU UNLOOSE FEAR.*

---

* Dr. W. Edwards Deming quoted in *The Deming Management Method,* by Mary Walton, New York, Perigee Books, 1986, p. 73.

Fear of Discrimination

This is the fear that we will suffer unpleasant consequences because of *who* we are or what we may do in our private life. We may fear that we will be denigrated or treated unfairly because of prejudices held by our superiors, colleagues, or subordinates. By their comments, their behavior, or the overall atmosphere, we may expect to be treated unfairly because of our race, gender, religion, national origin, age, handicap, or lifestyle. Certainly, there are many documented cases of discrimination in the workplace. People who identify with the prior victims of discrimination may well fear becoming victims themselves.

Fear of Harassment

Although the basis for harassment may be the same as the basis for discrimination, harassment is much more active and behavior-oriented. Discrimination may tend to be covert actions of denial, (deny access, promotion, employment, etc.). Harassment tends to be overt actions, (physical contract, verbal assault, written communication, etc.). Often the result is what the courts have termed "a hostile work environment." Victims of high levels of sexual harassment often speak of their fear of going to work. Harassment may take the form of physical threats and intimidation, taunting, unwanted touching, or varieties of sexual innuendoes and may generate fear of embarrassment or humiliation, of emotional distress, and, in some extremes, fear of physical assault.

Fear of Social Sanctions

We may fear that our socioeconomic origins have not prepared us for acceptance or effective functioning in the social interaction that accompanies our organizational activity. We may fear that we will be rejected because of the way we dress or speak or our social behavior. (This fear is linked to the fear of discrimination.) One company even found that some winners of their international recognition program feared going to the annual awards banquet because of their lack of social skills. Research has shown that a highly predictive variable of where we will end up in life in terms of our geographic, professional, and social affiliation is socioeconomic origin. This is after controlling for such potent influences as level of education, even advanced levels. It is still true to various degrees that "birds of a feather flock together, ..." and we tend to interact socially with those we perceive to be more like us, in ways that are important to us. It is worth noting that a common factor in employees who resort to workplace violence seems to be that they are alienated from the social support of friends and colleagues. In our discussion of participative management, we address the importance of providing a strong social identification by giving workers something to belong to. Also, we can fear that saying or doing controversial or unpopular things will lead to social sanctions. We may then remain generally silent or nonparticipative to avoid the possibility of "exposing" ourselves to these sanctions. We may fear that we will "slip up" in some little way that will cause us to be ostracized.

Fear of Success

As incongruous as it might seem, some people fear success. Many people simply do not picture themselves as ever having been or ever being successful. This becomes a self-fulfilling prophecy.

WE LIVE LIFE TO THE LEVEL OF OUR EXPECTATIONS.

Perhaps recognized success at current levels of responsibility will cause us to be assigned or elevated to additional responsibilities that will be beyond our capability. This would be similar to fear of becoming a victim of what is usually called the Peter Principle. In some organizations, we find that success leads to additional loading of work and/or responsibility. We may fear that success will subject us to demands beyond our resources, including time. It is not uncommon for there to be great disparity in workloads at colleges and universities, with much heavier demands being placed on those who have been successful in the past. Therefore, people can actually come to dread the negative consequences of being recognized for doing a good job.

Success can also produce enemies, particularly in an environment where competition for organizational rewards is high. We may fear that success will result in the negative consequences of jealousy, envy, or being identified as a "rate buster." In the most competitive environments, it can result in a widespread fear that cooperating with and supporting the efforts of colleagues will result in some form of loss. Therefore, new information, ideas, techniques, and so forth may be hoarded or concealed from others.

This list of possible sources of fear in the workplace is meant to be illustrative, not exhaustive. You may very well be able to identify other sources of fear in your organization. The salient point is that there are many sources of fear in the workplace, and we can expect to find some level of fear in every organization, although it may vary considerably across time in the same organization.

Signs of Fear in Organizations

In Chapter 2 we offered the 16 identifiable traits of a fear-based manager. Here we offer identifiable behaviors (or lack of) that identify the existence of fear in the organization. Aside from Ryan and Oestreich's finding that people won't speak out, we offer the following "dirty dozen."

Twelve Identifiable Traits of Organizational Fear

1. Increased telling of untruths
2. People hiding mistakes
3. People hesitating to exercise initiative and take risks
4. Productivity decreasing and "extra efforts" disappearing
5. C.Y.A. (cover your anatomy) becoming an art form
6. Increased passive/aggressive behavior
7. High AT&T (absenteeism, tardiness, and turnover)
8. Obsequious behavior
9. Blaming
10. Informing
11. Hostile interpersonal relationships
12. Overall demonstration of negativity

1. Increased Telling of Untruths

In high-fear, low-trust environments, punishment is practiced as a routine way of reacting to uncommon occurrences. This punishment takes many forms, such as

- ◆ Public embarrassment
- ◆ Silence
- ◆ Nonverbal displays of contempt
- ◆ Removal of privileges
- ◆ Exclusion from future high-profile assignments
- ◆ Verbal warnings
- ◆ Formal written censure

To avoid these punishments, workers/staff will tell untruths. At times these untruths are planned or they may be reactive, emotional, knee-jerk responses. This is common behavior with children and, unfortunately, is duplicated in adulthood. Children tell untruths to avoid negative reactions from their parents. When that same autocratic parental model is brought into the workplace, workers (adopting the role of children) will tell untruths to avoid negative sanctions.

Not all incidents of untruths are due to organizational fear; many individuals have lifelong patterns of demonstrating untruthful behavior. However, incidents of untruths increase in a Third Reich, high-fear, low-trust environment.

An interesting comment from George Mosher:

> When one of my daughters first went off to college, the dean of students spoke to parents and said, "Some of you at one time or another over the next 4 years are going to get calls from me or my staff and they are going to say that your kid is doing something that is not acceptable. Your kid is telling you that they aren't doing it and you're going to want to believe them in the worst way. But the fact is, that we don't make those calls before we really have our ducks in order. And most students, when put into a corner, will not tell the truth. Not only is that true of students, but I'm finding it's true of most people. If they really get put into a corner, they won't tell the truth." Ever since that statement I have kept my antennae up to look for those kinds of situations. As an example, if you look at the history of the presidency, Nixon was kicked out of office not for Watergate, but for the cover-up of Watergate. People get into half-truths, then they get themselves in a box, and ultimately, if you investigate hard enough, you will find they aren't telling the truth.

Lessening the fear and increasing the trust within the organization reduce the need and tendency for people not to tell the truth. While untruthful behavior will never become totally extinct, incidents can be dramatically reduced.

2. People Hiding Mistakes

Obviously, this issue is closely related to the telling of untruths and may be one of the issues with the most negative impact on today's organization.

In a high-fear, low-trust environment workers hide mistakes. They don't quit making mistakes (high fear may be increasing the number of mistakes), and when mistakes are made, rather than bring them to the attention of management for early correction, they are hidden, either to lie dormant and undetected or to move from mole hill to mountain to mountain range status. Why? As previously discussed, punishment is an issue. When mistakes are made we punish the offenders to teach them not to do it again. Not only do we punish to impress the offenders, we do so visibly so that the entire workforce will see what happens to people who make mistakes. The result is not an irradication of mistakes; rather mistakes go underground and unreported.

Example: If a worker makes a mistake and takes it to the manager for correction, the worker may be greeted with the statement and overall message of "Yes, you did make a mistake, and I'm going to teach you not to do that again. You will be written up, taken off the project, given days off without pay, etc." What do workers learn to do? To hide the next mistake; rather than report it, they hide it. While the mistake may not remain buried permanently, this behavior

◆ Avoids immediate consequence
◆ May buy the employee a couple of days before having to answer for the mistake
◆ May give the employee time to update his or her resume and begin networking before the boss finds out

In reality, the mistake may never be found. The boss will know that something didn't go right, but may never be able to pinpoint exactly what happened. Or, perhaps, the discovery of the mistake comes so late that it is counterproductive to even address it with the employee (like spanking the dog 3 months after you find the torn-up slipper — the dog has no understanding of why it's being punished).

In many high-fear, low-trust organizations workers become better at burying their mistakes than managers are at uncovering them, and this behavior of hiding mistakes totally transforms management. In truth, management cannot exercise the future-focused behaviors of planning, prioritizing, establishing goals, and evaluating the payoff of the current process.

Management must focus on the past, demonstrating behaviors of inspection and investigation and establishing error accountability.

**MANAGEMENT BECOMES INVESTIGATORY —
FOCUSING ON WHO MADE YESTERDAY'S MISTAKES
RATHER THAN WHERE WE ARE GOING TOMORROW.**

This investigatory behavior of management not only hinders productivity, it's a horribly expensive way of doing business. If employees learn that they can bring their mistakes to their leadership and experience this type of a response: "Yes, I acknowledge that a mistake was made. I appreciate your being mature enough to bring that to my attention. Let's address two issues: (1) How do we fix what's happened? (2) How do we avoid a repeat of this in the future? Let's be sure we learn from it and let's move on."

As we previously identified as number 11 of the identifiable traits of Third Reich managers, the higher you are in the organizational ladder, the greater the tolerance for making mistakes. The lower you are on the organizational ladder, the lower the tolerance for making mistakes and the greater the likelihood that the mistake will get you punished. From the top we hear, "We made a mistake. We're going to learn from it and we're going to move on." In the lower levels of the organization we hear, "You made a mistake. It's going to cost you. I will teach you not to do that again."

**KEY QUESTION: WHAT IS THE TOLERANCE
FOR MAKING MISTAKES IN YOUR ORGANIZATION?**

---

3. People Hesitating to Exercise Initiative and Take Risks

No rocket-scientist stuff here. When we ask people to exercise initiative and take risks, we are asking them to

- Make a decision
- Do something out of the ordinary
- Make something happen

Whenever any of us has the opportunity to make decisions, we don't always make the correct one. We make mistakes, you make mistakes, and the people who work for you make mistakes. So when we are exercising initiative and taking risk, there is a certain rate of probability that we may not do the right thing. If we had a history of punishing these wrong decisions, why are we surprised that people show low initiative and little or no risk taking? If you were my boss, I would rather have you be disappointed in me because I don't exercise initiative than punish me because I did and it turned out to be wrong. Many times when organizations perceive that they have employees with low motivation and they engage a consultant or outside source to help *fix* the employees, the root cause of the problem is actually with leadership. Would your people perceive that they are encouraged to exercise initiative and take risk or would they articulate their belief that they are criticized for doing it? There is a huge difference here. Can your employees/staff recite examples of initiative and risk taking that have been costly for them or for others?

In many high-fear, low-trust, Third Reich organizations people have learned that you don't exercise initiative or take risks unless it's the boss's idea. If it's your idea, it will be criticized; if it's the boss's idea, it's an absolute "brainstorm inspired by divine intervention." In other words, don't do anything unless you're told to because if you do, it will be wrong. The result is that employees will literally stand around waiting to be told what to do. Why? Because we've proved to them that if they do something on their own, there is a price to be paid. These same managers who create this environment would loudly chastise their people for being unmotivated, uncaring, and unwilling to work.

4. Productivity Decreasing and "Extra Efforts" Disappearing

Workers and staff will only do the bare minimum necessary to keep their jobs in high-fear, low-trust environments. There is little or no motivation to be a top performer and the resentment generated in such an environment renders workers/staff unwilling to do more than is absolutely necessary.

♦ They don't *want* to be the best performer.
♦ They don't *want* to produce the best quality of which they are capable.
♦ They don't *want* to make their boss look good.
♦ They don't *want* to make their organization excel.

They resent the way they are treated and this resentment is displayed with low levels of productivity and the unwillingness to do more. One graphic example of the way we experience this behavior is when employees commit themselves to doing everything by the book. They follow all policies and procedures exactly to the "T" and this results in huge slowdowns. When we hear of planned, orchestrated work slowdowns, what is really happening is that employees comply with the absolute letter of their guidelines. We heard of an example of some state agricultural employees who routinely conduct random inspections of vehicles returning to the mainland via bridges from offshore barrier islands. To demonstrate their resentment and rejection of the management style they perceived they were being subjected to, they developed the following strategy. Over a long weekend they began at noon on Monday to inspect thoroughly every vehicle that crossed the bridge, asking every occupant to exit the vehicle and closely inspecting the vehicle's contents. The resulting traffic jam was horrendous. A relatively short trip, even on a busy holiday weekend, took agonizing hours to complete. The agriculture department employees were merely doing things "by the book" and quickly made their point not only with the public, but with the management structure of their department.

5. CYA (Cover Your Anatomy) Becoming an Art Form

Valuable, productive time is unproductively utilized by protecting oneself from accountability and blame. The focus is not on what we need to accomplish but on proving that whatever happened wasn't our fault. Some examples of CYA behavior:

♦ Favorable measurements are predetermined. Significant amounts of time are spent even before a task or project begins. Negotiating the standard of measurement to ensure that no matter how bad the actual outcome, we can somehow be made to look good.

♦ Memos, E-mails, and FYIs of various forms are communicated in order to have written backup of agreements, communications, results, etc. Documentation for self-defense purposes has become a job activity of its own.

♦ Journals are kept, summarizing conversations, formal or informal, to be used later to protect oneself.

♦ Logs are kept, detailing activities of supervisors or peer employees; i.e., if I am being criticized for tardiness, I will keep a log of the daily arrival times of others in my peer group to establish that my behavior is the norm and not the negative exception.

Why are we consuming so much valuable time playing C.Y.A.? In the face of inevitable, pending punishment, we learn to defend ourselves, to deflect the blow. The result — lower productivity and higher costs.

6. Increased Passive/Aggressive Behavior

Passive/aggressive behaviors can be those of commission, e.g., sabotage, or those of omission, e.g., withholding support or information. We smile at people, verbally support their ideas and actions, and work behind the scenes (i.e., behind their backs) to disrupt what they are doing.

Commission:
♦ Deleting information from a computer program
♦ Writing anonymous letters to upper levels of management criticizing and accusing others of detrimental activities
♦ Damaging equipment
♦ Starting negative rumors
♦ Vandalizing
♦ Writing on restroom walls: prose, poetry, and artwork
♦ Publishing anonymous underground newsletters, reports, exposés, etc.

Omission:
♦ Intentionally not solving a problem — "letting the chips fall where they may"
♦ Intentionally withholding information from a manager or supervisor — it's not lying; it's just not telling the whole story
♦ Failing to take action to support someone else's efforts in a timely fashion
♦ Saying "I forgot"
♦ Inventing convenient illness or other reason for absenteeism during peak-demand periods
♦ Being unwilling to help others or go above and beyond
♦ Saying "It's not my job"

7. High AT&T (Absenteeism, Tardiness, and Turnover)

Absenteeism. People don't look forward to coming to work and will seize any opportunity, reasonable or unreasonable, to justify not coming. If there is a light dusting of snow on the ground, they are snowed in. If they have a sore throat, they stay home. If a family member has a crisis, they are always the one to sacrifice and stay home to work it out. When a car problem arises, they stay home rather than find alternative transportation. The bottom line is they don't look forward to being at work.

Tardiness. While there may be many reasons for repetitive tardiness, one of them is avoidance. People dislike coming to work in high-fear low-trust environments and may delay the inevitable as long as possible; staying too long at home in the morning, not leaving the restaurant until the absolute last minute, even hanging around the company cafeteria as long as they can to avoid going to work. Another demonstration of this avoidance is allowing everything else to take priority over an on-time arrival.

- ◆ Having to drive a neighbor to work
- ◆ Having to have work done on the car
- ◆ Having to run an errand on the way to work
- ◆ All of the other creative reasons employees dream up for being late

Turnover. Very simply, people who have options do not remain in high-fear, low-trust, Third Reich environments. If they are unhappy with and resentful of the way they are being treated, they choose to move on. Those who tend to remain are those who perceive that they have nowhere else to go or those whose options may truly be limited. One prediction is that with the change in health care laws recently enacted by Congress and signed by the president that allows employees with preexisting conditions to take their health care with them when they leave will result in an even greater exodus of productive people from Third Reich environments. This change in the laws removes a stumbling block that has restricted many people from making a desired job change, and some organizations are going to be shocked at the volume of the chorus of the long-standing country music refrain of "Take this job and shove it."

8. Obsequious Behavior

Widespread displays of obsequious, kowtowing behavior are sure signs that people with power are feared within the organization. Much of the activity is directed toward pleasing those who are in power whether or not the activity contributes to organizational objectives. When this sort of behavior is evidenced in an organization, it is based on real, not imagined, consequences of displeasing those in power. As we previously discussed, the Third Reich managers' insistence on unwavering, blind loyalty to themselves, as opposed to exceptional job performance and/or customer service, emphasizes, this culture of keeping the bosses happy and making them look good to avoid the fearful consequences.

9. Blaming

Blaming is a reactive response (*post hoc*) intended to distance oneself from responsibility for events that have already taken place. Written documentation is a formal, ritualized demonstration of blaming. Other common examples:

- ◆ "Don't blame me, it's not my fault."
- ◆ "It was the other shift's fault" (or department, team, group, etc. — any source of blame will do in a pinch).
- ◆ "Nobody told me. How am I supposed to know if nobody tells me what's going on?"

Why is blaming so prevalent? For many reasons; number one is that in high-fear, low-trust organizations someone must be singled out to be at fault. The focus is on who did it as opposed to what happened. Negative consequence is attached to the fault finding and it is without a doubt in everyone's best interest not to be the person who absorbs the blame. To avoid this, we blame others. Another key influence here is that blaming is also a great internal self-defense strategy. If we can successfully blame others, we never have to look in the mirror and take personal responsibility for the things that happen. Being an effective blamer has short-term payoff and long-term downside. People who blame don't grow, don't learn from their mistakes, and forfeit the trust and respect of those in their environment. High-fear, low-trust organizations institutionalize this dysfunctional behavior.

10. Informing

While blaming is a reactive behavior, informing is a proactive behavior, that is, distancing oneself from responsibility before the event takes place or before it has been discovered. In children, we call this tattletale behavior and most parents try to weed this behavior out very early in a child's life. In high-fear, low-trust Third Reich organizations this behavior is encouraged, cultivated, and actually reinforced. Favor is bestowed upon employees who inform. This generates distrust and disrespect, not only toward the organization and its leadership, but also toward members of the peer group as well. Employees will eavesdrop on conversations, rifle other people's files, perhaps listen in on phone conversations, so that they can be the first to "tip the boss off" to "what's really going on around here." Frequent demonstrations of this type of behavior indicate that employees are willing to sacrifice peer relationships to avoid punishment and curry the boss's favor. Informants eventually incur the wrath of their peers and become ostracized and isolated. Despised by their peer group and encouraged through their leadership, they are actually held in low esteem and respect. They have no point of group identification.

11. Hostile Interpersonal Relationships

When people cannot strike out at or respond directly to the source of the fear or the threat, they may displace their anger and resentment toward easier or less-threatening targets (each other). High incidence of verbal abuse, nonverbal demonstrations of resentment and anger, threatening behaviors, attempts at intimidation of fellow employees are all examples of this behavior. Total withdrawal or refusal to communicate is seen at the other end of this behavioral spectrum. This tends to splinter the group, and, in many cases, this splintering is eventually reversed as workers and staff unite in an effort to deal with the high fear and low trust. Unionization is a legitimate option once cohesion begins, but prior to that happening, it's not uncommon for employee groups to express their resentment in behaviors toward one another.

12. Overall Demonstrations of Negativity

This negativity is best seen as expressions of a cannot-do attitude vs. a can-do attitude. It is exemplified by identification with the prediction of absolute downside outcomes vs. expressions of probable positive results. This negativity is expressed by predictable and consistent disagreement with everything that is said. Such people make an art form of predicting impending doom and searching for disturbed negative meaning in positive reporting.

An example: An organization has significantly increased its spending on upgrading its plant facility, replacing worn-out equipment with new, painting and repairing the interior and exterior of their facilities, and investing in state-of-the-art technology. This positive activity was seen by employees as proof that they were "upgrading and pouring money into this place just to sell it."

> Improvements in organizations cannot occur without leaders who develop an environment of trust so that every employee is willing to take the risks associated with change in that organization.*
>
> Robert W. Galvin
> Chairman of the Executive Committee, Motorola

Cherie Carter-Scott, in her book *The Corporate Negaholic*, lists the following ten clues that corporate negativity, or as she describes it corporate negaholism, exists:

- ◆ People's behavior is motivated out of a desire to protect themselves, each other, or to preserve the status quo rather than fulfill the mission of the organization.
- ◆ People's individual compulsions, addictions, and neuroses begin to dominate and determine the strategy, activities, and even the direction of the company.
- ◆ Individuals turn the negativity they feel about themselves toward the organization that employs them.
- ◆ Employees spend the majority of their time criticizing or judging their co-workers, the management of the organization, the policies, or the way things are being done instead of taking constructive action.
- ◆ Employees act out the sentiment, "Why would I want to be part of an organization that would have me as an employee?"
- ◆ Individuals unconsciously work out their unresolved childhood issues (i.e., the pursuit of attention, recognition, approval, love, sibling rivalry, rebellion against authority figures, etc.) with their families in a work environment.
- ◆ The self-sabotage that individuals personally experience is transferred to the organization.
- ◆ Dysfunctional behavior contaminates employees, who in turn infect the customers, which seriously affects the bottom line.
- ◆ The "I can'ts" have taken over through a long, slow process, inculcating the majority of employees in such a way that they have become addicted to their own negativity.

---

*From foreword to *Teaching the New Basic Skills,* by Richard J. Murnane and Frank Levy, New York, Free Press, 1996.

♦ There is no consequence-management and, therefore, no incentive for individuals to strive for excellence and make a difference.*

While there is certainly anecdotal evidence of cases where fear has resulted in productive levels of activation or motivation, we believe that high, sustained levels of fear created by the leadership of organizations are more likely to lead to negative consequences for the organization.

Ryan and Oestreich in their book *Driving Fear out of the Workplace* state that their research "indicated that fear did have some place as a motivator but only under restricted conditions. Slightly over 10% of the research responses suggested that fear can be a positive stimulus but only if it is self-imposed; that is, when a person takes on a risk as a personal or professional stretch, fear may be a successful self-motivator. Another group of responses reflected the idea that fear could work in the short term but not the long term and even here there were deficits."

We agree that self-imposed fear can be a positive motivator. Fear can also be a positive motivator if its source is generated from outside the organization, from a competitor, or a deadline, for example, but internally generated fear, while it may accomplish things short term, will have, long-term, disastrous consequences. Going to the well of fear in rare extreme circumstances may have little negative consequence, but return trips to that well, or as a consistent strategy, are costly, unproductive, and destroy trust and respect. People who are preoccupied by fear are much less likely to take the initiative, to engage in risk taking, or to be innovative. They are more likely to engage in survival behaviors, those behaviors designed to protect themselves (CYAs). The overriding criterion becomes not what contribution will it make to organizational objectives, but rather what will be the consequences for me personally.

In addition, many people who employ fear as a management technique or tool wield it in the pursuit of personal, not organizational objectives. Long-term consequences, as already discussed, include lack of risk taking, little or no initiative or innovation, and a predilection for the absolute minimum effort or activity. The fear of doing the wrong thing can be paralyzing for the individual and the organization and overrides the quest to do the right thing.

---

* *The Corporate Negaholic,* Cherie Carter-Scott, New York: Ballantine Books, 1991, pp. 4, 5.

- ◆ Organizational goals and objectives are neglected in favor of self-protection or self-aggrandizement.
- ◆ Organizations with very high levels of fear can expect to lose their best people first (they have the most options).
- ◆ There will be higher levels of workplace stress in organizations where fear is prevalent. (As previously mentioned, in some areas, workplace stress is the fastest growing source of workmen's compensation claims. Stress also increases health care costs.)
- ◆ If the organization becomes widely known as a place where fear reigns, it will make recruiting and retaining a talented workforce more difficult.
- ◆ Loyalty to the organization will be reduced or extinguished.

All of these consequences will increase costs and reduce competitive capability. In other words, in a highly competitive economy, with increasing demand for talented, committed workers, can we afford to be an organization based on fear? We think not.

FEAR IS AN EXPENSIVE MANAGEMENT TOOL.

Chapter 5 will now look at current topics of organizational restructuring and how performance-driven leaders handle these challenges.

CHAPTER 5

RESTRUCTURING: DOWNSIZING, UPSIZING, AND RIGHTSIZING

We use coined, harmless-sounding terms, downsizing, upsizing, rightsizing, to describe how we take people's jobs away and inflict havoc on their lives and our organizations. No matter which term is used, all of these restructuring techniques share some common attributes and consequences. All of these efforts disrupt the organization and impact negatively on the employees who go and on the employees who stay.

Restructuring, especially downsizing, has been a very prominent force in the arena of business organizations of the 1980s and 1990s. A significant change in the use of downsizing has been to employ this tool when the organization is *not* experiencing financial crisis. A common motive ascribed to downsizing and other restructuring moves during recent years has been either to retain or to regain a competitive posture. In many cases, restructuring has taken place during high, even growing levels of profits.

Restructuring, in many cases, is a reactionary behavior that is being used to reduce bloated levels in an organization that has grown as a result of poor leadership and bad staffing decisions. Much of the job elimination has come at the expense of management. Middle management has been the level hardest hit in efforts to downsize, rightsize, upsize, etc. This, in and of itself, is a tremendous challenge for performance-driven leaders because the leaders' span of control increases dramatically and they must influence more people and, in some cases, tasks and functions with which they are not familiar.

George Mosher had some thoughts on avoiding layoffs:

> Our policy is not to lay off people, if possible, and we really focus on the managers to not hire unless they are willing to make that same kind of capital commitment. The starting salary is only probably half of the total cost of an employee, and if you multiply that starting salary times two, because the employee is not going to be at that starting salary forever, and multiply that by five, that's probably the capital investment you are making to add another permanent employee. So it's better to use temporaries or to do something else before you instantly knee-jerk react to hire people. What we are trying to do is keep the number of people down, and I see a lot of indication in this country that that's not happening. People sort of get regarded as pegs, and there's no loyalty because they've been treated that way.

When we hire without a thoughtful plan, or when we use promotion as a payoff to people who deserve to move up as opposed to creating positions only when the positions make a significant contribution to our core tasks, we create an obese organization that lends itself to downsizing.

Make no mistake, poor management has led, in many cases, to the need to downsize. Rather than applauding management for being willing to make the tough decisions and take decisive action in reducing the size of its organization, management should be judged harshly for the previous actions that made all of this necessary.

George Mosher added:

> Too many companies have asked "What does the employee deserve?" The result is they give them promotions to jobs that don't really exist. [Positions are created to reward employees resulting in a bloated level within the organization which doesn't really address the core responsibilities and adds to overall costs.] Then they discover that they have 20,000 too many managers. And it was all because Susie or John deserved the opportunity to grow. They hired someone to replace Susie or John in the real job, and now they keep busy because people will keep themselves busy, and costs become too high to be competitive. This whole structure that's been built up is very costly. We have worked very hard to say we are not promoting you just because you are doing a good job.

Like any cost-cutting technique, downsizing offers the allure of a short-term upward movement in profits, often dramatic. In addition, large-scale downsizing has frequently led to a favorable response in the stock markets, as investors reward what is viewed as hard-nosed management taking the bold steps necessary to increase efficiency (and earnings per share). There is evidence, however, that stocks of organizations that have engaged in large, especially repeated, job slashing have not outperformed other stocks over the longer term. At any rate, this short-term payoff is directed toward a narrow segment of the organization's stake holders, specifically higher management and shareholders, particularly executives who take the money and run and shareholders who take their profits in the near term.

However, cost cutting alone does not guarantee long-term competitive success. As several astute observers have expressed, we cannot grow operationally by cutting, nor will cost cutting alone expand market share. Life is much more complex than that. And while there may be some gains for some shareholders in the short term, there appears to be a number of significant negative consequences, both short and long term.

DOWNSIZING BRINGS SHORT-TERM GAINS AND SIGNIFICANT SHORT- AND LONG-TERM INCREASED COSTS.

Among the negative short-term consequences of massive and/or repeated downsizing may be disruption of customer relationships, some period of organizational chaos, diversion of focus from quality, stifling of initiative and creativity, reduction or stagnation in productivities, serious economic consequences for those who are downsized (fired, laid off, surplused, reallocated, etc.), and "survivor syndrome" among employees who remain in the organization.

When an organization is restructured, not only are people removed, but, by definition, organizational structure is changed. We begin to eliminate and consolidate, and often the first things to go are

- Compensation increases
- The training department
- The advertising department
- Customer service
- The "extras" that we do for our customers

All of these have significant short-term and long-term downsides. A horrible flaw that exists in the structuring mentality of many organizations is the idea that fewer people can continue to produce the same level of quality, efficiency, and productivity. This would be valid if it were true that an awful lot of people had been standing around doing nothing. While there may be isolated incidents, this is not usually the case. It doesn't take a mathematical genius to see that in the case of downsizing, rightsizing, upsizing, whatever, subtraction is not addition. Yes, restructuring can stop the hemorrhage of dollars. Yes, restructuring has an initial reduction in cost, but it comes at a significant price, and often that price is not anticipated or planned. Denial has taken on new dimensions as executive levels of organizations plow into restructuring like the proverbial bull in a china shop.

There are exceptions to every rule, but, unfortunately, in far too many organizations downsizing may lead to less efficiency.

DOWNSIZING EQUALS FEWER PEOPLE DOING LESS, LESS EFFICIENTLY.

Almost certainly, any large-scale reduction in force will result in customers coming into contact with new faces, voices, and personalities in the organization. Employees will be dealing with new (to them) customers. Sometimes, this may disrupt relationships built on mutual respect over many years. While some customers may respond positively to these new persons, some may not.

During almost all large-scale restructuring efforts, the organization enters a period of relative chaos as adjustment is made to new reporting, collaborative supporting, servicing, and information-flow relationships. Again, this adjustment may disrupt long-standing relationships, both formal and informal, that had been developed to facilitate a certain way (the old way) of doing business.

Of course, there will be no further input into quality improvement, innovation, or creativity from those who have been ushered out the door. Employees who remain on the job will also be distracted by the need to form new relationships, and have concern for their own jobs, and in many cases, an expanded workload. It may sound trite, but there are only so many hours in a day, and people cannot do more than they have time to do.

When faced with a restructuring reality, one of the first strategies of the performance-driven leader is to analyze the workload and the yields in productivity. We now have fewer people, and these fewer people cannot continue to do the same amount of work. The result is we have to "major in the majors," rather than "major in the minors". Careful thought and analysis must be given to identifying the truly critical tasks, those most important to the overall success of the department, team, or entire organization, and insuring these are given first priority. Fewer people cannot continue to do everything just as before. Make sure what is left undone are the less important, less critical tasks. Key questions must be asked by the performance-driven leader:

♦ What are we doing that really doesn't need to be done?
♦ What reporting can be eliminated or reduced, freeing up valuable time?
♦ Are we continuing in our pursuit of obsolete practices long after they are no longer necessary?
♦ How can our technology be used to free up people's productive time further?
♦ What are we doing that is urgent, but really not important?
♦ How do we reduce the crisis mentality that diverts our efforts into high-stress firefighting activities?
♦ What can we do to contain the workplace stress that will increase with escalating demands?

A proverbial 80/20 rule suggests that 20% of what we do gives us 80% of our true efficiency and productivity. The performance-driven leader focuses on identifying that 20%, doing it well, and as much as possible reducing the 80% of activity that appears important but truly is insignificant.

Because the workload has dramatically increased for surviving employees, productivity has likely stagnated or its growth significantly slowed. Too often the same or increased workload is heaped upon fewer people using the same processes as before. Where fear and a need to survive dominate the consciousness, "Quality will *not* be job one." When quality suffers, our relationships with our customers suffer. And while customers can be patient and understanding with the plight of our organization, their patience is not infinite. Many organizations have acknowledged that they have cut too deeply in restructuring, dramatically reducing their service to their customers, and have suffered significantly either in loss of business or, at the very least, in bad public relations. While most organizations benefit from a well-planned pruning of their customer base (reducing low-end, low-profit, inappropriately high maintenance customers), when that pruning begins to shear away the customers on whom our future growth development and survival depend, it is not a healthy strategy. How many organizations, through restructuring and reductions, antagonize the core of their customers?

Employees who are terminated (yes, it sounds much harsher expressed so!) will experience the very negative consequences of loss of income, loss of security, loss of esteem (from both self and others), disruption of social relationships, loss of identity, and in some cases, the possible loss of physical assets, such as their home. Loss of ability to fund retirement, children's education, and health setbacks is also a factor. Those who lose their jobs may also be required to undergo long periods of unemployment (with all its economic and social implications), underemployment, and/or relocation (which will disrupt family, social, school, and community relationships). It is no wonder that there is a relationship between loss of job/income and increases in domestic violence. In extreme cases, workers undergoing such stress may direct their violence toward the former workplace. Although not common, this can be quite tragic when it does occur. How displaced employees are treated is very important.

EMPLOYEES LEAVING THE ORGANIZATION SHOULD BE TREATED WITH RESPECT.

Neither bosses nor co-workers should make light of the loss being suffered by these people. Their loss should be recognized and acknowledged as such. Loss of our job is second only to the death of our spouse or child in its impact on our lives. Displaced workers should be given a chance to grieve their loss and possibly should be directed to counseling and other programs supported by the former employer. But grieving is not enough. Most responsible organizations provide a wide range of support to departing employees, generally under the heading of "outplacement services." Outplacement activities can and should, in our view, include counseling for emotional problems, substance abuse, family tensions, and other personal needs. But a broader view of counseling will provide advice on financial management, real estate sale, relocation, education and training opportunities. Other support activities can include training, job search procedures, interviewing techniques, resume writing, and skills assessment.

The employer can create and maintain job banks and referral lists. In some cases, the organization outplacing the individual can even provide short-term skills training designed to help the former employee transition to a new job.

Whatever level of support the organization can reasonably afford, it should be provided to displaced employees. On the large scale for dislocations that characterizes contemporary restructuring, the organization is not discharging people for fault. Those leaving have, in most cases, been good employees, dedicated and productive. Often the progenitors of the need to downsize have been failings on the part of management, e.g., lack of strategic vision, haphazard staffing and work design processes, overcommitment of resources, etc. Helping ease the pain of separation for previously valued employees speaks to the very character of the restructuring firm. How it treats its discharged employees will speak volumes to surviving workers, to customers, to investors, to prospective employees (yes, downsized firms will be hiring again, often sooner rather than later), and to critical elements of the political environment. For their years of faithful service, most displaced employees deserve respect and support. During the mid 1980s, one of the authors ran an outplacement center for ARCO. This company never hesitated to provide any requested support for its outplaced employees. Unfortunately, we focused almost all our efforts on those who were leaving. We generally overlooked the very real needs of those who would remain in the organization.

Implementation of Restructuring

How does the performance-driven leader implement restructuring?

- ◆ Communicate early and completely.
- ◆ Be truthful.
- ◆ Listen and acknowledge people's reaction.
- ◆ Care for the casualties — nurture.
- ◆ Reinforce appropriate long-term behavior.

Communicate Early and Completely

When bad news is inevitable, share it with the entire group as early and completely as possible. Don't hold anything back. If there's going to be a layoff (downsizing, upsizing, restructuring, rightsizing, whatever the euphemism of the moment may be), announce the true number of jobs to be cut; don't soften the blow with intentionally distorted low estimates. If we must amputate, do it all at once. Don't cut off the foot one toe at a time! Minimizing the true impact is a sign of leadership weakness and somehow assumes that people aren't strong enough to deal with the truth. Early and completely should go together. One organization told its employees, "Some 40% of you will be laid off. We will get back to each of you individually over the next 2 weeks to let you know who will go and who will stay." Imagine what this did to everyone's morale!

Be Truthful

Tell people the truth. If their department or position is vulnerable, don't offer false reassurances. If the facility is to be closed, don't tell them that it's just a downsizing and that some will be able to keep their jobs. In the turmoil of bad news, trusting the truthfulness of the leader's communication may be the only anchor that people have in a storm of fear and uncertainty. In any organization, there will always be the doubters those negative individuals who loudly proclaim that "management is lying to us, they aren't telling us the truth, and it's really going to be much worse than they said." Weak managers become "willing allies" in proving these people correct and in providing them with actual untruthful targets to attack.

Lani Arredondo has this to say:

> Trust is synonymous with truth. In my experience and observation, leaders make a big mistake when they lie to people. If you are telling me lies or if I perceive that what you are saying is a lie or a falsehood, that is an untruth that destroys trust because we don't trust lies. If an organization is facing restructuring and final decisions have not been made or there are certain aspects of timing that must be addressed, it may not be appropriate to go public with the information. In my view, at that point, the leader should say nothing instead of going to people and giving them false reassurances or false hopes like: "Don't worry, we are in great shape." "The company is growing." "We are not going to have layoffs." That was a big mistake AT&T made. They announced layoffs, they said that's the last of them, and then less than a year later, they announced another 30,000 to 40,000 jobs were being cut.
>
> I think we need to trust that people, in the majority, are more resilient or stronger than we sometimes give them credit for. We think we can't deliver bad news because people won't take it well. I think we need to deliver bad news when it's necessary to do so and then provide people with the tools and resources they need for dealing effectively with the bad news. As an example, I worked with an organization several years ago that was closing down a

customer service department in one of their local offices due to a regional centralization. There were 40 to 45 people who were going to be laid off. As soon as that decision had been made and finalized, the announcement was made to those people directly. At that same time they were given a schedule of training by outplacement services and consultants who were going to be personally available to help them with updating their resumes and building their skills. Number one, they were told the truth. Number two, they were provided with the resources and support for dealing effectively with the bad news. That's how you build trust.

Listen and Acknowledge People's Reaction

In the wake of bad news, people will respond in widely different ways. Some will take it in stride, some will become very angry, others will be very fearful about an uncertain future. All of these emotions are predictable and normal. Permit people their reactions. Don't expect everyone to greet the news with great enthusiasm! Don't berate, ridicule, or ignore their legitimate issues. Acknowledge that their issues are valid and, most importantly, help people to begin to identify their options.

LEADERS IDENTIFY OPTIONS.

Be attuned to the feelings of victimization.

VICTIMS ARE PEOPLE WHO PERCEIVE THEY HAVE NO OPTIONS.

People feel victimized by things happening to them when they think there's nothing they can do to correct them. Help people identify what options are available. The options are out there in many cases; people just don't see them. (Example: When downsizing is announced, help people to identify their options. How can they be included in the percentage of people who will stay? Can an increase in their productivity positively influence decisions in their favor? What other employment opportunities are available? What training do they need to prepare themselves to compete in the current job market?)

Care for the Casualties — Nurture

Once options are identified, the performance-driven leader will offer as much support as humanly possible to help the best options become reality. For example, if raises are being denied or compensation is being reduced, providing guidance on debt consolidation or budgeting could be very appropriate. Many organizations provide their employees with these skills even in good times, not just in the face of bad news. (These are skills that benefit employees, not only in the short-term, but throughout their entire lives.) If we are downsizing and people are losing their jobs, there are certain areas of information that are always appropriate:

- *Financial options* — Is there severance? Explain the laws of unemployment compensation (they vary from state to state). Are there other agencies that may help them during their short-term financial crisis? What are the benefit package provisions, etc.?

- *Job search* — Is there any outplacement service that will be provided? Teach people how to write an effective resume. Are there typing/printing services available? Teach networking skills. Are there videos/publications to guide them through this process? Can state employment agency representatives be utilized? Can we coach them on appropriate skills for interviewing? Most people go on very few interviews in their adult working lifetime. The prospect of having to interview for a job and present skills is intimidating to even the most highly qualified people. They question their ability to interview effectively. It's very difficult to be confident about skills you rarely use.

- *Counseling* — What can we do to help people keep a healthy balance when they are experiencing bad events? How can we help them to make sure that events at work don't travel to other areas of their lives? (It's all too common for job loss to end up in family problems.) What sources of help can we recommend? Are there employee assistance programs, faith affiliations, public health programs, etc.? Identify what's out there to help people during this short-term negative event.

Extending as much support as possible to the casualties of bad news is important for two reasons:

1. It's the right thing to do. Preparing people to deal successfully with their future is the right thing to do and is of paramount importance to a performance-driven leader. It's raising their worth and it's having them exit their experience with greater levels of skills than when they entered. Exploitation is using people's skills and giving them nothing in return. Growth and development is providing them with marketable skills that will enhance their future value.
2. It impresses upon those employees that remain that the leader and the organization will do everything within their sphere of influence and control to assist those whose short-term future has been disrupted. It's the difference between projecting a caring vs. a callous image.

The National Selected Morticians, a professional affiliation of high-quality, high-standard funeral homes, has a useful motto:

FUNERALS ARE FOR THE LIVING.

It's very important that the people who remain with the organization see those who are being forced to leave as being treated fairly and compassionately. When cuts are brutally inflicted with little regard for terminated people and their families, a horrible negative message is sent and results in a delayed exodus by those remaining. People whose jobs have survived do not want to work for a callous organization and begin their own job search. The people who do not move on are the lower producers and tend to be those with little or no options (not the people who will make us great!).

Reinforce Appropriate Long-Term Behavior

If leaders desire a long-term outcome from their employees, then it's appropriate to offer incentives for that outcome. For example, if a facility is to be closed, communicate the target date and what the organization will do for the employees who remain until that date in areas of eventual outplacement, training, and financial reward. Design severance and benefit packages that encourage people to leave at the optimal time. Some organizations use most of their resources to compensate those who leave first, having little for those who remain loyal to the end.

Ron Stewart was the head of the southeastern regional distribution center for Dana Corporation located in Athens, GA. It was an automotive and light truck parts distribution center and served clients who were involved primarily in the automotive after market business, selling replacement auto parts. The decision was made to close this facility, and Ron was the leader who, along with his leadership team, had to make the announcement of the plant closing and maintain productivity between the time of the announcement and the actual time of closing.

About the decision to close, Ron said:

> It was a strategic decision, looking at how we could more effectively distribute a product using cross-stocking methods and better transportation methods. These were the primary reasons. It had nothing to do with the productivity of the facility. Unfortunately, this particular facility was not in the best location for our future needs. It was a good location and had served us very well, but we looked at what we needed to do for the future, and it was not in the best place for us. I supported that decision. I was a part of creating the plan of how to change as we moved into the year 2000. I was a part of it and I agreed with the plan that the facility should close because it did not seem to fit the needs of the future, even though it was a very productive plant.

Ron said the following about making the announcement of the facility closing to the employees/staff:

> Unfortunately, in the workplace there are times that you have to convey bad news. I have experienced probably the worst news that you could ever tell any employee, and that is that they are going to lose their job because the facility is closing and there will be no more work in the future. When people go through layoffs and downsizing and those types of things, I think people tend to see that at least they might have a chance of coming back to work, or of finding work in the future as long as the facility is still going to be in place. But in this case, we had to tell people that the plant was closing — period.

We asked Ron what he had done to prepare to convey this bad news. He said:

It's not so much what we have to do in conveying bad news; it's what we have done up to that point to be able to convey the bad news. It's the management style over time that has taken place regardless of good news or bad news. The thing we did before the announcement was that we believed in a lot of communication, and in our communication we believed that we stayed within the highest ethical, moral, and legal standards that we could to convey information that we thought our employees needed to make good decisions in the workplace.

Additionally, the employees were given a 6- or 7-month notice, but it turned out to be much longer as the closing deadline was advanced at least twice. It was obvious that the decision was made to convey the bad news as early as possible to avoid surprises for the employees and prepare them to experience as little disruption in their lives as possible. We asked Ron what were the factors involved in timing the announcement of the plant closing.

There were probably three factors that were involved in this particular case. We were looking at the overall plan of our organization, and we had to keep consideration of our customers at the highest level. They are very important to us, and notifying them and getting them to understand was a priority. Also, there were the obvious employee considerations. We had strong relationships with our employees and, in some cases, we had as much as 18-year relationships with quite a few of our people. We felt very strongly that our employees deserved as much notification as possible, and as much support, help, and training that we could give them, both from the local standpoint as well as an overall organizational standpoint from the Dana Corporation. We wanted to support them in continuing their careers, we hoped successfully within another company in the local community, or perhaps even stay within Dana Corporation, if they chose to relocate. We felt that because we had done a lot of very good things (we had turned this facility in about 3 years from a very negative facility to a very positive one), we felt that the timing was such that we could give our people as much notification as possible without having really a lot of disruption in the workplace. We anticipated the initial reaction of disappointment; that employees would be losing their job because of the closing of the facility, but we felt we could overcome that if we did the right things and continued to do the right things for our people.

To announce the closing, a facilitywide, structured meeting was held so that everyone would receive the information at the same time.

> We said we would spend as much time with people as they needed. What happened, even during that day, was that people went back to work. They talked on the floor, and that was expected. But the next day it was kind of scary because it was almost business as usual. People did have questions and concerns, but they still kept them in the context of doing their job, doing it very well, and very productively, as opposed to being disruptive in the workplace or disruptive to others around them.

When we discussed productivity after the announcement, Ron said:

> We knew that we would go through an emotional roller-coaster ride when we announced it. There would be sadness, madness, high anxiety, perhaps some resentment. But I realize overall, as I look back, the drop in productivity was so insignificant, we were probably more critical of what we thought it was going to be, from a management standpoint, versus the reality. And I guess we kind of underestimated the people. The drop in productivity was basically negligible. And when you look at that particular month, it was at the end of the month when we announced it, we saw no dramatic drops, no decrease in productivity; it was almost like it didn't occur. Even though these people were losing their jobs, the effort was tremendous. They continued to improve on their productivity and to do the right things. Not only were they shipping the typical workload out of the facility, they had also picked up work from the other two facilities that were supposed to take on the customer base when we closed. The fact that people would still have that much commitment to the company and to the organization speaks a lot about them as individuals. I hope, it also speaks about the management and the things we had done to create the environment that we could announce a plant closing without experiencing a lot of negativity in the workplace. People continued to produce in a very positive environment. We maintained productivity, I think, because people perceived and understood our sensitivity to what was happening. It wasn't that we just

stood up and said this facility is closing, in a cold, unsympathetic way. People felt all of our compassion and empathy. I think they felt that since we were a team and we worked very hard as a team throughout the whole organization, it wasn't like we were picking on any one individual or one department. And we really didn't have anything negative to say about why we were closing. It was a legitimate business decision. We were closing because of a strategic plan and not because of anything or anyone that we could point fingers at, not because management had done a bad job or the people at the facility had done a bad job. People felt as if they were committed to continue to do their jobs and do them well, and that's what happened.

Ron addressed the continued productivity and how it was measured:

We had put a plan together in October, a 1-year plan, very typical as most businesses do. It addressed how we would continually improve our business, all of the financial areas, and productivity and efficiency. We had been doing very well and, in fact, in most areas we had anticipated about a 10 to 15% increase in the measurement, whatever it was, expense to sales or internal sales, return on assets, customer errors, etc. Up until February, when we made the announcement, we had blown all of those numbers away. It was just unbelievable. We made the announcement in February, and after the announcement in March the improvement continued. We did not continue on an incline like we were from November to February, but we still continued to improve. The improvement percentages dropped off some, but improvement was still there. We had a few blips here and there, but those blips were primarily due to other factors which caused our efficiency to go down, but nothing related to the productivity or the quality of the people and the job that they were doing.

Another example of our goal was to have two ideas per person per month. Up until we announced the closing, we were averaging within a range of about 3.4 to 3.7 ideas per person per month, with very close to 100% participation of all our employees every month. We also had about an 80% implementation rate of ideas each month. When we made the announcement, that dropped pretty drastically. That was one area that did. It dropped down to about 1.6 ideas per month, just slightly under our goal. But in March, we did make a rebound and we got back to over two ideas per person per month. The rate did drop some as we moved into the later months, not because I think employees were not wanting to participate and look at what they could do to improve the workplace and their job performance, but simply because we took the emphasis off the program because we felt we didn't want the employees to perceive that we were browbeating them, in a sense, to come up with ideas knowing that the long term was not there.

We asked Ron what they had done to help their employees through this period of transition and prepare them for their next career moves. We were also curious to know how they were able to encourage people to stay through the entire closing and not jump ship prematurely. Ron responded:

We didn't encourage our employees to leave or stay. What we tried to do was encourage our employees to evaluate the right thing based on their personal lives, their family, and so on. And we tried to work with each one of them as much as we could on a one-to-one basis, still keeping the group and the team in mind and why we were there — to serve the customer. We provided a number of training and development opportunities. We had planned to continue our ongoing training in the workplace, but once we announced the closing, what we did was change our training from a focus on our future business development to helping people meet their short-term needs of understanding what was happening to them and dealing with it from a personal level and a family level.

Ron went on to describe the training that was provided:

We provided our employees outplacement training through an outplacement service company that our corporation had utilized in the past. We provided them some additional computer training that we felt was necessary for them to continue to increase and expand in their knowledge of computer skills and to assist them in looking at other job opportunities. We felt that was a critical skill. We created a window for them to understand, from a different point of view, what was happening here in the local Athens community, for those who did not want to relocate or move out of the area. We invited the Chamber of Commerce in and they gave us some insight into the type of things happening in the community. We brought some other local business and industry leaders in who spoke on the positive things that were happening and the things that people could look for. We provided people with training to help them understand the highs and lows of what they were experiencing, and that was very helpful. Trinity Solutions in Peachtree City, Georgia was very helpful to us in that regard. The outplacement training service that we utilized had various things that they helped us with in dealing with the emotional roller-coaster effect and also in helping our people put together professional resumes and other information that they would need to go out into the workplace and, I hope, find another job opportunity. They actually went through resume-writing skills, interviewing skills, and other things to help them understand the hiring process, to help them package themselves as a top candidate in any situation they would apply for.

What was the employee response to this training and support? Ron shared with us:

The employee response was overwhelming. Almost 90 plus percent of the people, as they would come out of the different training sessions and the different meetings that we conducted, would tell us that they enjoyed it, that they learned something, that they had a better understanding, and that we gave them something that they perceived would be of value to them as they moved into the future. They were very positive about it and thanked us, as management, that we thought enough of them to take the steps that we were taking, and to encourage them to look at things in a positive way versus just from the negative standpoint of "This place is closing; I'm losing my job.' " We wanted everyone to see this in the proper perspective as a next step in their career.

We asked Ron to tell us about the incentives that were offered to the employees to stay long term through the closing. His response:

We really did not have any incentives that we offered the employees. Of course, they had our standard severance package that was a part of our written policies. They did have to stay to the end to receive their severance package. Some employees chose not to, but I think those people made good choices. They seemed to be leaving early for the right reasons. People were not just leaving for the sake of leaving. The only other thing that we really did as far as incentives was that when we announced the facility closing, we addressed the issue of our bonus, or gain-sharing, program. We realized that our crystal ball didn't work so well that we would know exactly how the measurements of the program would continue to go — whether they would stay the same or whether we would experience a decrease in productivity. Although we didn't expect a huge decline, we thought that anticipating a decrease was prudent. So as we stood up and announced the facility closing, part of the presentation we made to our people was we made a commitment not to hurt them financially because they were getting about 14.7% of their compensation each month in gain sharing. So we made a commitment to go back and look at the past 6 to 8 months and average out the gain sharing program, and that's what they would receive starting in March, throughout the whole process of the facility closing. We felt that was the best approach given that we knew we would probably have up and down months. We felt committed to do that because that's what our people deserved and it was not their fault that the facility was closing and we did not want to hurt them financially.

The successful closing of the Dana facility is an example of performance-driven leaders continuing to lead their employees and staff through very difficult times and continuing to

♦ Drive peak performance
♦ Raise people's value
♦ Work with people for success
♦ Prepare employees and staff for their growth, development, and survivability

Survivor Syndrome

Those who remain after restructuring, the survivors, will have significant emotional and professional needs as they struggle with the demands of developing new relationships, of shouldering an increased workload, of mastering new and unfamiliar tasks, and of dealing with survivor guilt.

Corporate downsizing and high numbers of jobless professionals are part of what leads a majority of workers to identify 1995 as a time of high stress in the workplace. Human beings are amazingly adaptable creatures with great capacity for change. However, everyone has a threshold point of stress which when attained begins to deteriorate performance rapidly. If the level and cumulative impact of the stressing forces continue unabated over extended periods of time, after coping attempts have been less than successful, performance can approach zero, being replaced by a survival mentality, focused on whatever might promise to save one from the next round of layoffs. Often, survivors have no idea why others were let go and they were retained. Feelings of fear, anxiety, resentment, and anger are common among survivors. They may need help in coping with their reactions. They will need access to information, to counseling, and to other support activities, such as an empathetic boss or a peer support group, to deal with these feelings and to get refocused on the positive aspects of being a survivor. New working relationships should be clearly laid out, and workers should be guided and positively reinforced as they develop these new relationships. They should also be assisted in recognizing and dealing with the loss of esteemed colleagues and comfortable (and often productive) relationships. The survivors may also suffer a loss of self-esteem and may perceive their new role as less prestigious or rewarding than their old. In some cases, they will be correct. In any case, survivors will experience a range of emotional responses from relief to anger and fear. They must be able to deal with these feelings so that they can refocus on new roles and new challenges.

A majority of executives in a recent survey responded that, following restructuring, they often found themselves working too many hours, being physically exhausted, and lacking adequate resources to fulfill their new roles. Before downsizing or other major restructuring, the organization needs to take a hard look at just how much increased workload survivors can be expected to absorb and still remain productive. Though we may, in fact, be able to do more with less, the answers to "How much more?" and "When is more too much?" will be critical.

Major restructuring will almost inevitably result in many remaining workers facing new roles which encompass unfamiliar tasks, perhaps ones for which they have neither the skills nor the requisite training. If the magnitude of these new and unfamiliar tasks is great enough, it can lead to a feeling of helplessness or perceived (or real) inability to adapt and master the new role. Information, training, and coaching are essential support activities at this time. Often workers can benefit from skills assessment and guidance in developing a realistic plan for acquiring the needed skills. Some may even need redirection and assistance in voluntary transfer, reassignment, or early departure. Not everyone will be cut out of the new cloth.

Although survivors may feel relieved to still have a job, they may also experience the guilt typical of those who have survived a traumatic event. Why am I still here when others who were just as bright, talented, productive, and highly regarded as me are gone? Is it fair for me to still have everything when they have lost so much? Could I have done something that could have saved their jobs as well as mine? Should I find some way to bear my share of the pain? The less information survivors are provided about the new structure and their place in it and about why some were chosen and others were not, the more likely that feelings of survivor guilt will develop. Early, open, honest, and continuing information can help. Also, recognizing, confronting, and dealing with these feelings will be of value.

SURVIVORS NEED HELP, TOO!

Although there has been considerable debate about the benefits of massive restructuring (one study suggests that up to two thirds of these efforts are at least partially unsuccessful), most observers express the belief that downsizing and other massive restructuring strategies will continue to be widely employed, though perhaps at a declining pace. There are also a number of suggested alternatives to downsizing, such as regeneration, redirection, even growth. Even if these alternatives are increasingly considered, they also are not without their own set of costs and consequences. If having considered all the alternatives and weighed the pros and cons, the organization decides to undertake downsizing, there are better ways to do it. At the very least, downsizing needs to be recognized and accepted as a major change event in the life of the organization, with all of the implications discussed in Chapter 3.

Planning for Restructuring

HAVE A PLAN!

Like all major management endeavors, downsizing needs a plan. This plan must be well considered, fully developed, and widely communicated *prior* to the advent of the actual downsizing. This plan must address a number of critical issues. One of these is whether the departure of specific individuals should be voluntary or involuntary. Each approach has its advocates and its advantages and disadvantages. Voluntary approaches often seem to be the path of least resistance, sparing managers from the really tough decisions about who goes and who stays. Also, in our culture, many will perceive the voluntary approach to be somehow more fair. However, a strong argument can be made that if the organization must endure the pain associated with downsizing, then it really calls for a selective, therefore, involuntary, approach.

Who goes and who stays will be determined by the current and future needs of the organization. This implies that management must have a clear set of objectives for the downsizing, a clear vision for the future activities of the organization, and a well-reasoned structure that will both accomplish the objectives of the downsizing and position the organization for future success. This will be no small task. The organization and those who will bear the pain, however, deserve no less from management. Top managers typically earn big bucks from downsizing. This is how they can earn it!

Conclusion

Workers, shareholders, the community, and other important constituents should be clearly informed of the reasoning behind the downsizing and of the benefits promised. Those who will be downsized must be informed, treated with dignity and respect, compensated for their losses to the extent possible, and assisted in their transition to new opportunities. For their years of loyal and productive service, they deserve nothing less. Attention must also be paid to survivors. They must have help in dealing with their feelings, in understanding both the reason for the change and the promise of the new order of things, in identifying and developing new skills that may be required, and in regaining a reasonable sense of job security.

There are those who argue that traditional concepts of organizational loyalty are outmoded. The idea that faithful service will be rewarded with continued employment is said to sap the organization of the flexibility needed to survive and thrive in the 21st century. And it creates unrealistic expectations on the part of employees who will be inevitably doomed to disappointment. However, if the organization cannot guarantee long-term employment, it can do much to aid the employee in the development and maintenance of *employability* through opportunities for education, training, skills development, and career/employability planning. (We specifically address the performance-driven leader's role in our subsequent chapters on training and communication.)

Many professionals are more loyal to their work than to a specific organization and this can be turned into a win–win situation. If we undertake downsizing in a capricious, arbitrary, and ill-planned manner, we may be smaller in terms of the number of employees remaining and we may be even smaller in productivity, innovation, creativity, and posture for future success. In situations viewed as arbitrary or unfair, it's often the best employees who will leave, as they have the most options.

In short, evaluate the costs and benefits of downsizing carefully. Develop a new vision and a transition plan. Treat everyone fairly and with respect. And pay attention to the survivors. Also recognize that effective downsizing will require increased resources devoted to communication and to training and development. Each of these will be discussed in detail in the chapters that follow.

CHAPTER 6

PARTICIPATIVE MANAGEMENT: EMPOWERMENT AND DECISION MAKING

In this era of revolutionary rule changes, when the old motivators of long-term job security, opportunities for upward mobility, and large, steady increases in compensation no longer apply, giving employees some measure of influence over their environment is essential to productivity and job satisfaction.

Empowerment

The king of buzzwords in today's organizational jargon is *empowerment*. Empowerment is supposed to unleash productivity by giving employees ownership of the process, ensuring that they buy in to the organization's ideas, and do more with less. Never has a word been so overly used and so totally misinterpreted. Make no mistake, the issue of empowerment is critical to performance-driven leadership; however, we must actually take the space to clarify its definition.

**EMPOWERMENT IS
THE MOST MISUNDERSTOOD WORD IN AMERICA TODAY!**

Management members often misunderstand the concept and many may feel severely threatened. They may fear that if they give more authority, responsibility, and control away to their employees and involve them in decision making, the result might be higher productivity, which would mean that managers might become obsolete, unwanted, and less necessary to the organization. Obviously, this response is based in the overall insecurity of a particular manager or management team and it is very predictable and understandable.

Management's fear of participative management initiatives is something that must be identified, articulated, and resolved. To ignore it is to do so at our peril. Third Reich managers rate self-preservation as the primary concern and factor it into all areas of planning and decision making. When that self-preservation is threatened in any way, strategies of stonewalling and increased control or intimidation are forthcoming. Instead of sharing authority, control, decision making, and responsibility, Third Reich managers consolidate their own power.

Some of management's concerns are legitimate, such as

- What if employees make decisions in their own self-interest and not in the best interest of the organization and its customers?
- What if employees exceed their authority and take actions and make decisions they are neither authorized nor qualified to make?
- What if the long-term financial stability of the organization is disregarded for the short-term focus of employee benefit and morale?

These are legitimate issues for managers to consider in their dilemma of empowerment and participative management strategies.

Employees and staff also misunderstand the concept and may feel threatened.

1. Throughout their working careers, employees and staff have primarily been implicitly told: "Come to work, do your job, keep your mouth shut, and go home. If I [your manager] want you to have an idea, I will tell you what that idea should be. If I want you to have an opinion, I will tell you what that opinion should be." Now management is saying to them: We *want* you to be involved in the process. We *want* your ideas and creativity. We *want* your answers to some of the significant problems that we are facing. This is a huge change for employees to absorb.

IMPLEMENTATION OF "EMPOWERMENT" IS A MONUMENTAL SHIFT IN CULTURE FOR EMPLOYEES AND STAFF.

2. Employees and staff have a legitimate concern about their abilities to accept more authority, control, and responsibility and to participate in the decision-making process. Having never been involved in these activities before, they have not developed the skills and do not perceive they have the scope of information to consider all of these things effectively. It is a legitimate concern for them to feel they may not have the tools necessary to participate at this level.

3. Employees and staff can be extremely skeptical about management's motives for empowering them with increased authority, control, responsibility, and involvement in the decision-making process.

WHY IS MANAGEMENT DOING THIS ???

It is very easy to develop the perception that management may be "setting us up." Employees may believe management wants them to make the decisions so that if something goes wrong, they will be held responsible and not management. Given this mind-set, why are we surprised that employees are very hesitant to become involved in this process, even when they are invited in? This fear is based on years of mistrust and exposure to fear-based management tactics. This is where the chickens come home to roost!

We cannot expect employees and staff to jump blindly into this body of water until they are convinced that they have identified all of the rocks and hazards that lie below the surface. And make no mistake, they fully anticipate a wealth of rocks and hazards!

What does *empowerment* mean? *Webster's Collegiate Dictionary* is not much help!

Empower — v.t. To give authority to; to authorize — **Syn.** See ENABLE
Ant. Prohibit, restrain.

We need to move beyond the limitations and murkiness of this misunderstood concept of empowerment and consider what participative management really means to the performance-driven leader.

Lani Arredondo (1991) offers her vision of participative management as providing employees with

♦ Control
♦ Community
♦ Confidence

Lani states "In an organization where you have a high level of trust and minimal levels of fear, these three factors are not only important, they are absolutely essential because they are *must haves.*" There are a number of reasons for this.

Control

All human beings want to feel that they have some control over their lives and over what happens to them at work. And when people feel that their sense of control is threatened, they either feel they have no control or they fear losing control. There are a lot of very negative ramifications to this. People will find fear-based ways to exercise control negatively: sabotaging projects, starting rumors, expressing resentments toward management or perhaps the whole organization. These are destructive ways of negatively grappling with or grasping for control. Leaders must look for constructive ways to furnish their people with some degree of control.

Certainly no one has 100% control, but leaders will look for ways that are constructive rather than destructive. Of course, that's what participative management is all about. It's that leaders are providing people some measure of control so that they feel that they are not robotic, they are not simply reacting to the demands of others, but they are able to live out their own lives and carry out some of their own interests and directions.

Community

Human beings are social creatures. We have a need to interact with each other, and we have a need for support and encouragement. That's what we mean by a sense of community. We have seen a breakdown of community in our culture as well as in our organizations. If we lack the sense of community socially in our neighborhoods, for example, then many people have that need for sense of community fulfilled in the workplace. In the past even if you didn't know your neighbors on either side of your home, you did know your co-workers who worked on either side of you. As there have been layoffs and downsizing, and there have been hostilities growing in the workplace because of divisiveness, these and other factors are affecting the breakdown of the sense of community in the workplace. Rather than you and I as co-workers caring for one another, supporting one another, covering for one another, working collaboratively with one another, we instead tend to be at odds with one another when we don't have that sense of community. Once again, a leader will look for creative ways to help build that sense of community in the workplace.

How does a leader instill a sense of community in today's workplace? Lani responds:

> I am a great believer in the concept that a leader is not so much someone who gives directions or instructions and mandates policies and procedures, but that a leader in large part is a behavioral model. In general terms, a first step in developing a sense of community in the workplace is to demonstrate that behavior yourself. In other words, leaders need to be approachable by their people so that they know that they can come to the leader when necessary. A leader needs to interact with people in the work group for whom they are responsible. And this interaction must be in a friendly, encouraging manner, not just going out and giving orders and issuing critical performance reviews. It's necessary to keep all of that in balance and make a point of offering positive feedback as well as the critical feedback when it is necessary. A big part of community is developing a relational environment and that starts with the leader's own behavior.

Confidence

Two people who were leaders in their respective fields offered these insights on the value of confidence. Helen Keller pointed out, "Optimism is the faith that leads to achievement. Nothing can be done without hope and confidence." And former tennis champion, Stan Smith, put it this way, "Experience tells you what to do. Confidence enables you to do it."

I know many people who have sterling credentials, skill, and competence — but lacking confidence, they don't achieve that higher level of performance and productivity of which they are capable. This is not only a loss to business and the organization, but perhaps, most importantly, it is a loss to individuals themselves. Most people know it. They have a "sixth sense," in a manner of speaking, that *something* is holding them back, keeping them down. That something is a lack of confidence. They function out of fear, rather than moving full steam ahead. With that gnawing sense that they could be more and do better, many people feel as a result frustration, internal conflict, stress, and distress. In the workplace, that often manifests itself in marginal performance, defensiveness, unnecessary conflicts or competitiveness with others, a negative attitude.

Leaders can do a great deal to foster or instill confidence: e.g., provide skill-development training, encourage mentoring programs, involve employees in tasks or projects that represent opportunities to experience success, regularly voice approval when someone does something. True leaders creatively find ways to promote or pull up the people they lead. In Chapter 7 we will address Lani's points of community and confidence. Here, we focus on control in decision making.

Decision Making

Much has been written, discussed, and lamented about involving employees in the decision-making process. It is a topic that is filled with confusion and fear, and one that must be addressed.

Michele Atkins shared an experience of hers.

> Recently I was at the airport by myself and decided to stop and have dinner on my way home. I was sitting in a restaurant and there were four men [managers] sitting at a table next to me who had obviously been there for a while and must have worked together in a manufacturing environment. They were having a conversation about their workplace and one of them said, "Let's face it, guys, the definition of management is the imposition of my ideas on my staff." They went on to say that they have a morale problem in their factory which is getting in the way of productivity and they were trying to figure out what they could do to fix it. The whole conversation was from the standpoint of what *they* could do, what ideas *they* could impose on their staff, and how *they* could increase productivity. I really think that concept is a dead concept. It's not working in this country anymore, and when people still try to do it, they experience reduced productivity. We are

dealing with grown-ups in the workplace and grown-ups learn differently from children, react differently from children, and the thing that most grown-ups need is to feel valued, to feel that their ideas count for something and that they're heard. In environments where that doesn't happen, I don't think those companies are doing well right now.

There is confusion regarding in which areas employees should be involved, in what decisions and where the boundaries should be drawn, and there is fear that employees' decisions could lead to disastrous results for the organization. There are three natural opportunities for involving employees in the decision-making process:

♦ *How* we are going to achieve our mission, goals, and objectives
♦ Hiring decisions
♦ Day-to-day issues

Decisions of How

The performance-driven leader's role is to communicate *what* we are going to do, *why* it is essential that it be done, *when* it must be accomplished by, and involve employees in decisions of *how* we are going to make this happen. This is the appropriate area for employees to have influence; it allows them input at their greatest level of expertise.

Let's look at four key issues of management:

1. *What* we do.
2. *Why* we are doing it.
3. *How* we are going to do it.
4. *When* we must accomplish it.

1. What We Do

If we have empowered employees, can they really decide what the organization does? The answer is simple — No. Those decisions are made at the highest levels of the organization (founders, ownership, board of directors, or even the governor or the president in the public sector). Employees or staff members have little or no input into what the organization does.

Example: If the management of a hotel practiced participative management and truly empowered its employees, could the employees meet and decide that they wanted to change what the organization does (provide sleeping and meeting rooms, banquet and restaurant functions, and other hospitality-related services)? Could the empowered employees decide they would rather be a hospital? "We have all these rooms, all we would need is some different beds, lots of medical equipment, some nurses and doctors, and we could be in the health care business!" Obviously, the answer is no. What the organization does is determined at the highest levels.

Participative management or empowerment is *not* about giving away decisions concerning what we do. This is determined by leadership and communicated to the employees/staff. George Mosher offers us an example of communicating the *what*.

> At the first of each year all of our managers are asked to provide me a list of the ten or so major objectives they would like to accomplish by the end of the year. It's very rare that I will change those significantly. This addresses what they feel the problems and opportunities are and we will tend to focus on their objectives within our standard growth and profit objectives. This is an example of how I map to empower. Once I accept the list, unless there's been a major change, this becomes what we are going to do during the year. Part of the reason I like this so well is that most people get trapped by the day-to-day demands and this forces them at least once a month to go back and fill out what percentage of the job they have accomplished in terms of their objective and which of the three or four things they are going to be focusing on in the next month. This reporting helps to get them back to focusing on what they agreed upon on a month-to-month basis.

2. Why We Are Doing It

Employees have no major influence over *why*. Why is determined by what we do (the process) and most importantly by the client, patient, or customer (internal as well as external), the people we do it for! If the importance of why we are doing something is not determined by the ultimate end users, we are creating something (a product or service) that will not meet their needs and we will quickly become obsolete.

**ANOTHER OF THE PERFORMANCE-DRIVEN LEADER'S
CRITICAL TASKS IS THE CLEAN AND CONCISE
COMMUNICATION OF *WHY* WE ARE DOING
WHAT WE'RE DOING.**

George Mosher:

> I believe that communicating the "why" is vital. One of the problems I have is I will get off on different stories that to me are giving some of the "why's," but I find that often other people confuse them. One of the things I have to do a better job of is getting the "why's" understood by people in their language. Because another fear that people have is not asking questions when they should because they don't want to look stupid or they think they understand and when they find out that they don't, they become reluctant to ask the question. But the "why's" enable someone to make the right decision if the facts are not lined up perfectly. If you can understand what the objective is, you'll start making the right decisions.

**"PEOPLE ARE MOTIVATED BY DOING
WHAT MAKES SENSE TO THEM."**

ANONYMOUS

That leads us to key issue number 3.

3. How We Are Going to Do It

This is the crucial building block of participative management.

**PERFORMANCE-DRIVEN LEADERS
INVOLVE THEIR PEOPLE IN ISSUES OF *HOW*.**

Leadership communicates what we are going to do, why we are going to do it, when it must be completed, and then turns to those actually doing the job, those with the most current, relevant experience, and asks the simple question, "How can we make this happen?" If you want employees/staff to take ownership, show initiative, and have high motivation, invite them to help determine the tactics and strategies of *how*.

Why does including them in the how drive ownership, motivation, and performance?

1. People tend to support that which they help to create.
2. People don't disagree with their own ideas.

Michele Atkins:

> Our staff understands that they are truly in charge of making de-
> cisions about how something happens. It's my job or the coach's
> job to tell them what we want to have happen, when we need to
> have it done, and why we are doing it. As long as I can outline
> those things for them, they can figure out how and they know that
> I'm not going to second-guess their decisions. They are doing
> wonderful work. A whole lot more work is being done now than
> in the past simply because they realize that nobody is going to go
> in and second-guess them. There is an increased level of trust and
> confidence, and that is manifested in staff meetings now where
> people feel more comfortable, people who used to sit quietly and
> doodle are now very, very comfortable saying "Wait a minute, I
> don't agree" or "I have a different opinion on that." It's a wonder-
> ful blessing to our agency.

Michele goes on to say:

> One of the things that I had to learn is that I don't have all the
> answers. I thought that that was part of my job and that somebody
> would look at me and say, "You are a failure if you don't have the
> answers." I now see my job as being (able) to articulate the ques-
> tion so that the question and the boundaries are clear. If that's all
> laid out properly, the staff can absolutely get the answers and
> generally it's a much more carefully considered answer than my
> normal needing to know the answer myself would be. I would say
> … frame the question properly with all the information then trust
> the organization's staff to find the right answer because it will
> happen.
>
> Participative management was a major change for us. The
> coaching team here was required to change their management
> behavior which is always an uncomfortable thing to do. All three
> of us had gotten used to being fairly successful at helping people
> to do it our way. Our style was clearly saying, "We're in charge
> and you get to do it this way because we say it's the best way."
> Part of what we had to learn was people can get where they're
> going, where we want them to go, in different ways. They may not

get there as quickly and they may not get there as cleanly, but when they get there, they will have learned. So what we had to learn was to be comfortable with letting the staff experience trial and error. And that took some huge hand-holding and behavior modification on our part before we were ready to deal with the staff. And it took a big "aha," somebody kind of pounding us over the head and saying, "What's the worst thing that can happen if they blow it? What's the best thing that can happen if they get it right?" And it took getting that "aha" before we could really move ahead.

4. When We Must Accomplish It

Again, decisions concerning issues of *when* (or time lines) are determined by the process (what we do) and the ultimate receiver of the product or service. If our time lines aren't responsive to the customer's needs, we are printing yesterday's newspapers tomorrow!

**PERFORMANCE-DRIVEN LEADERS MUST HAVE
EFFECTIVE, CLEAR, AND CONCISE COMMUNICATION
OF *WHEN* SOMETHING MUST BE ACCOMPLISHED.**

George Mosher:

> One of the things that I have learned is that I have not put enough deadlines on people. The result is that things are put off or people may be working on the wrong priorities. So one of the changes we are making is to institute more clear deadlines. I was recently reading a series of Civil War letters and something occurred to me which is going to be a part of my philosophy forever. In 1863, the week of the 4th of July, the Northern armies won six major battles. The reason was that each of the commanders independently said that he wanted to get the war over by the 4th of July. In the South, the 4th of July was not a major celebration. In fact, there was an avoidance or an attempt to ignore it so there was no sense that we are going to have our defenses in place by the 4th of July. And it gave the Northern commanders an opportunity to do everything that was necessary to make victory happen.

DEADLINES DRIVE PERFORMANCE.

In later chapters on communication, we will discuss techniques to en-sure that the communication of what, why, and when is successful. It is suffient to say here that the performance-driven leader strives to ensure that the communication is delivered clearly, in a manner appropriate to the people receiving the communication, and that the communication was clearly understood.

PERFORMANCE-DRIVEN LEADERS
USE FEEDBACK TECHNIQUES, VERBAL OR WRITTEN,
TO ENSURE THAT THE *WHAT, WHY,* AND *WHEN*
ARE COMMUNICATED EFFECTIVELY.

In Chapter 3 we offered the example of Kathy Foltner leading her people to the decisions resulting in reducing their hearing aid suppliers from 17 to 4. Kathy obviously used participative management skills to drive the deci-sion-making process.

She communicated what, why, and when (this technique is also called *playing the W's*):

♦ *What* — We are going to reduce our hearing aid suppliers from 17 to 4.
♦ *Why* — Issues of profitability, buying power, customer service, etc.
♦ *When* — Within 6 months.

And then she turned to her staff and said "How are we going to make it happen?"

When asked about the end result of using this participative management technique, Foltner replied:

> First of all, I have to say that with the exception of one person, everybody truly just went with it. There was enough flexibility with what we pared down to that it really didn't threaten anyone's comfort zone. There was one individual who was kind of upset that he couldn't do business with one company. He agreed to support the decision, but there were times when he wanted to use this one particular manufacturer. He resisted a little bit, and just

kept doing business with them. Every month I would get a computer report that would tell me exactly what each office sold by manufacturer. So I would give them immediate feedback saying, "Great!" One hundred percent preferred manufacturers or I would circle the ones that weren't so that everyone knew we had a tool for monitoring compliance. We allowed our audiologists to ease into the new program, but compliance was much quicker than I thought.

When asked if she was pleased with the result, she replied:

Absolutely. If I could have every change go that well, it would be wonderful! There weren't a lot of negative repercussions. I feel good about it, and they feel good about it. I said let's try this for 6 months and if it isn't working, we will consider changing it again. And I just checked with everybody a month ago and they are all happy.

Critical question: Can the how decision always be given away? Obviously, the answer is no, especially in highly regulated environments. In circumstances where the how decision cannot be given away, an even greater demand is placed on the performance-driven leader to define clearly the what, why, and when.

An example: Consider the fire department arriving on the scene of a building fully involved in fire. As the officer in command climbs down from the truck, is it appropriate to gather the firefighting team together to determine *how* to fight the fire? It's ludicrous to imagine involving the group in decisions of where we should position the equipment, who should perform what tasks, where the water targets should be established, etc.

**IN ENVIRONMENTS WHERE CRISIS IS PREDICTABLE,
THE *WHAT* AND *WHEN* ARE COMMUNICATED BY LEADERSHIP;
WHY AND *HOW* MUST BE ADDRESSED IN TRAINING.**

Although empowered employees cannot always be involved in decisions of how, seeking opportunities of "inclusion" make the "exclusion" more tolerable and acceptable.

Hiring Decisions

Another high-impact opportunity for the performance-driven leader is to involve employees in the hiring decisions for positions where they experience significant interaction. When new personnel are brought into their work group, employees should have some measure of control over who those people will be.

PERFORMANCE-DRIVEN LEADERS INVOLVE THEIR EMPLOYEES IN HIRING DECISIONS THAT INFLUENCE THEIR AREAS OF RESPONSIBILITY.

While ultimate hiring authority resides with the leader, it stands to reason that employees respond positively to influencing decisions concerning who will be brought into their working environment. Given the amount of time that employees spend at work, they have more exposure to their co-workers than they do their families! Chemistry is an important part of productivity.

A highly productive group can experience a significant drop in productivity if the wrong person is suddenly brought into the environment. Few things emphasize for employees their total lack of control or input than having someone dropped into their midst with whom they find it difficult to deal.

When employees are invited to influence the hiring decisions, they have a stake in the success of the new addition. There is much less evidence of the "new kid in school" syndrome, and new people find it much easier to assimilate into the group because of the welcome they receive. Training, both formal and informal, is engaged in willingly and enthusiastically to ensure success and to prove the correctness of the decision. The new person is treated with enthusiasm and encouragement and not grudgingly as an outsider.

Comments from Kathy Foltner:

> If you hire a person who doesn't step up to the challenge, it all of a sudden starts to affect the lives of other people because the new person doesn't follow through, doesn't get things done, forgets about things, isn't organized, and can't handle the workload. Regardless of what the causes may be, the unity starts to break down and you start to have other staff questioning whether or not that person should have been hired. When you involve the staff in the hiring decision, they are going to be willing and open to help train that person as well as give the person a break if the job isn't done perfectly. And if we don't hire the right person, it's a shared responsibility. We all made the decision together. We all chose this

person, and if it turns out to be a bad decision, we all missed the negatives together. I will do the initial interviewing and narrow the selections down to the candidates who are qualified to do the job and then I open it up to the staff and give anybody who would like to an opportunity to interview the candidates. The first time I did this I had three or four people out of the 12 who wanted to participate. I asked for their feedback and, in this case, all of the staff picked the same person, which made it easy for me. I supported that, I hired that person, but it was a decision that I really had to think about. This person wanted substantially more money than the other candidates and I wanted to support the group in their decision. I thought that it was the best decision to make and we made it and it has proved to be very good. I have gotten to the point now where I don't want to hire somebody unless each person has interviewed them because I know that when you get that buy-in, down the line the accountability for training, the result, the teamwork, and the overall results are going to be much better. The challenge is that some people don't want to bother with that. Some people just don't like doing it and truly don't care. They say that, but many times don't mean it. Out of my 40 employees I know for sure I have one who says whatever it is, whatever you decide, I will support it, and she actually does. I've heard that from many different people and they usually don't follow through with it. It's a cop-out. It's very easy to say I don't want to bother, but they are the people that you get the most resistance from. They come back and blame and complain, but they refuse to participate in the process. But overall, including the staff in hiring decisions has been very positive.

Obviously, training is a critical issue when including employees and staff in hiring decisions. *Do not* expose employees to hiring activity until they have been properly trained on interviewing techniques and the legal aspects of hiring (issues of discrimination, disability, background checks, etc.). The Third Reich manager won't allow employees to participate in the hiring process, predicting that "They will do something dumb and get us sued." Performance-driven leaders train their employee for effective participation.

Michele Atkins had these comments on involving her people in the hiring process:

In the past I would do all of the initial screening. I would get it narrowed down to the two or three people that we had an interest in and bring the other department heads in and they would ratify the decision that I had made. What we do now, is we let the position dictate the team that will do the initial screening. If it's a person who's going to serve in our program services area, that's somebody who works on outreach-volunteer management or Wishes, then that team will do the initial interviewing. The team members will screen down to three or so and we ask them to write their choices 1, 2, and 3, and in the absence of anything extraordinary, we will ratify the team's first choice. If it's not a ratification, then we'll come back and negotiate it. We would ask the team to list the key qualities that it is looking for in a person for this job. Then we would ask each member to rank each of the candidates with a rating of 1, 2, or 3. We would add those up to determine a leading candidate. Then we would ask the team to tell us what it was about each candidate that it thought was terrific. We would present some hypothetical situations and ask how each thought this person would handle these circumstances, and we have always had a clear winner. The decision was made by consensus. One of the values of that is if this person doesn't work out, there's no one that you can point a finger to or accuse of making a bad decision. And the group has to collectively have a stake in what to do about it.

Day-to-Day Decisions

There are opportunities for employees to be involved in the day-to-day routine of doing their jobs. As an example, scheduling elective time off can be a decision made collectively by the group instead of unilaterally by the manager (a specific example of this is presented in the next chapter). Scheduling of breaks, flextime, etc. are decisions that can be made collectively based upon what's best for the employees and the workload. Decisions on how the office or department should be set up, where desks, chairs, equipment, etc. should be positioned, who sits where, anything that affects the employees on a day-to-day basis that will allow them influence and control without affecting overall quality and productivity should be included.

In Chapter 7, we will offer some practical advice on the use of participative decision making.

CHAPTER 7

PARTICIPATIVE DECISION MAKING: COMMUNITY AND CONFIDENCE

The Steps of Participative Decision Making

Performance-driven leaders prepare and nurture their employees through a series of developmental steps:

1. Enabling
2. Clarifying boundaries (aligning authority, responsibility, and account-ability)
3. Creating opportunity
4. Providing feedback and agreements

Enabling

If we are going to involve employees/staff appropriately in the decision-making process, they must receive

♦ Effective training
♦ Complete information
♦ Pervasive knowledge

The fear-based manager is often heard justifying his or her lack of employee involvement in decision making by stating, "What if they make the wrong decision? What if they want to do something dumb that puts us out of business?" This reasoning results in employees being ignored in the decision-making process. In reality, if employees make a "dumb" decision, it is because the fear-based manager did not properly enable them in the first place. Employees must be taught to make decisions.

What happens when leaders do not enable their employees through training? Failure. Kathy Foltner:

> Why do organizations fail in participative management and empowerment? Without a doubt, it's training. If everybody decides that they want to empower their staff to do everything and tell them go ahead and make decisions, you may be asking a person who has never dealt with the situation to make decisions. By doing that, you're setting that person up for failure because the person doesn't have the knowledge base or the training to be able to make a quality decision. The manager then may become defensive and say to that person, "Well I told you that you could do that, but your decision was wrong. It was a stupid judgment. You cost the company hundreds of thousands of dollars or whatever." So then the manager steps back and says you can't empower people because they don't know how to make decisions. In reality, that's the manager's responsibility. Empowerment occurs when somebody is trained and then has the confidence and the knowledge base to do what's being asked. So it's my responsibility to train you. And I think in many cases that just doesn't happen. We ask people to become involved with things that they haven't been equipped to do properly.

All leaders want their employees to make good decisions and exercise common sense. For many managers, the definition of making good decisions and exercising common sense is "doing things the way I would do them."

If we want decisions to be made that are effective and consistent with our goals, objectives, and mission statements, employees must have a clear understanding of what those are. Employees don't have a crystal ball that allows them to read their leaders' minds.

Picture the decision-making process as a funnel.

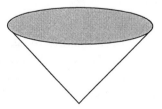

We become aware that a decision is necessary, we observe a situation, we gather relevant information and "filter" it through our decision-making criteria, and yield an appropriate decision. This filtering time may be instantaneous or the tissue may be considered over a longer period. If we seek consistent, appropriate, and realistic decisions from our employees, they must have knowledge of our decision-making criteria. They must fully understand what is in the funnel!

The fear-based manager, if pressured to involve employees in the decision-making process, will ask them to make decisions in a vacuum of information, then criticize their thought process and judge them harshly for not making the right decisions.

**PARTICIPATIVE MANAGEMENT DEMANDS
THAT EMPLOYEES BE GIVEN THE TRAINING,
INFORMATION, AND KNOWLEDGE NECESSARY
BEFORE EFFECTIVE DECISIONS CAN BE MADE.**

Clarifying Boundaries

Performance-driven leaders establish a clear understanding of the boundaries of participation. Decisions that are clearly the responsibility of the leader are identified. The decisions and accountability that will be the responsibility of the employees will be identified as well as those that will be addressed through joint consultative or collaborative efforts.

Fear-based managers make "blurring the lines of responsibility" an art form. They insulate themselves from possible accountability, always having someone to blame. Performance-driven leaders define these lines as clearly as possible. If employees do not have a clear understanding of the boundaries, their reaction will not be to exceed the boundaries but to do nothing. This avoids the risk of punishment and increases the errors of omission. James D. Thompson, an organization theorist, argued that true freedom of action can only be found within clearly defined and understood boundaries.

An important component of boundary clarification is the alignment of authority with responsibility. It is deadly to assign responsibility without letting go of the authority to implement decisions. And as we outlined in point 9 of Chapter 2, this is an identifiable trait of a fear-based manager.

IF YOU'RE NOT GOING TO GIVE AWAY THE AUTHORITY TO IMPLEMENT THE RESPONSIBILITY, DON'T GIVE AWAY THE RESPONSIBILITY.

In many organizations an illusion of participative management is created. This is accomplished by saying that employees can make decisions, but in reality, inviting them to "read the boss's mind." If the decision is just what the boss would do, then it is applauded and implemented; if it is different from the boss's thought process, the decision is criticized, rejected, and seized upon as an opportunity to prove that employees really aren't capable of making effective decisions. Employees do not attempt to make well-thought-out decisions; they merely play a version of "What do we think the boss would want us to do?" This is nothing more than an invitation to display "psychic abilities" and is quickly identified by employees for the distorted farce that it is. If employees are consistently successful at reading the boss's mind, they should start their own psychic hotline and begin to make some real money!

When performance-driven leaders clearly establish the boundaries of employee decision making, they must be willing to allow decisions to be made with which they may not totally agree. The performance-driven leader may perceive that the appropriate strategy is to head due north; however, the participative employees may decide to head slightly north by northwest. If the decision is reasonable and has a significant chance for success, the leader must allow the decision to stand and support it with a total effort. To interfere in the decision is to distort the participative management process and prove to the employees that we are merely giving lip service to participation. Should the leader ever intercede in the case of a potentially disastrous decision? Of course! However, when employees make decisions that are totally ineffective, the responsibility falls to the leader who has probably not prepared them with the appropriate training, information, and knowledge.

Michele Atkins:

> A friend of mine worked for a major corporation which has been through the reengineering process. I remember them working on a project where people were flown in from all over the world and they worked for months and months. And at the end of that time, they presented the results of their work to the corporate leadership.

And the leadership said, "Nope. You've got the wrong answer. Go back to the drawing board." That was hugely deflating and changed forever, for at least those people, the way they viewed participative management.

Accountability is a critical part of boundary clarification and is the third component linked with responsibility and authority. A successful decision-making process is assured when employees are held accountable for their actions.

Example: A performance-driven leader wanted to take the first steps in participative management and begin to involve her employees in the decision-making process. Not wanting to "throw out the baby with the bath," she searched for a way to manage the decision-making risk (giving the employees an opportunity for challenging participation without exposing them to an issue of such impact that a poor decision could do permanent damage to the overall group performance). The leader decided to transfer the authority, responsibility, and accountability for all decisions concerning "elective" days off to the employees themselves. If someone wanted to schedule vacation days, a doctor's appointment, any discretionary time off including "mental-health days," these would have to be approved by the entire group. Approval was to be based upon their ability to compensate for the loss of the employee's productivity (i.e., if a vacation is scheduled during peak seasonal activity, can we maintain our levels of production or service in the absence of the vacationing employee?).

A meeting was held to identify clearly that this responsibility was now shifting solely to the employees. No longer would they have to get their boss's permission for days off, and they would be held accountable for the quality of their decisions as well as overall productivity. As you can imagine, immediately after this shift of responsibilities, the employees had a field day approving each other's time off. All requests were granted (within the guidelines of written corporate policy) and decisions were made primarily on the basis of giving co-workers what they wanted in hopes of currying favor for one's own future personal requests. Productivity was marginally affected. The performance-driven leader allowed the decisions to stand even when not in agreement, knowing that a day of reckoning would arrive!

One of the requirements of this organization was that a very specific quarterly reconciliation or inventory had to be taken by the last Friday of each quarter. This was necessary for meeting internal control as well as fulfilling governmental compliance requirements. The inventory was begun at noon on the last Thursday of the quarter and completed by noon the next day. Friday afternoon hours were utilized for reconciling any problems. The completed inventory was on the leader's desk the following Monday for processing.

When the group faced its first inventory under their newly acquired responsibility, authority, and accountability for scheduling time off, a problem arose. Two of the group's members were going to be off during the inventory, leaving only three employees to do the normal workload of five. The three remaining employees approached the leader asking for help in completing the inventory.

They requested that:

1. Help be temporarily transferred from other departments (three people would be needed to replace the missing two because of their unfamiliarity with the process) or
2. Short-term replacements be hired from a temporary agency just until the inventory was completed.

The leader's response was very clear — the answer was no! "I will not burden or punish another department by taking people away from them to help you just because you have made an unwise decision. Nor will I incur additional unnecessary cost by hiring 'temps' because you collectively approved forty percent of your department members to be off during a predictable and consistent 'high demand activity.' "

Her remedy was to arrange for the three remaining employees to work late Friday and on Saturday to complete the inventory (extending the inventory deadline was not an option). Interestingly, the group contacted one of their "off" members and demanded she come in to help — the other member was unavailable! The inventory was completed and on the leader's desk Monday morning. Also on Monday morning, when all employees were present, a departmental meeting was held to establish a new, employee-driven policy change. The resulting document signed by all five members, read:

> Barring death, no one will be given permission to take vacation or any elective days off the last two days of any quarter coinciding with our departmental inventory.

The result demonstrates what happens when employees experience the component of accountability inherent in participative management. The performance-driven leader anticipated the problem and could have stepped in to correct it by admonishing, canceling the days off, and proving to the employees she had not truly given away authority, responsibility, and accountability. Instead, the employees were allowed to experience the brunt of their unwise decision and learn that the true criterion for making decisions was not self-accommodation, but overall departmental efficiency and compliance.

As in parenting, there are times when the child must experience a mild exposure to the meaning of *hot* to learn the importance of listening to Mom and Dad's command to "not touch the extremely hot burner on the stove."

That's what managing the risk is all about!

Creating Opportunity

Participative management has *not* been the norm in America. Employees have been taught, primarily through modeled behavior, to keep their ideas to themselves, do what they are told, and that innovation and creativity must be generated from the top — after all, that's where all of the organizational intellect really resides!

Employees have low levels of experience with participative management and initially do not possess the skills, knowledge, and information to participate in a truly effective manner. Couple this with the inherent suspicion of "why" we are moving toward this new management style, and reluctance or hesitation to participate is certainly predictable and understandable. The employees' mantra becomes "Why are they really doing this?"

IN A LOW-TRUST, HIGH-FEAR ENVIRONMENT, PARTICIPATIVE MANAGEMENT CAN INITIALLY BE PERCEIVED TO BE A "SETUP"; EXPOSING EMPLOYEES TO ACCOUNTABILITY TO JUSTIFY PUNISHMENT.

Because of this initial reluctance and hesitation, patience is a necessary virtue for the performance-driven leader. As we indicated earlier, employees are not going to jump enthusiastically into a body of water until they are sure they know where the rocks may be hidden below the surface.

Fear-based managers may begin to institute components of participative management, especially if pressured to do so from upper management, quickly seize on employees' hesitation or reluctance as proof of failure, and then quickly dismantle any working initiatives. This serves as proof to the employees that no matter what management says it's always business as usual.

REPEATED FALSE STARTS OF PARTICIPATIVE MANAGEMENT INITIATIVES ONLY DRIVE EMPLOYEES' SUSPICIONS DEEPER.

We interviewed a manager who voiced great skepticism with all aspects of participative management: "I've tried all of that stuff and it just doesn't work. I've asked them what they think we should do. I've asked them to make some decisions and all they do is look at me with blank stares; and if they do make a decision it is so outrageous and stupid I can't let it stand." When asked how long he had been trying this participative management "stuff," he replied, "At least 3 months now and it just doesn't work." He also went on to complain about the continued high turnover and low productivity that he was experiencing and proclaimed vehemently that "People just don't want to work anymore." At least not there!

PATIENCE IS A NECESSARY VIRTUE WHEN IMPLEMENTING PARTICIPATIVE MANAGEMENT.

In light of the employee's hesitation to participate, the performance-driven leader may need to create opportunities for participation (the previous days-off example is an example of creating an opportunity for involvement).

A performance-driven leader in the petroleum industry described his experience with employee resistance.

> We outlined very specific boundaries and circumstances where the employees would have complete decision-making authority. We trained them on the decision-making process, shared all relevant information, and were confident that they had the knowledge to make effective decisions.
>
> When decision-making opportunities would arise, I would communicate the circumstances and tell the group or an individual employee, "I want you to analyze this situation, develop at least three alternatives to address the issue, determine which of the

alternatives is the best, develop an action plan, and begin imple-mentation." Invariably they would look at me and say, "That's great, what do you think we should do?" I would repeat the in-structions again, very specifically, and then they would respond, "Well, if you were me (or us), what would you do?" They were extremely reluctant to make a decision or take an action, no matter how much I sought and encouraged their participation. I became extremely frustrated."

To correct this situation he was advised to create a teaching opportunity and make himself unavailable for consultation, forcing the employees to take decisive action on their own. He explains:

A decision had to be made concerning one of our suppliers. I realized if I didn't make the decision, if I took no action, a small "brush fire" problem would erupt. It wouldn't be a major problem, but it would necessitate making a decision and instituting some minor damage control [authors' note — an example of managing the risk]. I called the employees who would be impacted by this situation and outlined in detail the entire circumstances. I gave them some time to consider their recommendations and agreed to meet with them 2 hours later in the conference room. When the time arrived for the follow-up meeting, I didn't go. Actually, I sent a memo saying: "I'm very sorry I can't meet with you. I was just called into an emergency meeting of the Board of Directors. Please discuss your thoughts, identify three possible alternatives, agree on the best plan, and take the initial action before 5:00 p.m. Meet me first thing tomorrow morning to advise me of your decision."

They discussed the situation, had some stressful moments of disagree-ment, and ultimately agreed upon a reasonable solution. When the group met with the leader the next day and explained its decision and the reason-ing behind it, the performance-driven leader took the opportunity to extend very positive reinforcement and recognition to those involved, acknowledg-ing them for their willingness to take action and the "depth" of their rea-soning. He also seized the opportunity to offer training. "I was impressed with what they had decided and implemented; however, there were some things that I thought they may have overlooked. We reviewed these few points to ensure that when they were faced with a similar situation in the future, they would broaden their decision-making criteria to include these omissions."

From this positive experience the group gained confidence and was anxious for future challenges creating the opportunity to begin to break down resistance and reluctance. This two-way communication and debriefing of decisions made in a participative management environment is essential, and leads us to our next step.

Providing Feedback and Agreements

Many managers believe that just listening to employees' suggestions or complaints is enough to create a participative management environment. This is not true. If we just listen and respond with "Thank you for sharing" or "I'll see what I can do" or any similar inane statement, we merely leave employees with the feeling that they have been "handled."

**FEEDBACK AND AGREEMENTS ON FUTURE BEHAVIORS
ARE ESSENTIAL PARTS OF PARTICIPATIVE MANAGEMENT.**

Whether it is a complaint, idea, decision, or whatever, the employee deserves feedback on the result. If we listen without feedback, we send the very demeaning message that the employee's communication was meaningless, inconsequential, and that we have dismissed it "out of hand." This only drives negativity and anger and contributes to overall resentment.

**RECOGNIZE EMPLOYEES BY OFFERING VERY SPECIFIC
FEEDBACK ON THEIR INTELLECTUAL CONTRIBUTIONS.**

- ◆ If a decision is made correctly, offer specific information on *why* it was a good decision.
- ◆ If a decision is made that is incorrect or inappropriate, do not just criticize and correct it; explain *why* so that adjustments can be made in the future.
- ◆ If an idea is offered that cannot be implemented, offer an explanation of *why* the suggestion cannot be used. This communicates to employees that you value their intellect even though their idea cannot be used, and helps them broaden their thinking for future input.

♦ If employees lodge a complaint and if nothing can be done to resolve it, offer an explanation of *why* it cannot be corrected. This communicates to employees that you do take them seriously even if you can't support them with an action.

♦ If the answer is no — follow up with an explanation. "The answer is no because I'm the boss and I say so" is the classic response of the fear-based manager. This communicates to employees that they are not worthy of an explanation and that their issues are not important.

FEEDBACK RAISES THE VALUE OF THE RECIPIENT AND PRESENTS AN UNPARALLELED TEACHING OPPORTUNITY.

The end result of successful feedback is mutual agreement about how we will react in the future.

♦ Do we agree that we will consider these additional factors in future decisions?

♦ Do we agree that future recommendations will include cost limitation considerations?

♦ Your complaints are valid and we realize there is nothing that can be done at this time. Do we agree that we can continue under the current circumstances?

The performance-driven leader establishes agreements which are the basis for future action and behaviors. Are these agreements always kept? Of course not. We live in the real world, not the perfect world. What do performance-driven leaders do when agreements are not kept? They use techniques for inviting explanations from employees, not defensive reactions. We will discuss these and other communication techniques in Chapters 8 and 9.

Community

There are a number of ways that performance-driven leaders can help to establish a community with their employees/staff.

- Leadership consistency and fairness
- Cross-awareness training
- Belongingness
- Universal celebration
- Connection to the outcome

Leadership Consistency and Fairness

Few things foster unity like the consistency and fairness of the leader. While this is much easier said than done, it's important to cultivate these two attributes.

Consistency

Consistency basically means the leader's behavior and reactions are predictable and consistent, with mature patterns. The leader's reaction isn't based upon whether the leader is having a good or bad day; employees won't bear some form of punishment because the leader has had a previous bad event or be surprised by the leader's overreaction to an inconsequential event. All these reflect patterns of inconsistency. The performance-driven leader has a baseline behavior that isn't affected dramatically by whether things are going well or not. If performance or quality slips, the performance-driven leader will predictably and consistently address those issues without panic or rage. This includes addressing individual poor performance or behavioral problems within the group. The entire group will not be punished for the indiscretions of one individual; i.e., good leaders will not change their overall policies and invoke oppressive rules just because one person has gotten out of line. The performance-driven leader will deal with that specific person on an individual basis.

Fairness

The performance-driven leader creates an environment of fairness. Favoritism, real or imagined, is neither encouraged nor practiced. The rules apply to everyone fairly. Fear-based managers apply the policies and rules to everyone but themselves and their "pets." We learned of one fear-based manager who applied enormous pressure to his people to reduce overall travel, lodging, and entertainment expenses. He forced his people to stay in low-budget no-frills motels and to keep their meal expenses to an unrealistic minimum. All entertainment had to be approved by him in advance, and it was not uncommon for him to disallow a percentage of the entertainment costs, forcing the employees to cover that portion out of their own pockets. However, when he traveled, he stayed in four-star hotels and anyone who traveled with him was permitted to do the same. His entertainment was extravagant and governed by "costs be damned." This unfairness caused huge resentment among his people. Leaders are not exempt from rules, nor are their buddies or personal pets. As we all know, there are some rules and policies that must be enforced to the letter, some that can be "bent" by exercising judgment, and some that can be totally ignored. The key is fairness to all, not privilege to the few.

Cross-Awareness Training

Cross-awareness training does not necessarily mean training someone to the extent that they could do another person's job. Obviously, such cross training is very valuable when possible. It's good for the employee; it's good for the organization. As we know, many jobs can't be cross trained; however, all jobs can be cross-awareness trained. This means exposing people to other people's jobs to the extent that they have a basic understanding of what is being done. It helps them to view issues from the other person's vantage point and helps them to appreciate why certain things must be done in a certain way; i.e., if a worker becomes aware that not responding to a request for information on a timely basis or not providing that information in total creates a significant amount of work and stress to someone else, the worker's willingness to comply is certainly greater. Helping employees and staff to walk a mile in another person's shoes helps them to have a better understanding of what's going on in their environment.

Example: We met a manager from a software development company. She shared with us that one of her most significant challenges was coordinating the efforts of their outside salespeople with their inside research-and-development people. These two groups seemed to be always at war. The research-and-development people perceived that the salespeople were always loose cannons, making promises to customers that were unrealistic, making demands on their department that weren't possible. It appeared to them that the salespeople were intent on making their lives very stressful, and for blaming them for low sales, lost accounts, and customer problems. The salespeople believed the research-and-development people were put on

Earth just to make their life miserable! They perceived they were always being asked for information that was tedious and time-consuming to obtain, and totally meaningless. They perceived that the research-and-development department was in place merely to say *no* to every one of their requests and ideas, and that it was truly an impediment to sales (which was the lifeblood of the organization).

To negotiate a peaceful settlement in this ongoing war, the manager developed a program of cross-awareness training. The research-and-development people were all required to spend at least 2 days each quarter in the field accompanying a salesperson during a normal sales call cycle. Obviously, they were there to provide technical back-up and, more importantly, to observe the sales process. Actually experiencing what it was like when a customer would look the salesperson in the eye and say "If you want our business, this is what you will do; if you don't, we will find a competitor" or "We need a product that will do this for us, and if yours won't, we'll find someone whose product does." It was important for the research-and-development people to see that the salespeople, for the most part, were merely being responsive to customer needs and demands.

All of the salespeople, on a rotating basis, were required to spend a minimum of 2 days every 6 months in the research-and-development department; not to develop the skills actually to discharge those duties, but to become aware of the demands and requirements of those jobs. It gave the salespeople a much better and more complete understanding of what information was necessary, why it was necessary, and the "hassles" that were created when the information wasn't forthcoming. It also helped them to appreciate some of the limitations and restrictions under which the research-and-development department functioned and to realize that the department really was there to partner with them, not to punish them.

The leader went on to share with us that the organization was experiencing a much greater rate of cooperation between the two departments. The customers were benefiting from a more collaborative effort and it made for a much more peaceful environment.

Belongingness

Performance-driven leaders work hard to make their department, group, or team a unique entity, something of which they can be proud. As we have discussed, they do this by giving everyone some measure of control over their environment and also giving them some form of group identity. As the impersonalness of our entire world increases, it's not uncommon for people to not know their neighbors, to have a dwindling social support system, and to live far distances from their families. Many employees and staff look to their co-workers for at least the elementary structure of a support system. It is not the role of the organization to be all things to all people. However, performance-driven leaders do as much as realistically possible to bring their people together. Some suggestions follow.

Rituals

Allow rituals to develop whenever possible within your group. Some examples: celebrate everybody's birthday with a cake, a card, some very inexpensive gag gifts, etc. (Large groups may celebrate all monthly birthdays collectively, etc.) One group meets once a month immediately after work to go out to a local restaurant for dinner. (They try to choose the worst restaurant in the area and not the best, and spend the rest of the month talking about how bad the meal was, joking and cajoling each other, and then voting at the end of the year on which worst restaurant they liked least.) Rituals are fun and a necessary ingredient to bonding. If you think of a group in your life to which you have felt particularly bonded, whether the group be family, collegiate, athletic, social, or military, each one of those groups did things that you felt were unique to that group. College fraternities, sororities, and other fraternal groups are an example; they have handshakes, sign language, and passwords that are unique to them and that are an important part of bringing the group together. The performance-driven leader encourages rituals to develop as long as they do not lower the dignity of an individual or a group. Any behavior, intentional or not, that lowers dignity must receive an immediate negative reaction and be barred from every happening again.

Group Identification

George Mosher had some interesting thoughts on this:

> I think what the average employee is really [looking] for is to be a part of a winning team. If we have units that are not performing, they begin to get afraid, perhaps legitimately, as to what their future is. When people are a part of a performing organization, they feel linked up. They want to contribute and they know they are not going to do it by themselves. So to be with a company that is successful, or has a good reputation, or is respected, makes

them feel better, and that's why companies like IBM were always able to hire the really cream of the crop, because you went in to work for IBM feeling like you were already a winner because your perception was they didn't hire just anybody. They hired people that would help them grow.

We extend this feeling of success to our temporaries. If we hire temporaries, they will feel they fit in almost immediately. Ours is not a company where temporaries are looked upon as second-class people. It's a company where they are welcomed and made to feel more at home than they do in their typical assignment. They are a part of the team, at least while they are here, and they don't just sit in left field. Being a part of something that's success-ful is important.

Universal Celebration

Fear-based managers always represent their group when it comes to rewards and celebration. When their department achieves, they receive the rewards, are acknowledged at the awards banquet, and get their picture in the news-letter or newspaper. The people who certainly contributed to the accom-plishment of the task are not included. The performance-driven leader, on the other hand, looks for every opportunity to celebrate "with" their people, not at the "expense" of their people, such as

♦ Joint recognition at meetings and banquets
♦ Group celebration for goal achievements
♦ Group photo opportunities
♦ Provision for specific achievers to be recognized (not just be repre-sented by their manager)

One company president was being honored by a supplier as "Customer of the Year." Rather than travel to the banquet alone to receive the honor, he took with him the seven employees who actually used the products supplied by the company honoring him. He said, "I do not actually use the materials. While I'm honored that they have selected us as their customer of the year, I feel that the people responsible should share in the experi-ence." Seven people, not usually accustomed to traveling at company ex-pense, enjoyed a 2-day "Trip of Recognition." That is an example of uni-versal celebration. (So is buying a pizza for a group that is doing well —

food is very motivational to us and is always a part of any significant celebration!)

Connection to the Outcome

If employees are to take pride in their performance, ownership of the process, and make appropriate decisions, it is critical that they be connected to the outcome. Clearly stated, they must see their results or observe the fruits of their labor.

Picture a worker standing at a piece of equipment for 8 hours each day manufacturing a rubber gasket or machine part, etc. The results of his efforts are collected, taken for inspection, never to be seen again. If asked what happens to his "stuff," he might reply, "I have no idea; it ends up in the shipping department, I suppose." An airplane mechanic working on a flight line may become bored and slowly begin to lose sight of the lives that depend upon her doing a competent job. The production worker needs to experience the outcome he produces, i.e., show him exactly what happens to the piece he produces (where it fits on the car or lawnmower, or the suit onto which the button is ultimately sewn). The mechanic should have the opportunity to meet the flight crew depending on her; to walk through a full airplane just prior to takeoff; to visit the terminal and view the people boarding the plane.

A social service agency that provides independent housing for retarded adults experienced an interesting phenomenon. While some of their employees were extremely happy, dedicated, and self-fulfilled in their jobs, others displayed attitudes of "Ho hum, I only work here." Investigation of this circumstance discovered that the employees who had personal interaction with the agency's clients experienced the greatest level of job satisfaction. Those with the least exposure to the clients did not perceive their jobs to be particularly rewarding.

The corrective action was to develop opportunities for clients to visit the office; even remote personnel (those whose jobs typically offered the least client contact) were given specific client-related tasks. As an example, environmental service personnel were invited to conduct training classes for clients on proper cleaning techniques, scheduling frequency of cleaning, etc. Being connected to the outcome may also mean observance of what happens in the next department (the internal customer).

**THE PERFORMANCE-DRIVEN LEADER
FINDS CREATIVE WAYS TO ENCOURAGE EMPLOYEES
TO EXPERIENCE THE RESULTS OF THEIR EFFORTS.**

Confidence

The three primary opportunities to create confidence are

1. Training
2. Opportunities for success
3. Recognition

Training

Few things instill confidence in workers more than the opportunity to receive training along with the opportunity to put that training into practice.
The issue of training is so critical and complex that we are dedicating two
entire chapters to cover it in depth. Training affirms the value of an employee. It says you are worth our investment in you; we are willing to give
up your production to help you learn and grow; you are capable of achieving. The vast majority of workers want to be trained to do new things. The
appeal of learning is universal.

Opportunities for Success

We discussed creating opportunity earlier in this chapter, and, in fact, creating opportunity has the additional benefit of creating confidence. When
people are given the opportunity to perform and succeed, their confidence
obviously grows. We will be revisiting this issue again in our discussion on
training. One key observation at this point: it's very important that when we
train someone to do a task, we give them the opportunity as quickly as
possible to perform the task successfully and reinforce the learning. One of
the mistakes we make in training is that we train people on skills that they
won't be using immediately. While their enthusiasm for the task may be
high after training, if they are not provided the opportunity to reinforce the
learning and successfully discharge the task, the initial enthusiasm and

performance wane quickly. Confidence tends to be destroyed, not enhanced. When we provide training, the opportunity for reinforcement and success and must be made available on a timely basis.

Recognition

Again, recognition is such an important part of performance-driven leadership that we dedicate an entire chapter for discussion. The point of observation here is that we train people, we give them an opportunity for success, and we must also give them the appropriate recognition that they deserve. Confidence is not built in an environment where people do not perceive that they are recognized for having performed well. Confidence is generated when the leader, who you trust and respect, reinforces within you the fact that you have performed well. Recognition to the fear-based manager is silence. Recognition to the performance-driven leader is timely and very specific.

We conclude this information on participative management with an excerpt from the ancient Chinese teaching entitled *Tao Te Ching* (meaning, "The Way and Its Power").

> *A leader is best*
> *When people barely know that he exists.*
> *... Of a good leader, who talks little*
> *When his work is done, his aim fulfilled,*
> *They will say, "We did this ourselves."*

Now, let us turn to the topic of communication.

CHAPTER 8

COMMUNICATION

Communication is an eternal challenge for all of us, and certainly for the performance-driven leader. No matter how well we perceive that we communicate, it is an area in which all of us can improve our performance. Communication problems are high on the list of every organization as areas for improvement. There is always the issue of what to communicate, when to communicate it, to whom to communicate it, and, most importantly, how to communicate it effectively. If we communicated better in our lives, we would have fewer divorces, fewer wars, and, certainly, fewer organizational problems.

Even when motivated by the best of intentions, leaders forget to communicate or don't consider the entire web of who needs to know. In many circumstances, leaders "forget" to communicate follow-up information; that is, there is a task or a crisis at hand, it is handled, and we move on. Once the issue is resolved; the leaders perceive the information to be as important as yesterday's newspapers, and they push it out of their minds. They don't realize the negative impact this has on the rest of the group because no one knows what the conclusion was. People may continue to believe that the issue was never resolved! When people discover they have been "left out of the loop" and weren't told in a timely basis, resentment is high and may create a negative emotional response. Third Reich managers use communication as a weapon, withholding information from some, providing information to others, and, always in a carefully managed form, withholding key facts or issues to their advantage. In a Third Reich environment, some people know a lot, some people know a little, some people know nothing at all, and no one knows everything or possesses totally accurate information. The less information we have, the more we speculate, and that speculation is usually counterproductive.

IN THE ABSENCE OF INFORMATION, PEOPLE WORK IT OUT FOR THEMSELVES — NEGATIVELY.

Ron Stewart:

One of the biggest issues facing any organization today is fundamental communication, and it's very important to understand all parts of the communication, not just from a management view looking down into the organization, but also from the other side of your organization looking up to management. The worst thing that can happen is that employees have fears, perceptions, good or bad, and management ignores them because they don't communicate the same or they are not skilled communicators. Just as we need managers and supervisors who communicate effectively, we have to take care of the weaknesses of people communicating up to management. Somehow we must get everyone on the same page, singing the same tune.

Many companies have different levels of education. I've had an opportunity to supervise all professional people as well as to lead people with a lot of varied levels of education, some not even having high school diplomas. You have to understand the environment that you're in and that's very critical because how you communicate to a bunch of engineers who are all 4-year, master, or doctorate engineers is going to be much different from how you communicate with people who may have a high school education. What you expect from those people in their communication is certainly going to be different. You don't expect all of those various levels of education to communicate in the same way. We have to understand that an important part of communication is listening and find ways to bridge the communication gap so that we're understanding each other and not just talking at each other.

In response to the question, can communication be taught, Ron replied: "Yes, I think so. I believe communication can be taught. I think we put a

lot of emphasis into the verbal communication and sometimes we emphasize it too much. There are many ways to communicate — visual, written
as well as verbal — and all different types of communication are very
important."

There are two primary issues of communication:

♦ Actively presenting or delivering the information, and
♦ Listening or receiving the information.

The challenge for the performance-driven leader is to a large degree cultural
because we have tended to equate communication exclusively with delivery
or presentation of information. Somehow, we equate good communication
with good "talking." Usually when people perceive that they are good communicators, they perceive that they are good talkers (that is, they have a
better delivery style, better command of the language, or somehow possess
a self-attributed ability to get people to listen to them). The Third Reich
manager focuses exclusively on the delivery of information and "demands"
to be heard. Performance-driven leaders realize that what is said in communication is at best only half of the challenge. The "results" of the communication are what really count.

In communication, it's not what's said, but what's heard, received, and
understood that really matters.

LISTENING IS THE LEAST-PRACTICED SKILL IN AMERICA.

We don't listen to each other, we just wait to talk. The communication
challenges facing the performance-driven leader include

1. Command of the language
2. Presentation skills
3. Barriers to reception
4. Listening deficiencies

Command of the Language

It's been estimated that there are 600,000 words in the English language.
The vocabulary of an average person in the workplace may be 5 to 10% of

the language, or 30,000 to 60,000 words. This estimate is based not on how many words a person may use, but on how many words the person would understand or be able to reason through when heard in conversation or read in written communication. If everyone within your organization were considered to be on the high side of this average vocabulary, it would mean everyone would have command of approximately 60,000 words. That would leave 90% of the language, or 540,000 words untouched. Imagine if everyone in the organization knew a different 10%! Everyone in the organization would know words that no one else knew. It would take years to play the "If you know what this means" game, and everyone would know and use words the meaning of which the rest of the organization would not have a clue! Further, there are 5000 words in our language that have more than one meaning, and there are 500 words that can be defined a total of 14,000 different ways. No wonder we have communication problems!

For example, let's look at the word *crazy*. If I said to you about your friend Jane, "I met Jane and she is crazy," what am I really saying about Jane? In a social context, referring to Jane as crazy can be a high compliment. It implies that she is fun to be around, humorous, unpredictable, and that it's a pleasurable experience to be in her presence. In a clinical sense, calling Jane crazy is very critical. It implies distorted brain function, inability to maintain consistency, and instability. *Crazy* is one word that runs the gamut from positive to negative meaning. In a social sense, it's one of the highest compliments we could pay someone. In a clinical sense, it's one of the most critical and demeaning things that we could possibly say about anyone. Here's the key. Who determines the meaning of the word *crazy* when it is used in communication? I, the person delivering the communication, may have a clear understanding of what I am trying to say, but it's you, the receiver, who has the final influence on determining the meaning of the word.

MEANINGS ARE CONTROLLED BY THE RECEIVER.

The performance-driven leader exercises great caution in word selection, invests the time for clear explanation, and, as we will discuss later in this chapter, utilizes the tools for clarifying feedback to ensure that use of a word is properly understood.

As we become even more culturally diverse, the command of the language becomes increasingly critical. Different words have different meanings to those from different ethnic groups, religious backgrounds, and even regions of our country. The phrase "bad storm" conveys different meanings to someone in Miami, Florida and someone in Fairbanks, Alaska!

The varied meaning of words is complicated even more as we utilize shortcuts to communication through the use of slang, idioms, colloquialisms, jargon, etc. In our fast-paced world, we use shortcut phrases and assume that everyone understands the phrases the same way. That is a dangerous assumption.

Presentation Skills

It has been said that of our ability to communicate that we must be able to effectively send a message:

♦ Words provide only 7% of the meaning of the communication
♦ Voice inflection (or tone of voice) provides 38%
♦ Nonverbal messages provide 55%*

IT'S NOT WHAT YOU SAY BUT HOW YOU SAY IT!

When what you say is different from how you say it, how you say it will always win. The Third Reich manager understands these "communication truths" very well. The voice is raised, the posture is aggressive, and the communication is "Do it now because I told you to and I am the boss." The words are almost inconsequential. While taking care to select words that have the greatest negative influence, the true impact of the Third Reich manager's communication is in voice inflection and body language. This whole issue of presentation skills, while having been overlooked in the past, has risen to the forefront as we focus on effective communication. An example is the "bedside manner" of medical practitioners. A physician who is eminently qualified to diagnose and heal may be considered unacceptable by patients as a result of ineffective use of these communication tools.

The challenge of the performance-driven leader is to ensure that proper word selection is aligned with consistent vocal qualities and nonverbal communication.

---

*Nido Qubein, *How to Be a Great Communicator,* Nightingale Conant, audio presentation, 1988.

Barriers to Reception

External (Noise Levels, Competition for Attention/Concentration, etc.)

If an employee is engaged in a task and intent on concentrating to ensure completion of the task, it is difficult for a leader to communicate with that person effectively. External considerations also include where communication takes place. Locations can be intimidating. The Third Reich manager attempts to create intimidation by communicating with an employee in a surrounding where the employee is uncomfortable. Picture the Third Reich manager summoning employees to the boss's office, inviting them to sit in a straight back chair, towering above them, pacing, and communicating "displeasure of the moment" through voice, setting, words, and body language.

Internal (Lack of Concentration and Selective Listening)

If people are preoccupied with other issues, then obviously their listening is distorted. Compelling distractions can be neutralized. Some techniques for doing so include

- ◆ Pausing for effect. (Stop talking until receivers become aware of the silence and refocus their attention. An example is the "pregnant pause" that precedes radio broadcaster Paul Harvey's "... and the rest of the story ...")
- ◆ Repositioning yourself to move closer to them (in a nonmenacing posture) or to achieve better penetration of their line of sight.
- ◆ Requesting that they take notes. (When you suggest to someone to "write this down," it's amazing how many people do!)
- ◆ Rescheduling. If employees are truly preoccupied with a current event, crisis, concern, etc., acknowledge their reality and ask them when would be a good time to continue the conversation. In many cases, this request alone will intensify their focus on the communication and may actually result in an agreement to talk about it later. This reinforces the "partnership" of the communication and acknowledges their issues as being valid.

Listening Deficiencies

Selective Listening

Kathy Foltner:

> I have been committed to improving communication for many years and looking for tools to enhance the transfer of information. I would get very frustrated. I'd take 100% of the responsibility, but I would still get very frustrated: that when I would sit down with an employee and talk about something, perhaps something good, perhaps something bad, that sometimes the employee would walk away and I would hear from somebody else that the employee's interpretation of the conversation was very negative and it wasn't even close to my intention or understanding of the conversation. And I would think, How could the employee get that out of what we talked about? And I've learned the importance of listening in communication. Our listening is tainted, or enhanced, by our past and by our past experiences. We are always going to be listening through our past filters. And what we have to realize is that we have people working for us that we don't know outside of this work environment. Sometimes you know personal things about your employees, but a lot of the time, you don't. And all of their listening, every single thing you say to them is going to be affected by their past and by their past experiences. It could have been their past experiences with a big sister, their mother, a previous female boss that I may represent to them. And I can't take responsibility for that. Communication is not one-sided. It's something that we share equally. I think we both have 100% responsibility to communicate in a way that we can hear each other. And it's important that we talk to each other in a language that can be understood. Listening is an important part of communication.

Selective listening is a significant barrier to effective communication. Selective listeners hear only what they intended to hear. Example, employees who perceive the boss is always criticizing them, selectively hear only the criticisms offered by the boss. In a typical conversation the boss may make three very positive statements, five or six very neutral statements, and one critical statement. The employee hears, and can recall, only the critical statement. Selective listening is easy to spot in others and hard to identify in ourselves. Denial is rampant. In reality, we all have selective listening (certainly some with more intensity than others). Selective listening has its roots in our value systems, our interpretation of what is really going on around us. People who judge themselves harshly and doubt their own competency selectively filter through communications and hear only critical comments which reinforce their perception. Conversely, people who have inflated opinions of themselves may disregard any critical comment and seize upon only those statements that reinforce their inflated self-worth. Since it is receivers who determine the final meaning of the communication, their selective listening becomes their reality.

What does the performance-driven leader do to overcome these listening barriers? There are two primary tools:

1. Positioning of the communication
2. Effective feedback

Positioning of the Communication

Positive Information

Let's look at a situation where the performance-driven leader wants to communicate a very positive message to an employee (such as a compliment for a job well done or to relay a positive comment from someone else in the organization or from a customer). The key to assuring that the positive message is accurately received is allowing it to stand alone. The message should not be buried among other pieces of information or muddled by other references. The communication should be clear, concise, and very specific. It should always be transmitted with total focus on the receiver. This communication should never be a throwaway, casually tossed off or embedded among other mixed messages (part of a laundry list of things to be discussed).

During a high-level staff meeting, the head of the customer service department shared a compliment that she had received concerning one of the staff members from another department (accounts receivable). Apparently a customer was confused over some billing that was unclear. The payment had been delayed, and when the accounts receivable representative called concerning the past-due amount, she was able to assist the customer very quickly in clearing up the paperwork problem and expediting the payment. This avoided any late charges or disruption of future shipments. After the meeting, the leader of the accounts receivable department specifically went to the staff member who was involved said:

> Sharon, I really need for you to put down what you are working on and focus on what I'm about to say. During our management team meeting this morning, Ruth, the head of customer service, shared with all of the department heads a comment she had received from the people at the XYZ Company. They were very complimentary to you. Apparently you were able to help them work through a problem and expedite their payment. They felt a problem, which could have taken a couple of weeks to sort out, was handled in two quick phone calls. So much of the good work you do goes unnoticed, customers usually don't bother to call when they are happy. When someone is kind enough to do just that, I want you to know about it. This is just another example of the excellent work you do.

This communication was very clean, straightforward, and stood on its own with no extraneous information "mixed in." Notice also the absence of qualifiers or cancelers, such as "but" or "however." It was a very clear, concise communication of positive information. Third Reich managers would probably have somehow converted the recognition to themselves, not passed it along to the employee, or included it with a whole mishmash of other information so that the impact would be blurred or lost.

**POSITIVE MESSAGES SHOULD
STAND ON THEIR OWN WHENEVER POSSIBLE.**

Negative Information

The positioning of negative information that must be communicated is extremely important. Negative or critical comment is something that none of us wants to hear and we all have a natural self-defense system that deploys when we hear it coming. The key is to present negative/critical messages in a manner that is not hurtful, menacing, or threatening (all hallmarks of the Third Reich manager). The model we recommend for positioning negative/critical information is not new, but perhaps a further explanation of the process will be helpful. The positioning is compliment, critical comment, second critical comment (if necessary), compliment.

	(1)	(3)
HIGH	Positive Compliment	Positive Compliment
	(2)	
LOW	Critical Comment	

Before a critical comment is introduced, it should be preceded by something positive or complimentary. The reason for this is very simple. It opens the hearing process. Let's face it, when somebody says something nice to us we tend to turn up the intensity of our listening. Extending this self-knowledge, we realize that once we open someone else's listening we can insert a critical comment. A second critical comment is possible (if necessary), and should *not* be followed by any more. Two critical comments is the limit for one conversation! Obviously, the insertion of too much critical information may result in receivers shutting down their listening. It is crucial to follow up with another positive comment for two reasons:

1. To reopen the hearing process, and
2. To leave the conversation on a high note.

Rarely do we want to leave a conversation with the receiver being down because the last comment was critical or negative. (One of the major visible differences between the performance-driven leader and the Third Reich manager is how people feel upon exiting a conversation. The performance-driven leader leaves them up and the Third Reich manager leaves them down.)

This positioning technique is not new and has been called a "sewage sandwich" by some (positive stuff on the outside, bad stuff in the middle, or a high, low, high). Some people may perceive that it is predictable; anytime a leader says something positive they expect it to be followed by "a kick in the shins." While this unfortunately may be true, it indicates the practice of positioning positive information "on its own" isn't being followed. If the only time an employee/staff person hears something good is when it precedes something negative, the negative is going to be predictable. A positive message must sometimes stand on its own. If people never hear only the good, the bad will always be anticipated.

Here's an example of the proper positioning of critical information:

Mike, you did a good job presenting your information at the meeting yesterday. You were well prepared, your information was very clear, and everyone was able to grasp your ideas very quickly. One area that needs to be addressed is timing. We had agreed upon a 10-minute time limit and the presentation went almost 25. I would be happy to help you prepare for the next meeting, if you would like. We have to be sure that we keep our time commitments. My concern is that people will develop a knee-jerk resistance every time you get up to speak. Uh oh, here comes long-winded Mike again! And I also thought the questions you were asking of the other department heads during the latter part of the meeting were very insightful. You were demonstrating an excellent depth of knowledge.

Notice that the critical information concerning excessive timing, the offer to help, and the identification of a potential downside is placed between two complimentary statements.

Effective Feedback

To ensure that selective listening does not distort the accuracy of the communication, the performance-driven leaders will use an effective feedback technique. They will invite receivers to restate, in their own words, their understanding of the communication. While the model for this feedback technique is not new, an expanded explanation of the process will be helpful. In eliminating the problem, many leaders struggle with implementation. Let's take the previous conversation with Mike. After the communication, the performance-driven leader will invite Mike to repeat back what his understanding of the communication was, listening very intently for both the positive comments as well as the critical. If Mike is a selective/ negative listener, he will probably have heard only the critical comment and might display a negative reaction. If Mike is a selective/positive listener, he may not have heard the critical information at all, hearing only the positive/ complimentary. If he cannot restate the conversation accurately, it provides an excellent opportunity to repair the miscommunication.

There are three key considerations:

1. Proper presentation of the feedback technique
2. Refraining from judgmental comment
3. Repetition and celebration

Proper Presentation of the Feedback Technique

Many leaders have tried to use feedback techniques with negative results. Comments such as "You are treating me like a child" or "I feel stupid doing this" are not uncommon. The receiver may demonstrate some negative emotion, and usually this is the result of an improper use of the technique. Typical misuse of the technique are such statements as: "Did you understand me?" "Did I make myself clear?" "Are you following me?" "Did you get it?" To each and every one of those the receiver replies, "Oh, yeah" or "Sure." This agreement may be offered merely to bring the conversation to a quick conclusion, and there is no way of knowing whether or not the communication was understood at all.

Another entry in the hall of fame of bad feedback techniques is the communicator who asks: "You don't have any questions, do you?" or "Is there anything you didn't understand?" The answer to these inquiries, as we all know, is: "Oh, no. No questions. I understood everything. Everything is perfectly clear." The reason is that receivers do not want to appear to be stupid or incapable of keeping up with the conversation. So rather than risk public embarrassment, they will acknowledge total understanding when they know in their heart of hearts, they don't have a clue.

The only way to determine what they understood is to ask them to repeat it back in their own words. Here's the trap: this can be offensive if it's done in an aggressive manner. For example, if you were to say, "Mike, I want to be sure that you understood what I said. Would you repeat back to me what you understood our communication to be." He would probably have a negative response. Why? Because the total responsibility for the effective communication rests solely on his shoulders. The implication is the communicator did everything perfectly and now we are going to "test" to see if the receiver was "bright enough" to understand the communication. A negative reaction is almost guaranteed! How can we do it effectively? By using an assertive vs. an aggressive communication style.

AGGRESSIVE COMMUNICATION IS DOMINATED BY "YOU" MESSAGES AND INCREASES NEGATIVE REACTION.

ASSERTIVE COMMUNICATION IS DOMINATED BY "I" OR "WE" STATEMENTS AND DECREASES NEGATIVE REACTION.

The dominant use of the word *you* invites defensiveness. The dominant use of the words *I* and *we* signals partnership, collaboration, and shared responsibility. An assertive use of the feedback technique would sound like this: "Mike, *I* want to be sure that *we* have communicated effectively. Please help check *me* out. Would you repeat, in your words, what *we* have just communicated." This alternative places responsibility on the communicator's shoulders and removes negative pressure from the receiver.

Refraining from Judgmental Comment

If the receiver cannot repeat back the information accurately, obviously the communication was unsuccessful. This is cause for celebration, not negative comments or admonitions. Think of the problems that you have avoided by discovering the miscommunication early! The Third Reich reaction to the miscommunication would be: "Well, I'll repeat what I said again, but please, pay attention! I sure hope you will do a better job of listening this time!" (Intimidating and demeaning.) The appropriate response would be: "Obviously, *I* didn't do a very good job of communicating. Thanks for helping *me* discover that. Let's try the communication again and see if *we* can do a better job this time." Tone of voice is important, here, to convey sincerity rather than sarcasm. There is no blame to be placed for the miscommunication. Communication is a two-way street. If the message wasn't clearly conveyed, it could be the receiver's listening problem or it could be the communicator's presentation problem. Who knows? Who cares?

FIX THE PROBLEM, NOT THE BLAME.

It is not uncommon for the receiver to repeat back an incomplete message; that is, Mike could say, "Well, what I heard you say was that my presentation went too long, you are unhappy with that, and other people don't like it when I talk at the meetings because I take too long." Obviously this statement is, at best, partially correct. It includes negative judgment that was not there originally (the assumption that everyone is already "turned off" by the length of his presentations) and does not reflect accurately the two positive comments. (This could be an indication of a selective/negative listener.) The good news here is this would provide the performance-driven leader an opportunity to make the appropriate correction. "Mike, I don't believe I said I was unhappy, nor that everyone else had already formed opinions that you were too long-winded. And I also told you there were a couple of things I thought you did really well. Let me give you those again." (Repeat the process until the message is accurately restated.)

Repetition and Celebration

Generally, only one restatement is necessary, and if it takes more than that, repeatedly, it can be an indication of some other, more significant problems. One strategy to use if it takes more than two restatements to achieve a successful conclusion is to ask the receiver to write down the information. You might want to say to Mike, "Mike, do *me* a favor and quickly write down the points that *I* am going to make." If for some reason there is a listening blockage in place, seeing it on paper may drive the message home more effectively. Once the communication is concluded successfully, be sure that you celebrate. Let receivers know you appreciated their willingness to participate in this technique and you are really pleased that you had a good communication. Emphasize that working hard to communicate clearly avoids misunderstandings and problems later.

One productive result from frequent successful use of this feedback technique is that people will automatically begin to pay more attention to your communication and concentrate on accurate listening because they know that their participation is expected and will be verified. Some will begin to listen better because they know there will be a test!

Note: When should this feedback technique be used? *Anytime* there is a significant communication or one that has performance expectations as a result. When in doubt, use feedback.

Resistance to What's Being Said

There are three primary strategies to use when the receiver is resisting what's being said. They are

♦ Reassurance
♦ Delay
♦ Questioning

Reassurance

If receivers of a communication feel threatened by what they anticipate will be said, emotions will run high and their listening will be impaired. When defensiveness is high, listening is extremely low. Reassure receivers at the very beginning of the communication that this is not a threat and is not about them, that this *is* a business discussion and not personal. "We are making observations not criticisms." Give receivers time to calm down, regain whatever composure they may have lost, and take a few deep breaths. In general, this should be enough to position them to receive the information accurately. The more defensive the listener, the more reassurance that is necessary.

Delay

If receivers' emotion continues to run high and they seem to be unwilling or unable to reduce their defensive reaction, then it's appropriate to delay (delay *not* postpone). By delaying we merely agree to have the communication at another predetermined time. It is very important for the performance-driven leader to establish a specific time for the communication to take place. It's not "whenever," "later," or "as soon as it is convenient." It is a specific time.

> Jason, it appears that this is not a good time for us to have an important communication. I suggest we delay this until 3:30 this afternoon. Let's meet in the break room, have a cup of coffee, and then decide where it's best for us to talk.

Be aware of the potential trap of the delay turning into a postponement. This is not uncommon, especially if the communication we are planning is unpleasant or may cause some negative reaction. It's easy to procrastinate and avoid those conversations merely by putting them off and never really finding the time to "get around to them." A delay is short, rarely more than 4 hours, and overnight delays are to be avoided at all costs.

The timing of communication is extremely important. There is no magic formula and time can be your ally or your enemy. It may be best to have a conversation early in the morning so that you have the opportunity to correct misunderstandings or reactions throughout the entire day. It may be best not to have a communication with an employee just before we break for the day when the employee's mind may be on commitments after (chores, picking up the kids, etc.). It is unwise to have a partial conversation just before quitting time; then the employee can take parts of the incomplete communication, think about them all night long, and create a web of resistance and emotional barriers. A favorite technique of the Third Reich manager is to tell an employee just before quitting time on Friday that "I am very upset about something. We have a major issue here. I want to talk with you first thing Monday morning" (with an ominous tone in the voice). This puts the employee in a position to obsess all weekend, trying to figure out what is going to happen Monday morning. (This technique should be outlawed under the "cruel and unusual punishment" clause of the Constitution.)

Questioning

An effective technique to break down any resistance to what's being said is the appropriate use of questions. Lani Arredondo had some interesting observations:

> When someone is demonstrating resistance to what's being said, I suggest that rather than going into a "talk-to" mode (sending a message to them that they can defend or resist), slip into an "ask mode" (where you want to receive from them). For example, if I am communicating a point and I sense defensiveness or resistance, there's no point in continuing to talk. It's best to go into a receiving mode, so I will ask a question like "Perhaps I'm not making my point clear enough" or "Are there some other ways that I might put this?" or "How could I get this across to you?" You might try: "If you were going to communicate this to someone else, how would you do it?" Essentially what I'm asking the person to do is "help me out here." When you ask good questions, you are prompting a response, inviting them to be an active partner in the communication.
>
> The potential hazard here is that many people have a tendency to slip into closed questions. We'll ask questions like do, have, will, can, and these generally yield yes or no answers. It's important to frame questions in the form of open questions. I suggest that you remember the "w" when you ask a question in terms of who, what, when, where, and how. When you ask open questions, they prompt a response and a couple of things can happen. First of all, the response you get gives you more insight and information. The root cause of their resistance may be exposed and we can begin to address their issues. Also the very form of open questions suggests a greater degree of interest, on your part, in what the other person has to say. As an example, if I were to say "Do you think managers can learn leadership skills," you can answer yes or no and the form of that question doesn't indicate a lot of interest on

my part. But if I were to ask that as an open question and say, "In your view, *what* are the ways in which managers can improve their leadership skills," that suggests I have an interest in hearing your answer. You will notice that I didn't ask *why*. When you ask *why* questions, you will either get a "because" answer or an "I don't know" answer, or the person may interpret that you are being challenging and that you are testing them. I urge people to eliminate *why* questions and frame them in the form of *what* or *how*.

For example, if I am in a leadership position and I say to an employee "Why did you do that," that will put them on the defensive. But if I open that up and say, "Well, Susan, what were your reasons for doing it that way," that is a more neutral form of questioning and again it indicates that I really want to have an understanding of what her rationale was.

In Chapter 9, we turn from making sure people listen to us to making sure we listen to them.

CHAPTER 9

LEADERSHIP AND LISTENING: IDENTIFYING WHAT TO COMMUNICATE AND CONTROLLING RUMORS, GOSSIP, AND THE GRAPEVINE

Listening Skills

Communication is a two-way street. The Third Reich manager perceives it to be a one-way process: "I talk, you listen, you do." Performance-driven leaders realize the importance of listening and the importance of developing highly productive listening skills. Listening is one of the most important things we can do to build high trust and to reduce fear in an organization. Listening raises people's worth, honors their intellect, and acknowledges their ability to think and not just do.

LISTENING HONORS PEOPLE'S INTELLECT.

Lani Arredondo:

> I think if you ask most people, "Do you listen well?" they would say, "Oh yes, I listen well." But if you were to ask a person they were in conversation with, did they listen well, the person would say, no, they didn't. I think most people would agree that we do not listen as well as we could or we should. Listening is by far the

most significant aspect of communication. When I talk the focus is on me, but when I listen the focus is on you. If you want to build powerful, loyal relationships with people as a leader, if you want to build influence with your people, if you want to build loyalty from your people, one of the most powerful things you can do is send them the message that they count, that they matter, that they are the focus of attention and not you. Listening helps you to establish that.

Picture in your mind someone that you hold in very high regard, that you trust, and with whom you feel a very close connection. If you were to list all of the reasons why you hold this person in high esteem, probably among the first three things that you list would be that the person listens to you. The person doesn't always agree (it would be a boring relationship if agreement were total), but acknowledges that your thought process is valuable and makes you feel that your ideas are worthy of consideration. Few things enhance people's esteem more than being "listened to."

People who have been in the presence of what they perceive to be "people of greatness" often come away in awe of how those persons listened to them. People who have met presidents, popes, prime ministers, authors, scientists, and many others of great renown, even though the meeting may have been brief, come away with the impression that for the few precious minutes they had with that person, they received total focus from them. They were heard, and for those few brief moments, they were the only people on Earth. When people are in your presence, bringing you their issues, do they feel like they have your total concentration? Is your focus totally on them, and for that brief moment are they the only person on planet Earth? Unfortunately, with the fast-paced, demand-driven environment in which we compete, we impress people with the fact that they are one of five or ten things that we are thinking of at the very moment! We have conversations while we are looking around the room, finishing the report that's lying on our desk, dialing the telephone to start another conversation before this one is even brought to conclusion. The performance-driven leader learns to eliminate distractions and focus intently on the person who is the communication partner of the moment. Is it easy? No, of course not. Easy, no; necessary, yes!

**"LISTENING IS ONE OF THE FEW SKILLS THAT HAS
THE POWER TO CHANGE RELATIONSHIPS."**

DEBRA SUCH

Active Listening Techniques

- ◆ Commitment to listening
- ◆ Listening to report
- ◆ Summarizing
- ◆ Taking notes
- ◆ Nonverbal attending

Commitment to Listening

Listening doesn't just happen. You have to make a commitment to concentrate on and absorb what is being said. The most-effective way to develop this commitment is to affirm your awareness that nothing is more important than listening. You are committing in order to affirm the value of the person to whom you are listening and to affirm that you refuse to continue to insult and demean people with your poor listening habits. Committing to yourself, "I am going to become a better listener" is a huge step in beginning the process. You have to make the commitment; you are in control.

Listening to Report

Listening to report is the technique of positioning yourself to listen as if you were going to have to give a detailed report to someone else later. As you begin a conversation, say to yourself, "I am going to focus and concentrate on what they are saying and recall it to a degree that I could factually and accurately replay this conversation for someone else later on." This is a very simple technique and merely requires that you concentrate on the need to listen and that you prepare yourself at the beginning of each meaningful conversation.

Summarizing

Summarizing is a variation of the feedback technique we discussed earlier. Many of us use this technique instinctively, and it consists of repeating back to senders what you understood them to say whether they invite you to or not. This accomplishes two things:

1. It impresses upon them the fact that you are listening intently.
2. It ensures that you are understanding the communication correctly.

It is interesting that when we are in communication situations where we realize that the accurate transfer of information is critical, we will instinctively use this technique of summarization, for example, if we are in a strange city and asking for directions. Someone gives us directions, "Go three blocks, turn right, go three blocks, turn left, turn right at the blue building, turn left at the pink building," etc. What's the first thing we do? We repeat back the directions to make sure that we heard them accurately. Why? Because we know that there is an imminent "downside" to misunderstanding this communication. We are going to be lost within minutes if we haven't processed it accurately. To avoid this pending downside, we instinctively summarize for accuracy. When we are involved in a significant conversation in the workplace, while the downside may not be as imminent as in the above example, it is important for us to summarize to the sender to demonstrate active listening techniques, as well as to assure accurate understanding. Summarizing provides the person delivering the communication with the opportunity to correct any miscommunications before they become problems.

How do we summarize?

+ "Let me be sure I understand."
+ "I want to be sure I'm clear."
+ "What I heard you say was...."

Taking Notes

Taking notes during conversations is an excellent active listening technique because it forces you to concentrate enough to write a summary. For example, when someone comes to you with what either of you believe is a significant communication, say "This communication is important and I want to be sure I remember it accurately. Would you mind if I took some notes?" Occasionally you will find someone who will object to your note taking because the information is very sensitive or the person doesn't want a written record. Those circumstances are very rare. Most people will be very impressed that what they are saying is important enough for you to write notes. Your notes are not word-for-word transcription, but an outline or summarization to aid you in the recall of the information, giving you a written reference to help you at a later date. This is an excellent technique to use when talking on the telephone. Many people are bored or distracted when they are on the phone and may be involved in other tasks at the same time (reading reports, signing memos, balancing checkbooks, etc.). People on the other end of the phone quickly realize that they don't have someone's full attention and it sends them the message that the call is not very important. They begin to say things like: "Hello, are you still there?" "Have we been disconnected?" "Is someone else there?" Saying to them — "This is an important call. I'm going to take some notes to be sure that I'm following accurately. If there's a hesitation in my response it's because I'm writing as we are talking. Is that okay with you?" — forces you to concentrate and impresses on the person on the other end that you are listening actively.

Nonverbal Attending

Much has been written about the importance of nonverbally attending to the people with whom you're communicating. While most of us are aware of this information, a quick review is always helpful. Furthermore, knowing it and doing it are two different things.

- ◆ Face the person with whom you are communicating.
- ◆ Maintain an open posture.
- ◆ Maintain eye contact (keeping your eyes open is a good idea!).
- ◆ Nod appropriately to any salient points.
- ◆ Maintain similar positions (both standing, both sitting, etc.).
- ◆ Keep your mouth shut so that you are not interrupting.

We interviewed one leader who told us that when he focuses on listening, he puts the knuckle of his index finger in his mouth. While this may look silly to some, it may appear to be a behavior of high concentration to others. In reality, he sticks his finger in his mouth so he won't start talking and interrupting! He said, "There are times when I walk away from conversations with teeth marks embedded in my knuckle, but at least I know I listened and didn't just dominate the conversation."

What to Communicate

What to communicate is always a judgment call for the performance-driven leader. Each of us needs to make our own decisions about what information is appropriate. We should all be familiar with the 80/20 rule developed by the Italian economist, Vilfredo Pareto. We mentioned it in an earlier chapter, and it certainly applies to communication. The rule: 80% of what we need to know is contained in 20% of the information available to us. It's important that we communicate that 20% of core information to everyone around us. Determining what to communicate and actually transferring the information are challenges for every organization and issues with which every organization struggles. Invariably, important information is not communicated. People are "left out of the loop" and problems are often blamed on "nobody told me." While Third Reich managers withhold information by design and manage the information flow to accomplish their own agenda, most communication problems are errors of omission and not commission. We do not sit down and systematically decide to whom we will deny information. We just don't think through the communication process properly or take the time to implement it completely. Many leaders, out of frustration, will say, "I don't have time to communicate everything to everybody." And while this is a legitimate observation, the retort is, "You always find time to go back and fix the problems that the lack of communication creates." The problems created are numerous, from poor performance, missed deadlines, customer neglect, and the more human issues of hurt feelings and the impression of being left out.

The performance-driven leader will never be perfect in the communication process. No matter how sincere the commitment and the effort, there will always be something that will be overlooked. This should not lead us to give up or not to try.

The guidelines are as follows, communicate as much information as humanly possible. Obviously the core 20% of critical information needs to go to everyone within the organization and it must be communicated on a timely basis. The best way to communicate is face to face in meetings with written backup as is appropriate. The last thing any organization needs is more meetings!! It's been estimated that 90% of all organizational meetings are a waste of time and proof of this can be observed in any organization on any given day. The correction here is not to distort the communication process by eliminating meetings, but to become much more efficient at managing meetings.

It is not enough to communicate information in writing where it will probably be buried in someone's in-box. Some people process their paperwork religiously; others do not. Some people check E-mail regularly; others do not. Some people are not good at assimilating just the written message; they also need to hear it verbally. Verbal presentation with the opportunity for questions and feedback, backed up in writing, is the most effective way to communicate as much information as possible.

WHEN IN DOUBT, GET THE INFORMATION OUT. ERR ON THE SIDE OF COMMUNICATING TOO MUCH!

Perhaps your people will come to you saying, "Hey, I don't need all of this stuff. I don't need to know all of this information." That is a good problem to have. It is easily corrected and establishes the environment of open communication. People don't perceive that they are being denied information. Trimming of information will certainly be necessary, but err on the side of too much information at first. Too much information never incurs the same level of damage as not enough. Let them tell you what they don't need. Let it be their idea. Do not be perceived as denying information.

Michele Atkins:

> There is a staff perception, and I don't think it's unique to our staff, I think it's true in every staff, that they are entitled to every bit of information on every decision. My read on this is to have enough information so that they don't feel that they are ever going to be surprised. Grown-ups don't like being surprised. I certainly don't, and I want to accord the same respect for the staff. One of the things that was profoundly troubling to me in the early days was that there was a perception that we had a hidden agenda and that I was not being entirely truthful and that somehow I was looking to set a trap somewhere and there didn't appear to be much trust. Trust, obviously, has to be built. Now a couple of years into our reengineering phase, the trust seems to be so high that if I don't communicate completely on an issue, the staff can say, "Yeah, you forgot to tell me that, but I know how much you have on your plate and that's okay. I really don't feel left out." My read on this is if you continue to use a communication style which says, "Here's all I know about it, here's what I'm thinking I might do, I would love your input," and then inform them about the decision when it's made, there are going to be huge rewards to that. There are clearly certain issues the staff should not have input into. Perhaps managing a true crisis, safety and security of staff, these and others are issues that you just simply don't tell people because it would

not make them safe to have the knowledge. But beyond that, there are very few things I'm not comfortable sharing.

Proprietary Information

The communication of proprietary information is always an issue. Management typically is extremely sensitive about the information that is made public because it fears that somehow the information will end up in the wrong hands. Is there proprietary information that shouldn't be universally shared? Of course! However, it is an extremely small proportion of the total. How much information in your organization is really too sensitive to share with employees? In reality, it's very little.

Management's fear that employees may somehow misuse the information is usually groundless. Key question: If one of the workers is provided with important information, who is the worker going to share it with? Rarely does the worker have exposure to competitors, etc. The risk of exposure is usually limited to the very top echelons of the organization. The dreaded leaks rarely happen in the lower levels. It's the executives and leaders who mingle with others in the industry. Trade associations, professional groups, etc. are the greatest potential opportunity for an inappropriate transfer of information and meetings with these people aren't attended by the people on the shop floor!

George Mosher:

> Although we are a privately held organization, we try to run an open-book company. All employees get a copy of the monthly letter submitted to the Board of Directors so they know how the company is doing and they feel informed as to what's going on. It's about a one- or one-and-one-half-page letter. It addresses sales figures but not necessarily all of the charts, and it will go down to the dollar profit and dollar sales.

When asked if he feared this information getting into the hands of a competitor, he responded:

> What are they going to do with it? So they would know whether we had a good month or a bad month. Actually I would rather have my competitors be profitable. It's much better to compete against profitable competitors. And it's important for employees to know that they are a part of a profitable and successful winning organization.

Kathy Foltner also feels it's important to keep employees and staff informed on all aspects of the business. They are given copies of weekly reports that address sales, expenditures, earnings. They are compensated based on the overall performance of their offices, and she feels that they need to know where they stand at all times. She says:

> They have their budget numbers, all of that stuff, right there in their offices. They are told it's confidential, but I guess they could be mailing it to my competition and I would have no way to control that. I have to trust them. If they want to work for a competitor, they could take it with them, but so what? If you take my budget, what are you going to do with my budget? You would know how much we sold per year and which months were up and down. I withhold very little information because what makes our success happen is the team, the leadership and the team. And if you're missing parts of the puzzle, you can't be a contributing member to the team. Withholding information causes far more problems than sharing it.

Sharing as much information as possible builds trust and commitment. It communicates to all employees and staff members that they are valued, that they are trusted, and that they play a major role within the organization. For all employees in the organization, their job is as important to them as the president's or the CEO's. Don't they have a right to know what's going on within the organization where they have chosen to invest their effort, their future, and their security? Nothing positive will be gained by withholding information.

Critical Issues

Among the issues that are most critical to communicate are

- ◆ Goals
- ◆ Progress
- ◆ Results
- ◆ Crisis updates
- ◆ Pending change
- ◆ Pending issues
- ◆ All sides of an issue

A few of which we'll discuss specifically.

Goals

Goals that must be communicated to the entire organization include long term, short term, organizational, departmental, and individual. How can you be expected to achieve something if you don't know what it is you're expected to achieve? In his 1989 book *The Seven Habits of Highly Effective People,* Dr. Stephen Covey lists as one of the habits "Start with the end in mind." The entire organization needs to know where we are going. It's a favorite trick of the Third Reich manager to blur goals or not communicate them in an attempt to coerce people into achieving them. The thought process is, "If I don't tell them what the goals are, I can get them to do more." Rarely if ever does this result in goal achievement. It's also not uncommon for various layers of management to inflate the goals as the goals are passed down through the organizational ranks.

For example, the executives of an organization may project a 7% growth. They believe this is reasonable and attainable and base their financial projections and budget on this number. They communicate this goal down to the next level (the directors). The directors perceive that if they want to get a 7% increase, they better inflate the goal for their people to 10%. While they don't anticipate achieving the 10% increase, they do expect to reach the 7%. Their people will work hard, but they will fall short in the attempt. So they communicate the 10% goal to the next level (department heads). The department heads, believing that they have a 10% goal, perceive that they must inflate the goal to 13%, hoping their people will achieve the 10% while chasing the unrealistic 13%! By the time these goals get to the employee/staff level, they may be up to 14 to 15% (double what the executives were looking for). The employees and staff take one look at these goals and realize that they are totally unachievable. The first question they ask is "What are these people smoking during their lunch breaks?" They quickly dismiss the goals as unrealistic, fantasyland projections and don't even attempt to achieve them. The result is no one tries for any kind of an increase. Setting unrealistic goals often elicits responses of learned helplessness and results in no growth whatsoever.

This process of step-by-step inflation of goals is not a successful technique. Even if it were successful, what the various layers of management have done is successively invite their people to a banquet of failure! If the 7% goal were achieved, the executive and director level would take pride and satisfaction in goal achievement and everyone else in the organization would be basking in failure. To compound the problem, employees and staff would sense that the executives and directors were pleased, while knowing that their department head and individual boss were not, and would read all kinds of unfairness and confusion into the process! Should we be surprised when employees would not take future goals seriously?

The performance-driven leader establishes realistic and attainable goals and outlines the benefits of successful goal overachievement. "We are projected for a 7% increase in productivity. If we exceed that, this is what the results will be for you." In this way, we are not using our goals as a ceiling of performance, but rather a threshold in measuring achievement.

Past and Pending Issues

Obviously, no leader has a crystal ball with which to see the future. However, there are many pending issues that can be anticipated. It's important that these be communicated on a timely basis. Discussions on the pros and cons of various strategies, along with the reasons they have been implemented, are important information to be shared.

We talked with the CEO of a $20 million manufacturing and sales organization. He shared with us that every 4 months (three times a year) for the past 5 years he has conducted companywide meetings to keep employees informed. These meetings are held on Saturday mornings at a hotel close to the plant. Attendance is voluntary and he said that the first few meetings were attended by approximately 50% of the employees. Now every employee attends and, if someone is absent, it's due to a "crisis of the moment" and not resistance or apathy. His meetings have a standard three-part format:

1. These are the significant issues we have faced and decisions that have been made in the past 4 months and here's why.
2. These are the issues and changes that we are anticipating in the next 4 months or beyond. (He attempts to cover all sides of the issues, takes care not to prejudice a particular position or decision, and presents as much fact and detail as possible.)
3. Any questions or comments?

The employees/staff feel that they are kept well informed and when issues do arise of which they have no knowledge, they tend to feel it's an isolated incident that has fallen through the cracks and not the result of a specific intention to withhold information or evidence of a hidden agenda.

He goes on to explain that during the question and comments portion, there is nothing that is considered out-of-bounds. Anyone is free to question any decision, offer any thoughts or comment in any way on anything that relates to the business. Employees have learned that there will be no retaliation and that a true "punishment-free communication environment" exists. Any employee is free to say anything he or she wishes. The rules of the road, however, are that all will address each other with respect and dignity and everyone will conduct themselves as adults. He states:

> I would not permit someone to stand up and say that a particular decision was, "The dumbest thing they have ever heard" or "Whoever made that decision must be an idiot," or to talk about mine or someone else's Momma. That is neither adult behavior nor treating each other with respect. However, any employee is free to stand up and say, "I'm not sure I understood this decision. I'm not sure it's clear to me. Could you explain it a little more and help me understand the reasoning behind it?" I will carry on those types of conversations all day long. One of the results of these meetings has been a lessening of the informal criticisms of management (employees talking behind the managers' backs) and a reduction in the activity of the rumor mill.

The Informal Communication Highway

Every organization hosts the "superhighway" of informal communication: *rumor, gossip,* and the *grapevine.* This informal communication network will never be totally obliterated. However, it can be managed and reduced if leadership is willing to make a commitment to share information with the entire organization. Everyone in an organization wants to be "plugged in," "part of the loop," or whatever the euphemistic term of the month is for "knowing what's going on around here." Everyone wants to be a part of the "in-crowd." The difference between the in-crowd and the out-crowd in any organization is quite simple. The in-crowd gets information accurately from management on a timely basis; the out-crowd gets information from rumor, gossip, and the grapevine. Rumor, gossip, and the grapevine are always slanted toward fear, always slanted toward reducing trust, always lower moral, and are antimanagement in tone. Have you ever heard a rumor that made you feel good?

**RARE ARE THOSE RUMORS THAT RAISE OUR MORALE OR
THAT MAKE US FEEL GOOD ABOUT WHAT'S HAPPENING.**

The rumors that do make us feel good are usually truly negative reports that we somehow take perverse pleasure in hearing (when we hear of the demise of someone that we are happy to see demised). We may hear that someone is finally getting "what's coming to them" and we may take some pleasure in that report. In reality, it's a rare rumor that brightens our outlook.

Consider the example of the Third Reich manager who goes to a department head meeting. Upon return to the department, the manager will generally have a conversation with his or her "pets of the moment." The conversation starts out with "Don't tell anyone I told you this, but here's what's going to be happening." The pets swear confidentiality and the Third Reich manager shares *some* of the information with them, obviously withholding anything perceived to be sensitive or risky. The pets, who have sworn secrecy, then go to their buddies and say, "Don't tell anyone I told you this, but here's what I just heard from the boss." They share their confidential information, obviously withholding anything they perceive to be sensitive or risky. This pattern repeats itself in a cascade of information until it finally gets down to the lowly out-crowd, and the information they receive in no way resembles the initial information that was communicated at the beginning of this process. We have all played the game of "telephone" as children, where we assemble in a circle, someone whispers a statement to the person sitting next to him or her, and as the statement goes around the circle, it experiences a huge distortion. By the time it returns to the originator, it isn't even close to what was initially said. That's how rumors usually are created. If the only radio station on your dial that comes in loud and clear is the rumor, gossip, and grapevine station, why are we surprised that the Third Reich manager deals with high fear, low trust, low morale, and negativity!

How do you neutralize this informal communication superhighway? By sharing information equally with everyone at the exact same time. Everyone hears the same information. Everyone has the opportunity to ask questions and everyone has the opportunity to hear the same responses. One person isn't told one thing and another person another. The nature of human beings ensures that there will always be rumor and gossip. However, when we create an environment of low fear and high trust, rumors are more likely to be brought to the leader for clarification, rather than reacted to or passed on. When employees report the latest rumor they have heard, the performance-driven leader listens, clarifies, and, most importantly, doesn't react. In contrast, the Third Reich manager who gets wind of a rumor begins an "inquisition." The person bringing in the rumor is placed in the untenable situation of having to disclose the source, which causes embarrassment for the person and denial and negative reactions from the source. Does shooting the messenger ring a bell? The result of this is that Third Reich managers very quickly dry up all their sources of information and they don't hear the rumors because everyone, other than their cultivated informers, is afraid to disclose information because of the feared reaction.

The performance-driven leader

♦ Takes care not to overreact
♦ Has department or teamwide meetings to address the rumor if it is substantial enough
♦ Follows up to see if the rumor persists

This behavior ensures that the leader will continue to be plugged in to the informal information superhighway as a result of not punishing the people who share what they've heard.

A component of sharing information is honesty.

**"ONE OF THE BIGGEST ISSUES FOR PEOPLE
IN THE WORKPLACE TODAY IS BELIEVING THAT
THE WORKPLACE IS NOT OUT TO HARM THEM
AND THAT THINGS THAT ARE SAID ARE TRUE."**

MICHELE ATKINS

Ron Stewart:

> I think sometimes you have to tell people what I call the *ugly honest truth*. That is, telling people the truth as you know it to be even when it isn't pretty or comfortable. If we are dealing with an issue that is confidential, the right answer is to tell people "I can't answer that because it's something that's confidential." You shouldn't tell them some B.S. answer that leaves them walking away saying, "I know what he really said but what did he really mean." We should

just say, "It's confidential and I can't tell you that. When I can, I will." I think sometimes we forget that in our communication.

There are times when the performance-driven leader has to say, "I don't know." Acknowledging a lack of information is far better than remaining silent and saying nothing. If there is a huge rumor circulating through the organization, by ignoring the rumor and pretending it doesn't exist leaders make some very powerful "silent statements."

♦ Their silence is perceived to affirm the reality of the rumor.
♦ Their silence implies that they are withholding information.
♦ Their silence implies that they know the rumor is disturbing to their people and that they just don't care.
♦ Their silence sends the message that "You aren't worth my time, I don't value you highly enough to inform you of what is going on."

Obviously these are very damaging and counterproductive messages. Michele Atkins:

> One of my answers to building trust is when you don't know, say you don't know. Communicate that there is no hidden agenda. Early in our experience, when I would go in and say "I don't know," I would hear what I call the ladies room gossip going on, which is "She really does know, she's just playing a trick on us." As people have been with us long term and have demonstrated their ability to change and grow with the organization, they now trust implicitly when I say, "I don't know." They know I mean it. When I say, "I'm thinking about something, what do you think?" they know I'm gathering that kind of information. They no longer fear the hidden agenda.

Performance-driven leaders bring their people together to say, "I'm hearing the same rumor that you are. I don't know what the truth really is. I will do everything that I can to find out the truth, and when I have fact, I will report it back to you immediately. Please understand I will not come to you with the latest rumor of the moment. I will only come to you with fact, and it's very possible that you may hear something before I can confirm it. I don't want to be in the rumor business; I want to be in the fact business. And as soon as I know, you will know." This expression of truth reinforces the trust in the relationship. Ignoring rumors only induces fear and reduces trust. And, make certain it happens! When you know, communicate it to them.

It is a foolish leader who believes that "sensitive organizational issues aren't leaking out." If it has been discussed or put in a memo, regardless of the classification of confidentiality, it is being discussed throughout the organization, rampantly and inaccurately. The discussions are slanted toward fear, away from trust, against morale and against management.

Bad News

How do we deliver bad news when it is necessary? Let's face it, it doesn't take a lot of talent to be the bearer of good news, always telling everybody that things are going well! Some managers will hide their discomfort with bad news and their inability to communicate it properly either by prolonged silence (even in the overwhelming presence of bad indicators all around them) or by maintaining a smile and reassuring everyone that things will be fine. (Nero fiddling while Rome is burning.) "Don't worry.... Everything is great.... Nothing to be concerned about!" Often, while the contorted face, the wringing hands, and other nonverbal cues send a more accurate message, such managers tell us not to worry. However, they certainly are upset!

In Chapter 5 we discussed the communication of bad news. For review, how does the performance-driven leader communicate "bad news"? There are five specific guidelines:

♦ Communicate early and completely
♦ Be truthful
♦ Listen and acknowledge people's reaction
♦ Care for the casualties — nurture
♦ Reinforce appropriate long-term behavior

The most important of these is, when bad news is inevitable, share the news with the entire group as early and as completely as possible. Don't hold anything back. For example, if there are to be no raises for the next full year, don't tell people, "We will review this policy quarter by quarter." If you say that and raises aren't forthcoming at the quarters, by not dealing with one piece of bad news, you will then have to deal with *four* pieces of bad news. People will continue to live in disappointment, generating anger and ongoing resentment.

The performance-driven leader realizes that adults have a great capacity for dealing with truth if truth is offered. It is the deliverer of bad news, not the receiver of bad news, that struggles with truth.

CHAPTER 10

THE PERFORMANCE-DRIVEN LEADER AND TRAINING

Training is one of the most important issues facing the performance-driven leader. As we discussed in Chapters 6 and 7, we cannot incorporate aspects of participative management or invite people to become more involved in their jobs and in decision making unless we effectively train them to do so. Training is something that every organization acknowledges as critical. However, too few really treat it as such. Training receives a lot of lip service, but is often not supported with appropriate budgets and planning. Few things that the performance-driven leader does are more important than training, but the importance of training is often lost in the shuffle. Because training is an activity that yields delayed payoff and is not necessarily "urgent of the moment," it's easy to deemphasize. The squeaky wheel gets the grease, and the delayed squeak of poor training tends to be heard later in terms of long-term loss of productivity, quality, and competitiveness. Training deficiencies tend to be cumulative rather than "in your face" confrontational. In times of downsizing, budget cuts, or crises, training budgets and entire departments may be on the bubble. When things are going well, we fund the training effort; when things aren't going well, that's one of the things we cut. Interestingly, training during the bad times is probably one of the most important things we could do, but our judgment tends to be clouded by more immediate needs (cost cutting, etc.).

When General Dwight Eisenhower, in the midst of the turmoil surrounding preparations for the D-Day invasion of France, was asked how he kept his focus under the pressure of such a large number of complex activities, he replied that "I try to remind myself that what is most urgent is seldom most important, and what is most important is seldom most urgent." We must constantly remind ourselves that while training may not present itself as our most urgent activity, it is certainly among the most important.

Organizations make a typical series of errors in their training efforts. Most train too little and attempt to cover that fact by hiring only experienced personnel. They make a horrible assumption that the people they are hiring have been trained well. Why should we assume that someone else, another organization, was willing to do and do very well that which we are unwilling to do at all? When we hire only "experienced" personnel, they bring with them their bad habits as well as their good. A big portion of initial training is actually "untraining" or the breaking of old, unproductive bad habits. When we don't train properly, we basically say to a new employee:

- "We want you to train us."
- "We hired you because of your experience."
- "We want you to do it the same way you've always done it."

One of the biggest identifiers of this condition is how often we hear from a new employee, "Well, that's not how we used to do it at the ABC Company" or "We did it much differently over at the XYZ Company and it worked much better." When we hear statements such as these, it can be a significant warning that our training is deficient and that employees perceive they are there to fix us.

It is not uncommon for employees to resist initial training. They may believe

- They know all there is to know.
- Their training and experience is superior to what you can provide.
- They want to impress you with their current knowledge and skills.
- Their old way is "comfortable" and they would rather not have to adopt new behaviors.

This resistance cannot be allowed to shortcut the training process. George Mosher offers an example:

> We hired a new manager. He was familiar with one type of computer system and he wasn't familiar with the system we were using. Both systems were capable of doing the same thing and probably the new person was correct that the other system was

newer and more state of the art and was easier to use. We wanted to use our computer systems as we had developed programs to be interchangeable and if we let people develop their own computer programs, then we would have some form of babble.

The performance-driven leader is open to ideas and suggestions from new people and certainly encourages them to allow us to learn from their past experience. However, before they begin to introduce "the old way we used to do it" or "the better way they did it over there," the leader insists that they learn to do it our way and then if change is appropriate, we will all change. They must learn it our way first, and then we will entertain changes to our process.

When we don't train properly, we also send a negative message with horrible impact:

♦ "You are not important enough for me to train."
♦ "I have other much more important duties to address."
♦ "The job you are doing really isn't important enough to spend time ensuring that it's done well."

Lack of training lowers the self-worth and self-esteem of an employee. It underscores the lack of value or importance the organization places in them.

Some organizations train too much. We see this especially in heavily front-end-loaded training programs. An example: We hire new employees to join our organization and they are subjected to 6 weeks of intense initial training. Not only are they trained on the initial tasks they will be doing when they assume their new responsibilities, they are trained on tasks and techniques they may not be doing for the next 24 to 36 months. Typically, the result is early strong performance (because the initial tasks were reinforced by actually performing them) and a downward spiral of performance as introduced but unreinforced tasks are undertaken. While they were taught the delayed tasks during training, they were not given the opportunity to learn and reinforce them by actual application, and the training becomes lost. We judge the employees harshly and tell them of our disappointment. They were obviously taught these skills but weren't capable of sustaining the learning, and we show our disappointment with reduced ratings on performance appraisals which negatively affect compensation, promotability, etc. While 6 weeks of initial training may be appropriate, it's probably not appropriate all at one time. An effective alternative method is the "just-in-time" (JIT) method that is shown in Table 1.

TABLE 1
Just-in-Time Training Model

Time of Service	Length of Training	Training Presented	Tasks Implemented
Initial hire	2 weeks	Training on initial tasks, tasks performed within first 90 days of employment	Immediate consistent completion of tasks initially trained
90 days	1 week	Review initial training and present training on phase 2 tasks just prior to assignment of responsibility	Consistent completion of phase 2 tasks
9 months	1 week	Review phase 2 training and present training on phase 3 tasks just prior to assignment of responsibility	Consistent completion of phase 3 tasks
15 months	1 week	Review phase 3 training and present phase 4 tasks just prior to assignment of responsibility	Consistent completion of phase 4 tasks
24 months	1 week	Review phase 4 training and present training on phase 5 tasks just prior to assignment of responsibility	Consistent completion of phase 5 tasks

Totals: 2 years of employment; 6 weeks training.

As you can see, a total of 6 weeks of training was presented. However, it was not presented all at once, but as a preplanned, phased program over two years. This allows the training to be presented in manageable modules with quick reinforcement by completion of the trained tasks.

Our goal in this chapter, as well as in Chapter 11, is to underscore the importance of training, acknowledge the deficiencies that exist in most organizations, and help the performance-driven leader to use training to

- Ensure efficient performance
- Prepare employees and staff for change
- Identify and implement training as a mechanism of motivation
- Raise the net worth of employees and staff by increasing their inventory of skills

The Third Reich Manager and Training

The typical Third Reich manager views training as a *reactive* behavior. Reactive training is training that is instituted only when we have experienced a problem and is focused on teaching employees to do exactly what they are told or to "fix" what they have done in error. Another aspect of reactive training is providing compulsory training that is designed strictly to hold the organization harmless for the acts of its employees. For example, many training programs are offered on sexual harassment issues, diversity in the workplace, nondiscriminatory hiring practices, etc., with the sole intent of the organization being able to prove that it provided training for employees and should not be held responsible if an employee violates the law. This training is basically provided to allow the organization to distance itself from the acts of its representatives. This training does not have a basis in growth and development, but merely in self-preservation. While these issues are critical to today's workplace environment, the focus should not be merely training to C.Y.A. (cover your anatomy "corporately"), but to guarantee high quality, efficiency, and productivity through compliance.

Proactive training, training that encourages employees to take the initiative, make decisions, and exercise good judgment, is foreign to Third Reich managers and not a part of their overall training initiative. The Third Reich manager is often intimidated and fearful of other people's input and decisions, feeling that if others thought processes are accepted, it would diminish their own, so they are loath to offer training that would encourage such a potential outcome.

Third Reich managers have a somewhat convoluted interpretation of training. Training tends to be

- Something that they don't want to do
- Something that is not "real-world" based
- Something that is done only to be in compliance with company policy

---

**THE THIRD REICH MANAGER'S DEFINITION OF TRAINING
IS "LOSS OF PRODUCTION TIME."**

Third Reich managers are usually reluctant to involve themselves in the training process because it requires them to keep their skills current and sharpened (if you're going to train it, you had better be able to do it). It forces them to complete the tasks "by the book" (you can't train on short-cuts — employees will figure these out for themselves).

The performance-driven leader pursues and supports training opportunities, realizing that, without training,

◆ Employees will not grow and develop
◆ Changes cannot be properly implemented
◆ Competitiveness and efficiency are dramatically reduced

Six Training Truths for the Performance-Driven Leader

1. The performance-driven leader is committed to self-education.
2. The performance-driven leader realizes that training is a leadership function.
3. The performance-driven leader is committed to leading change by effectively training for change.
4. The performance-driven leader is committed to analyzing the vision, mission, goals, and objectives of the organization and aligning appropriate training to support those outcomes.
5. The performance-driven leader is committed to being an active partner in the training process.
6. The performance-driven leader assesses the limitations of training.

Truth 1: Self-Education

As we have already identified,

LEADERSHIP IS ONE OF THE LEAST-TRAINED SKILLS IN AMERICA TODAY.

An unfortunate reality is that you, the performance-driven leader, are being held responsible for successfully using skills for which you have not been effectively trained. Leadership is not being trained in our schools and is rarely being trained effectively in our organizations. Organizations may not be capable of or willing to provide the leadership training that is necessary. Leadership training has primarily degenerated to OJT (on-the-job training) which is, in actuality, an "invitation to fail for a specific time." Leaders in America have been digging huge holes from which they have to unbury themselves as they commit the errors which are inherent in a program of learning strictly by failing. Leadership training, when provided, has been focused on

♦ Command-and-control-style management
♦ Compulsory programs provided so the organization can distance itself from responsibility (discrimination in hiring, price fixing, collusion, etc.)

In actuality, most leaders have developed their skill by merely modeling the behavior of their previous bosses.

Where Do Performance-Driven Leaders Turn to Receive the Training They Seek?

Congratulations! The fact that you are reading this book and have gotten at least to this point in Chapter 10 is evidence that you are committed to increasing your inventory of skills. There is a wealth of leadership material on the market today if the performance-driven leader is willing to dedicate the time necessary to learn. Without question, a portion of every day must be dedicated to learning through self-driven development. Take advantage of the written material that is available. Books by accomplished leadership gurus such as Tom Peters, Stephen Covey, Peter Senge, Ken Blanchard, and others (see Bibliography at end of book) are readily available through libraries and book stores (hardback and paperback). We also recommend:

♦ *The New Leader: Bringing Creativity and Innovation to the Workplace,* Gregory P. Smith, Delray Beach, FL: St. Lucie Press, 1997.

- *Leading People,* Robert H. Rosen, New York: Viking, 1996.
- *Leadership I.Q.,* Emmet C. Murphy, New York: John Wiley and Sons, 1996.
- *Leadership by Encouragement,* Don Dinkmeyer and Daniel Eckstein, Delray Beach, FL: St. Lucie Press, 1996.
- *The Leadership Challenge,* Koules Posner, San Francisco, Jossey Bass, 1995.

To enhance your training and presentation skills:

- *How to Present Like a Pro: Getting People to See Things Your Way,* Lani Arredondo, New York: McGraw-Hill, 1991.

Management and Leadership Development Seminars — Seminars such as these are offered throughout the country. Recommended sources are

- Local colleges and universities that offer courses on various aspects of leadership development
- Professional training organizations. We recommend groups such as
  - Trinity Solutions, Peachtree City, GA (1-800-368-1201)
  - Career Track, Boulder, CO (1-800-334-6780)
  - The American Management Association (1-800-262-9699)
  - The Forum Corporation, Boston, MA (1-800-FORUM11)

Alternative Training Technologies — There are a number of excellent audiotape and videotape training resources to help performance-driven leaders advance their skills. We recommend catalogs from

- Career Track, Boulder, CO (800-334-1018)
- Nightingale Conant Corp., Chicago, IL (800-323-5552)
- Dartnell, Chicago, IL (800-621-5463)

How Do Performance-Driven Leaders Assess Their Own Training Needs?

The first step is self-assessment. Rate yourself in the following areas:

	Current Level of Skill		Improvement Needed	
	High Low		Yes	No
1. Are my technical skills current and efficient?	High	Low	Yes	No
	1 2 3 4 5			
2. Do I stay up-to-date on the technical developments and terminology of my industry?	High	Low	Yes	No
	1 2 3 4 5			
3. Do I have competent communication skills, both verbal and written, that allow me to communicate successfully to all levels within my organization?	High	Low	Yes	No
	1 2 3 4 5			
4. Are my organizational skills sufficient to allow me proficiency in planning and prioritizing?	High	Low	Yes	No
	1 2 3 4 5			
5. Do I maintain a neat and efficient work area as an example to others?	High	Low	Yes	No
	1 2 3 4 5			
6. Are my computer technology skills appropriate to support the current technology within my organization?	High	Low	Yes	No
	1 2 3 4 5			
7. Are my mathematical skills appropriate to ensure success in my organization?	High	Low	Yes	No
	1 2 3 4 5			
8. Am I current on laws and accepted practices concerning hiring, harassment, discrimination (of any kind — age, gender, race, religion, etc.), and firing procedures?	High	Low	Yes	No
	1 2 3 4 5			
9. Do I understand and implement measurement systems to allow efficient tracking of results?	High	Low	Yes	No
	1 2 3 4 5			

Key Questions:

1. What skills do I need to successfully achieve my next career move? ____

_____

_____

2. Would my current skills be attractive to a new employer? (If not, what do I need to improve?) _____

_____

_____

My Personal Skill Development Action Plan:

Skills to Be Developed	How Will I Acquire Them?	Date the Learning Process Will Begin
1. _____	_____	_____
2. _____	_____	_____
3. _____	_____	_____

GAIN COMMITMENT FOR YOUR TRAINING AND SKILL DEVELOPMENT DURING THE PERFORMANCE APPRAISAL PROCESS.

One of the best ways to ensure that your training will be ongoing is to negotiate skill development through the performance appraisal process. A big part of any appraisal process is not just what you can do for the organization, but what the organization can do for you! Clearly, identification of how it can help to increase your inventory of skills is an appropriate commitment to seek. Opportunities for promotion may not be as prevalent within your organization as they once were, and if you are going to compete for those fewer opportunities, you have to

1. Demonstrate your willingness to learn
2. Demonstrate the results of that learning
3. Identify the advantages to the organization of supporting your learning

As the percentage of yearly compensation increases shrinks, an additional way of enhancing your total compensation package is the addition of the training component. Let your immediate supervisor know

- What skills you want to develop
- Why you want to develop them
- How you want to receive the training (when, where, etc.)

- How the training will benefit the organization as well as you personally
- How the training results will be measured

Performance-driven leaders assume responsibility for their own training and development. If training isn't being offered, pursue it personally. Do not blame others or allow yourself to become a "victim" of poor skill development because of the lack of the organization's training efforts. In the final analysis, you and you alone are responsible for your own skill development. Your skills will feed you for the rest of your life. When you assume the challenge of self-education you eat better!

Truth 2: Training as a Leadership Function

Few things for which the performance-driven leader is held responsible should assume a higher priority than being actively involved in the training function. As we will see later in our discussion of training and development, successful training encompasses a blend of various training techniques and may involve input from a variety of people. This should all be done under the careful influence of the performance-driven leader. Unfortunately, it's very easy for leaders to take their eye "off the ball" and assign lesser importance to their role in training.

- *It's easy* to let someone else be responsible for training.
- *It's easy* to become preoccupied with other tasks, not giving the appropriate priority to training.
- *It's easy* to let your skills erode to where training effectiveness is diminished.

The performance-driven leader is truly an exceptional "teacher/trainer." We have all heard the adage (*ad nauseam*), "Catch someone a fish, you feed them for a day. Teach them how to fish, and you feed them for a lifetime." Unfortunately, much of training today in America has become: show someone how to catch a fish one time, then watch them starve and criticize them for being skinny! We will address the critical components of effective training in our next chapter. At this juncture, we identify five performance pointers for the performance-driven leader and the training function:

1. The performance-driven leader actively participates in training.
2. The performance-driven leader actively practices JIT training.
3. The performance-driven leader avoids the practice of OJT.
4. The performance-driven leader practices shared experience training (SET).
5. The performance-driven leader eliminates punishment for trainees.

The Performance-Driven Leader Becomes
Actively Involved in Training

The performance-driven leader demonstrates and reinforces any and all training that has been received. Three points:

1. The leader's performance legitimizes the tasks being trained; the leader proves that it can be done by the book or the way "we trained it." If this point is not made early in the training process, it's very easy for the trainee to hide behind the wall of "training isn't real-world based." It's easy for the trainee to draw a distinction between theory and reality. Training is then disregarded and the quest to find the appropriate shortcut has begun.
2. Demonstrating the training establishes the leader's proficiency. It becomes very clear the trainee is not being asked to do something leaders cannot do themselves. It is very difficult to influence and lead people performing tasks that the leader is not capable of accomplishing. One of the realities of downsizing is that in many organizations we have leaders who have assumed responsibility for functions which they have never actually done or of which they have little knowledge. This may be unavoidable. Today, leaders are assuming a broader range of responsibility, and as management jobs are being eliminated, the remaining leaders are experiencing an explosion in their span of control. The performance-driven leader must become as familiar as possible with unfamiliar tasks. If knowledge of the task is not increased, it's very easy for the performance-driven leader to be led down the primrose path by employees who may distort information in their own best interest. How does an employee/ staff person maintain respect and develop trust for a leader who either cannot perform the task or has no clue what it's about?
3. Actively demonstrating the training establishes the performance-driven leader's legitimate right to critique and help the trainee grow through

constructive criticism. If it's perceived that the leader can't do it or doesn't understand it, the critiquing is not perceived to be legitimate and the employees develop high rates of resentment. "Why are you telling me that I'm not doing this correctly when you can't even do it yourself?" is an accurate and painful refrain in many organizations.

The Performance-Driven Leader Actively Practices JIT Training

As we discussed earlier in this chapter, it's important that training not be "front-end loaded" to the point we are training too far in advance of the actual use of the skills. Ideally, training should be timed to be presented just before an employee begins to perform the new task. Do not train too early or in technical terms that are above the employees' level of comprehension. Impress them with your knowledge and ability, don't attempt to baffle them with blabber or "B.S." (whichever term you prefer).

The Performance-Driven Leader Avoids On-the-Job Training

The term *on-the-job training* has in many cases become a camouflage for allowing training to degenerate to

- ◆ Worker training worker
- ◆ Short-term "observation" training only
- ◆ An invitation to fail for a specific period of time

OJT is the equivalent of pushing people into a swimming pool to see if they know how to swim. What basically happens is we select long-term, high-performing employees and have the trainee follow them around and "watch them work." This is perhaps the most inefficient and expensive training method possible and it's a trap we fall into because it is "easy" to implement. Let's look at the hazards involved with OJT.

Worker Training Worker — We tend to select our best, long-term performers and have the person being trained observe them. There is no guarantee that just because someone is a top performer he or she is also a top teacher/trainer. The individual may possess the ability to perform the task, but not to teach it. The athletic arena is chock-full of examples of high-quality performers, "hall of famers" who could perform at superstar levels but likely couldn't teach someone else to do it. The ability to perform and the ability to train are separate skills (as is the ability to lead). When they are combined in one individual, it is a cause for celebration. Before we assume the training ability, we had better establish an effective mechanism for assessing its existence. Don't assume that just because someone can do it well that he or she can teach it effectively. If, in fact, we are going to use a worker to train a worker (that is, a designated trainer), we must institute a "train-the-trainer" program.

The ability to train is a separate and distinct skill that can be learned. It is not instinctive or inherent from birth in your best performers. If the performance-driven leader cannot actively become involved in training, the decision to use a worker/trainer needs to be implemented with care. The decision should not be based on "I don't want to do the training" or "I'm too busy to do the training." In reality, that decision is usually rooted in the manager's own insecurity. "My skills aren't sharp enough to do the training and I don't want to embarrass myself" or "My skills have eroded to the point of ineffectiveness and I don't want that to be exposed" are too often the real reasons we turn to worker/trainers. Worker/trainers can make a valuable contribution to training, but it must be a planned contribution and not the leader merely waiving responsibility for training. The training responsibility should not flow downhill, degenerating to the point of letting someone do it because no one else wants to. When we select a worker/trainer, looking to the top performer may not be the best strategy. We need to blend performance and teaching skill, and that may be found in someone other than the top performer.

On-the-Job Training Can Intimidate the Living Daylights out of the Trainee — You take someone who is new to the function or whose performance you are attempting to correct and assign the person to observe the top producer. In reality, the person being trained may never achieve the observed top level of performance and certainly won't reach it in the short run. The only thing that you may accomplish is to impress upon people being trained the depth of their lack of skill or the inevitability of their failure. "I'll never be that good," "I'll never be able to perform at that level," "There's no way I'll ever be able to do that" are statements often heard after a session of observation.

We talked with one leader who recounted his experience with OJT early in his career:

> In one of my first jobs after I graduated from college, I was sent
> to another state to observe one of the organization's top perform-

ers for 3 days. I watched this guy work and he was a master. He was a very nice guy, very proficient at what he did, and it was obvious that he had a skill level far, far above the norm. While I was tremendously impressed with his ability, I also realized that I couldn't come close to performing at this level. I became convinced that I had made a terrible decision in my job selection, and I was never going to be able to achieve his level of success. I decided I probably ought to start looking for another job. On the plane ride home, I sketched out a new resume and began the search to find a job I would be capable of doing. It took my boss weeks to get me back mentally from my experience with OJT. In reality, I eventually reached that level of performance and was considered on a peer level with that person who trained me, but I can honestly say that the OJT did far more damage than it did good.

Worker Training Worker Punishes the Organization by Reducing the Productivity of the Top Performer Doing the Training — If workers are going to do an effective job of training, they need to perform the task at a slower rate so that it can be observed. They should take the time to explain both the sequence and importance of what's being done and to answer any questions on a timely basis if they are going to do a credible job of training. This obviously will reduce their level of production. Not only is this an ineffective way of training, it also reduces the overall performance of the team, department, group, etc., so we pay a very heavy and expensive price for this form of training (but it's *easy!*).

The Quality of Training May Suffer — Top performers are probably not performing the task "by the book." They have learned, over the years, shortcuts that work for *them*. When our top performers shortcut, rarely do we perceive this to be a problem and correct it. For most managers, the guide is "do it our way unless your way works better." If your way works better for you, is quicker, and maintains or exceeds our level of quality, then do more of it! Rarely do we correct top performers unless the quality of their work becomes a hindrance. When we have worker training worker, the "by-the-book training" goes out the window and we train on the shortcuts. "This isn't how they will tell you to do it, but I'm going to show you the real-world way of getting it done. My way works better." In reality, their way works better for *them*. It is *not* the appropriate message to send to the person being trained.

Another point to consider: top performers selected to do the training (or to be observed) may be reluctant to do a complete training job. They may perceive they have a stake in making sure the person being trained never knocks them from their pedestal of top achievement. "Do I really want to show this person everything to help them be a high achiever? I don't mind them doing well, but I sure wouldn't be happy if they out-produced me. Maybe I'll show them 85 or 90%. I don't think I'm going to show them 100%." This could be a very real issue for the top performer who has the desire to remain on top.

OJT and worker training worker are methods that perhaps look appealing on the surface, but below the surface may be a lot of submerged rocks that will damage or sink the ship.

The Performance-Driven Leader Practices Shared Experience Training (SET)

OJT invites trainees to observe a task for a specific period of time, then do it unsupervised on their own, and "fail their way to success" (we hope). SET training, on the other hand, is a blend of

♦ Classroom training
♦ Job observation training
♦ Performance practice
♦ Critique of performance
♦ Follow-up/feedback

In the next chapter we will offer a format for the SET training model. Our goal here is to establish the fact that SET training is heavily involved in two-way communication, by

♦ Understanding expectations
♦ Seeing the job being performed
♦ Practicing it under the guidance and observation of the leader
♦ Receiving a blended critique of positive and negative observations
♦ Monitor the trainees' progress when they actually go out on their own with planned follow-up/feedback sessions

We don't push trainees into the pool to see if they can swim. We practice the various strokes, breathing and kicking techniques, address their fear of the water, and then swim beside them to make sure they have achieved at least a minimum level of confidence before we let them venture into the deep end on their own. We then meet regularly to throw our new "Flipper" a fish to make sure the learning is reinforced and continued.

The Performance-Driven Leader Eliminates Punishment for Trainees

In many organizations, we punish people for the training they receive. How? By not lowering our short-term expectations or adjusting their workload in their absence. If people go to a training class for 1 day or 1 week, when they return, they are greeted with a backlog of all of the work that didn't get done in their absence. This requires them to work harder, longer to "catch up," and their stress level is elevated to new heights. Then, we wonder why people are reluctant to receive training and why some see training as the equivalent to a trip to the dentist. Part of the cost of training is factoring in the temporary loss of production while the person is being trained. No rocket scientist stuff here: If workers are going to be gone, we need to find a way of absorbing that loss of production without holding them accountable for it upon their return. It's not only training that is punished in this way, we similarly punish vacations, illness, days in the field, equally without discrimination. When people say they can't afford to take a vacation, it may have no relationship to money. It's an expression of the "horror" that will await them upon their return. We take vacations to get away and recharge our batteries and return to a mountain of work that negates the vacation within the first 8 hours we are back in the workplace.

Performance-driven leaders plan training to the extent they can reassign the workload, lower the expectations (short term!), and avoid the typical price paid by employees for receiving training.

Truth 3: Effective Training for Change

The two key issues here are

- There is nothing new without training
- Leaders and workers must receive the same training

There is Nothing New without Training

The point has been made several times throughout this book that if we're going to ask people to do things differently, we must equip them with the abilities to actually do the things differently. We cannot institute a new procedure without training people how to do the new procedure. New tasks without training are a significant contributor to stress in the workplace, resentment, and poor performance. We commit a grievous error when we assume that everyone knows how to do it the new way.

The changes we are facing today are due in part to

♦ The explosion of new technology
♦ The changes in global and domestic competition
♦ The development and growth of workers and staff
♦ The realities of downsizing, reengineering, and restructuring
♦ The elimination of the traditional "carrots" of motivation and job satisfaction

All these require that new skills be trained and learned. The paradox is that in this environment of revolutionary and compelling change we are often too busy to train, can't afford it, and, in reality, haven't thought the process through completely to know what it is we are supposed to be training! When Americans put men on the moon, they were trained far in advance to ensure success and safety. We didn't just get them there and then try to decide what to do with them once they had arrived.

NOTHING NEW WITHOUT TRAINING.

Michele Atkins:

> Planning training is part of our budget process every year. We put out a memo to all of the staff, saying we are about to do budgeting: what are your perceived training needs for the upcoming year and what training would you like to receive? And, everybody puts a lot of requests on the table. It's interesting that it has become a value in our culture that you get to do this. They view training, not as an imposition, but as a treat, as an opportunity. And then, we go back and negotiate with them. If I have one person who's specialty is desktop publishing and that person wants to take three thousand dollars worth of courses next year on desktop publishing we may go back and say, okay, you get to pick one course. What's the one that you most want to do? Additional training can also be used to reward high achievement. Some of our training is predetermined and imposed, but we make as much as possible elective. Because these are grown-ups that we are dealing with I think they get to have a say in what they are going to learn.

Leaders and Workers Must Receive the Same Training

Consistency of training reinforcement is a huge problem in most organizations today. Workers attend training sessions, receive excellent information, and when they return to the workplace, it's "business as usual." The terminology they have learned is not consistently used within the workplace. The techniques they were taught are not reinforced (many times because the manager has yet to be taught the new techniques), and the training quickly dissolves.

It's imperative that leaders and employees/staff receive the same training. The training does not have to be done all at the same time. Leaders may receive training and cascade the training down to the various levels of employees or staff.

Employees who receive training in a Third Reich management environment are often greeted by these phrases when they return to work:

♦ "Welcome back to the real world."
♦ "You do it the way I tell you to do it and let me worry about the training department."
♦ "I don't care what they taught you in training class, here's how we do it here in my department."

Even the best-intentioned leaders cannot reinforce what they don't know. The presentation of training must be all-encompassing. In a healthy environment, the leaders are the first to be trained, not the last, and training received in the classroom is reinforced consistently in the workplace. This cannot happen unless everybody receives the same training.

Truth 4: Evaluation

As mentioned in Chapter 9, in Stephen Covey's 1989 book *The Seven Habits of Highly Effective People,* he lists as his second habit "Start with the end in mind." There could be no greater first commandment of training. Before we begin any kind of training program, we have to ask ourselves what it is we are trying to accomplish and how we structure a training program to address the vision, mission, goals, and objectives of the organization. Training programs can become obsolete quickly because they don't change along with the changing focus of the organization. Our mission changes, our goals change, our objectives change, but oftentimes our training program does not.

It's the same training program that we have been presenting for the last 10 years! We cannot afford obsolete training. The only way to ensure against obsolescence is to have frequent, ongoing, and effective assessment of where we are going and then evaluating the skills we must train to get us there.

There are seven steps in this process of evaluating our training:

1. Assess
2. Enable
3. Align
4. Train effectively
5. Evaluate and reinforce
6. Measure success
7. Review

Assess

There are three key questions to address:

1. What are we trying to accomplish? — Are we attempting to accomplish new goals, changes in our procedure, implementation of a new process or new tasks? Are we attempting to improve a current process or task, etc.?
2. Why do we want to accomplish it? — Are we addressing issues that matter? Are we trying to accomplish things that are critical to our core responsibility? Are we majoring in the majors (the tasks to insure success) or majoring in the minors (spinning our wheels on noncritical pursuits)? Are we adding disproportionate importance to relatively unimportant goals, etc.?
3. When must we accomplish it? — What are the deadlines? Is this short term driven by crisis? Long term driven by planning? What are the time dimensions and the time expectations?

Enable

The critical issues are to

1. Evaluate the skills that will get us there and
2. Train those skills.

What are the specific skills that will take us where we need to go? What is it we need to train? The following diagnostic tool may help us to look at the tasks to be accomplished, the skills required for success, how the skills will be trained and how success will be measured.

Training Diagnostic Tool

Task to Be Accomplished	Skills Required for Success	How Will It Be Trained	How Will It Be Measured
1. _____	_____	_____	_____
2. _____	_____	_____	_____
3. _____	_____	_____	_____
4. _____	_____	_____	_____

This diagnostic tool should be implemented from three different information points:

- The performance-driven leader
- Human resource professionals
- Employee/staff responsible for success

The views from all three of these information points may be different and the successful course of action will probably be a distillation of these three opinions. It is important that we don't train on existing "job description" only, but that we train on "current job reality." Job content changes often, while job titles and descriptions remain the same, and our training may be ineffective because it hasn't kept pace with the changes. For example, we may be providing training to customer service specialists that may not address the challenges they are facing. We may not be training them on communication skills and conflict resolution, while we are training them on the proper way to fill out a customer complaint form! Employees who are successfully completing the task are the best source to diagnose skill demand and often are the least heard. An excellent exercise in your quest to build an effective training program is to assess your current top performers.

- What skills contribute to their success on their current tasks?
- How did they learn these skills?
- Can they teach these skills to others?
- How can we effectively provide training and follow-up?

To further ensure that your training is meeting current skill demand consider:

1. What do we want to accomplish (our goals)?
2. What is our current level of performance?
3. How do we close the gap between 1 and 2?

Your training program becomes identifying and teaching the skills to close the gap.

Align

As previously discussed, training must be consistent with leaders and employees/staff. Leadership must be exposed to the new training, understand why it's being done, and be very clear on the follow-up that is necessary. Leaders' consistency in reinforcing application of the new training will be crucial to a successful outcome. They need to be the first on board in this process, not the last.

Train Effectively

In the next chapter, we will address effective training techniques and review the SET model.

Evaluate and Reinforce

The progress of the individual should be observed and evaluated with corrective feedback offered as well as recognition for success or "successful approximations." Of critical importance here is that we reward and recognize "interim successes." Encouraging words should not be withheld until trainees successfully accomplish the entire task. As they *begin* to adapt to new behaviors, as they *begin* to get a portion of the things right, as they *begin* to demonstrate their willingness to learn the new technique, recognition and rewards should be forthcoming.

For example, think of a child who is learning to walk. Does the child have to walk completely across the room or be able to run laps around the outside of the house before the child earns positive reinforcement or encouragement? Of course not. What happens is children, on wobbly legs, venture forth with that first precious step. They take one step and go down on their nose or their diaper. Immediately they receive a flood of positive reinforcement. Children may not understand the words, but they understand the very positive and very encouraging message. Is it any surprise that they can't wait to get back up and try it again? After each attempt, each "failure," they receive the message of "You did good. Do some more." And, as we all know, it's a short matter of time until they are walking all the way across the room and running laps around the perimeter of the house! They are encouraged to keep trying and are reinforced even when they are not perfect. Think of how this applies to the workplace. We train people in a new task and criticize them every time they make a mistake. They don't receive appropriate reinforcement and encouragement until they have performed the task perfectly (if they ever get to that perfect level). In reality, they may never receive positive reinforcement at all. The learning curve is accelerated when we reward and recognize interim successes.

Measure Success

The overall success of the training program must be measured. Are the goals that we set at the very beginning of the process being met by the bulk of the group that is exposed to the training? Inherent in this step is having a very clearly identified and agreed-upon measurement system. The question, "How will success be measured?" must be addressed before the training begins. For example, if our goal is to increase quality, it can be measured by

- Tracking the reduction of warranty work
- Tracking the reduction of internal rework
- Tracking the reduction of customer complaints
- Tracking the reduction of work rejected by the quality control department

Measurement is critical to management and overall success and this certainly applies to the training function. Our reluctance or inability to track results wastes dollars, time, opportunity, and results in lack of overall goal achievement. The measurement of training must go much deeper than evaluating how much the trainee enjoyed the session; it must not evolve to whether or not it was a "feel-good" experience.

One caution: measuring the results of your training program can also have the effect of raising levels of fear. Why? Because most employees/ staff have an inherent distrust of measurement systems. The reason is very simple. They have either seen or been the target of a measurement system that was used to "get" somebody, or to punish. A huge challenge for the performance-driven leader is taking fear out of the measurement system by constant explanation and reassurance that the intent of the measurement system is tracking training effectiveness and not individual performance.

THE MEASUREMENT SYSTEM IS NOT A WEAPON TO BE USED AGAINST EMPLOYEES.

George Mosher:

> We measure for errors in our organization. One of the things is that any error typically costs more than someone's salary for the day. So, the sense of being too busy to do it right or not doing it properly is extremely costly. Essentially you have to pay at least twice to ship damaged/defective furniture or product back that was initially shipped in error. That's a hard concept for some people to accept. As you work hard to cut errors back this can produce fear in people because as we start measuring for errors, which we do, people can fear the measurement system. It's for training, but it's also fearful for people.

When asked if this fear of measurement diminished over a period of time, George responded,

> Definitely. I think the longer people are in, they become less fearful of little things and may become more fearful of bigger things; like if I'm not able to keep up with the growth of this company as opposed to the day-to-day fear that the boss is going to be angry at me for making mistakes.

Review

In any training situation, there is an initial grasping of the new skill and then a natural and predictable erosion of performance (familiarity breeds contempt — the more we think we know about something, the less we tend to pay attention to it). It is always appropriate to have a basic, fundamental review of the tasks that have been trained. All of us have forgotten more about our jobs than we will ever remember. We are never so competent that we cannot benefit from a review of fundamentals. The timing of the review needs to be planned during the initial step of enabling. The time lapse between initial presentation and the review and the frequency of the review sessions will vary from organization to organization, task to task, and will depend on the outcomes desired.

Truth 5: Active Partnership

Effective training requires that partnerships be formed between the performance-driven leader and other training professionals within the organization. (It's possible that in some smaller organizations, the performance-driven leader is the training department!) It is an unfortunate fact of life that there is often an antagonistic or adversarial relationship between on-line managers and the training department. Training departments are frequently viewed as lacking real world experience and orientation which hinders their credibility. Frontline managers and workers frequently hold the training department and its activities in low regard. However, it doesn't have to be that way. We recommend the performance-driven leader adopt a "CAT" strategy.

Create
Alliances with
Training departments

How can we create these alliances and partnerships with training?

1. Acknowledge the valuable role the training department and other training professionals play within the organization.
2. Become an active participant in assessment and feedback programs (not to criticize but to evaluate what we're doing well and what we are not).
3. Break down the barriers that exist between training professionals and frontline managers. Work to change the organizational paradigm that the training department is not really based in the real world.

Obviously, the establishment of these alliances takes willing partners. While there are exceptions to everything in life, most training and human relations professionals are very anxious to collaborate and increase the overall positive impact of training on the organization.

Third Reich managers delight in the widening separation between training and frontline management. It gives them a ready scapegoat; someone to blame. If their department isn't performing, they can blame it on training;

"I can't help it. Don't blame me. That's what the training department is telling these people to do. Go fix training. Don't be jumping on my back." Understandably, many times the training department will fire its "defending salvos" and blame the frontline managers for not implementing the high-quality training it is presenting. If such antagonisms exist, a truce must be declared and relationships forged that identify what we have in common — goals, skill development, and outcomes.

Truth 6: Limitations

As we acknowledge the importance of training, we must also address the fact that training is not a cure-all for all organizational ills. While the importance of training cannot be overstated, we also need to see training as a piece of a picture puzzle and not the whole picture. When tasks are not being successfully completed or employees are performing poorly, there are a number of factors that come into play.

Reasons for Nonsuccess

Reasons	*Remedy*
1. Employees don't *understand* or *don't know* how to do the job	a. Communicate expectations b. Train in the skills necessary to do the job
2. Employees *cannot do the job;* they may not possess the physical or mental aptitude to perform in a satisfactory manner	a. Better selection in the hiring process b. Reassignment to a different job c. Dismissal for nonperformance

---

**NO AMOUNT OF TRAINING CAN OVERCOME
THE INABILITY TO DO THE JOB, OR
LACK OF PHYSICAL OR MENTAL APTITUDE.**

---

3. The employee does not have the *resources* to do the job in a satisfactory manner	Leadership must provide the resources necessary to enable the employee to perform in a satisfactory manner (training obviously cannot overcome the lack of resources and the correction is not the responsibility of the employee)

	Acquiring resources is a leadership function
4. There are *barriers* (real or imagined) interfering with the employee performing the task in a satisfactory manner	Management must either (1) remove the barriers or (2) determine strategies for overcoming the barriers (barrier removal is not a training issue and the correction is not the responsibility of the employee) Barrier removal is a leadership function
5. The employee *refuses* to perform the task in a satisfactory manner (ATTITUDE!)	Management must institute a program of goals and controls. a. Goals: Clear and measurable short-term goals must be negotiated with the employee b. Controls: Must be increased, such as reporting, monitoring, observations If the institution of a goals-and-controls strategy is not quickly successful within the short term, the next step is to progress to the disciplinary program defined by company policy If the performance is allowed to continue unaddressed past the short-term deadlines, the poor performance is reinforced and is very difficult to overcome Reward and recognition may also play a part in this attitude challenge, and we will address these in Chapter 12 The performance-driven leader must demonstrate a consistent, predictable, and fair (yet low) tolerance for poor performance

WE RECEIVE THE PERFORMANCE
THAT WE ARE WILLING TO TOLERATE.

As we can see of these five major reasons for lack of success, training is appropriate in only the first instance. Training cannot "fix" every situation, nor should it be "blamed" in a reactionary knee-jerk response when things aren't going well.

In Chapter 11, we'll look at the areas impacted by training.

CHAPTER 11

TRAINING: GROWTH AND DEVELOPMENT

We will now address five specific areas that impact the performance-driven leader's effectiveness in successfully utilizing training to improve job satisfaction and job performance and to achieve organizational goals.

1. The value of training
2. The three types of training
3. Seven areas for training opportunities (ATOs)
4. The critical issues of learning
5. Training resources

The Value of Training

As we have already discussed, training increases people's net value; it raises their worth to themselves and to the organization. In this era of the loss of the traditional motivators — guarantees of job security, promotability, and big raises — training becomes one of the key motivators. Why? Because it

- Increases the employee/staff's inventory of skills
- Prepares them for future growth
- Prepares them to do the job more efficiently and effectively
- Prepares them to make positive contributions to the overall working environment

♦ Raises their awareness of organizational issues and opportunities
♦ "De-demonizes" change

Michele Atkins:

Training operates at two levels:
   ♦ Training of the individual
   ♦ Training of the group
On an individual level it's different for every person. Some of it is company imposed. I may say to a receptionist, as an example, "You need to receive some additional training on phone skills." That's me saying you need this. The other is the employee saying, "I would like to learn this additional skill because I think it will make me better at my job a couple of years from now." I think there are times in people's professional journey when roadblocks are in the way because they've been doing something for so long in one way and now suddenly they have to go in a different direction. Computers are a perfect example of this. People my age (early baby boomer) who entered the workforce when they were in their 20s understandably are reluctant to learn a computer because it's frightening. When you have people in that circumstance the best thing you can do for them is put them in an environment where they get the training they need and help them to succeed at it. Receiving training and being successful are two different issues, and that training has to be good or they will throw up their hands and never try it again. For all of the staff, one of the questions that we always ask is, "What do you want your job to look like 5 years from now?" It's interesting that a lot of people have very clear visions of what that will be. Many times they perceive moving into management or moving their career along. We sit down and talk about what are the courses going on in the community, where they think they can get that training, when the training would be available, and what we have to do to make that happen.

In the areas of group training, I think the issues are different. There are certainly times when an entire group, particularly a group going through reengineering or major change, needs to confront some of the issues that are in the way of the group doing their jobs. As an example, many grown-ups hate confrontation and some will go to extraordinary lengths to avoid it, but in any workplace there are times when confrontation is going to happen. For our group, learning to deal with that was very important, and we have begun group training on positively dealing with conflict and confrontation. It's important that the group all receive the training at the same time so that everyone has equal skills and no one is perceived to have the advantage of having learned techniques that no one else has. We're not perfect at it yet, but at least we are aware that we have challenges in dealing with confrontation and the awareness has been raised that we need to do something about it. That's a long step in the journey. At least now they can say, "Oh, this is one of those confrontation things and we don't do that well. Maybe we ought to pay attention to this." So I think when any organization is looking at training issues, it has to address individual growth and identify what it is it wants the group to accomplish.

Training should be a significant and permanent presence in the organization. Most organization members should be involved in some type of training and development. If we can offer training in skills that make it easier to do one's work well and if we can offer training that helps each person develop for the next job (either with us or with someone else), we will increase productivities, quality, satisfaction, and feelings of security.

Is training always welcomed? No, of course not. Michele Atkins:

When we began our conflict resolution training, I knew that for this group it was going to be a difficult thing. There was huge anxiety going into that. I began to communicate why I thought it was important that we receive this training and that it was truly a function of reengineering. After we began to discuss what training we were going to provide, many people started coming in, closing the door, and saying, "Yeah, it's okay for everybody else but it's not okay for me." They were implying that everybody else had problems dealing with conflict but they didn't feel that they needed to dedicate the time to the training. It was important that I stood my ground and said, "You've got to do it and we're going to do it. This will benefit all of us." Part of what the leader has to determine is whether this is normal resistance to change, which many people don't like to do, or is there really an issue here that's going to get in the way? I think it's perfectly normal, particularly when you get into something as big as reengineering, when people are going to be inherently distrustful, and the leader must understand that in the beginning there's going to be some normal resistance to training and change. Part of what the leader has to do is figure out what's the norm and what's outside the norm.

A leader must assess the training that is being done, and if the training isn't being successful, for whatever reason, I believe that a leader has to step in, change it, stop it, redesign it, refocus it, or whatever. But inherent in that decision to reassess the training is also the commitment to continue. People will test limits. In a former life I used to teach 4 year olds and there's a lot of similarities. Four year olds always test limits. They always seek to see if they can act out sufficiently to make teacher or mom and dad change the way they normally react. That's the job of 4 year old — to test limits, to figure out what the parameters are to their life. When I see a staff being challenged to change some basic behaviors, they're also going to act out to see where are the walls, where are the parameters. The leader's job is to understand this and reinforce the boundaries. If the leader says, "Things are going to change" or "Reengineering is going to happen," then it had better happen or you've lost the battle. You'll never be in charge again.

Resistance to training, as is true of resistance to any change, is very normal, and performance-driven leaders use their skills to reduce resistance and to implement successful training and change.

The Three Types of Training

There are three types of training:

1. Orientation/awareness training
2. Workplace competency training
3. Growth-and-development training

Orientation/Awareness Training

This is the type of training that prepares employees to begin work in a new environment or to adopt a new task. This is the training new people receive when they join the organization or when they transfer to a different location or different department. Orientation/awareness training is the presentation of policies, procedures, logistics, and basic rules of the road. Included in this initial training are introductions to co-workers, safety instructions, explanations of benefit packages (medical/dental forms and booklets), and so forth.

Good orientation/awareness training helps the new person to fit in more quickly and reduces the litany of questions that is usually forthcoming in the first few weeks.

Workplace Competency Training

This training prepares employees to do their job and to function productively in the workplace environment. It is very specific training on the exact tasks the employee will be doing and includes such things as team building, communication, customer service skills, etc. Workplace competency training encompasses a broad spectrum of skills, and is not limited to just the specific technical skills (that is, which button to push, which form to fill out, etc.). It addresses the interactive skills that are necessary for success in dealing with co-workers, customers, and suppliers. Workplace competency training is both a part of the initial program to introduce the employee to the skills that are necessary for success and an ongoing process as we introduce new challenges, identify areas where additional training will enhance performance, and implement in periodic reviews of fundamentals.

Growth-and-Development Training

This training prepares employees for organizational, professional, and personal growth. It may come from outside of the organization, as we encourage and assist in funding college degrees or other external study programs, or it may be done internally to prepare people for certifications and licensing, as well as to teach the skills necessary to prepare them to move upward or even to lateral positions within the organization. Growth-and-development training is very motivational and can be used as part of the reward system to increase people's value when they have achieved. Growth-and-development training is generally not associated with new people and is focused on developing the longer-term productive employee/staff member. Growth-and-development training can focus on enhancing the employability of the worker, softening the impact of loss of job security.

Seven Areas for Training Opportunities

As we begin our discussion on training opportunities, and the type of training that we should be providing, we need to address the issue of training assessment. How do we determine what training is appropriate at what time? We asked the question of Ron Stewart, "How do you assess what training is necessary for your people?" Ron's response:

> The best way that I found to do that is to try to get to know and understand your people. I think that's a big part of it. The way I've approached it from a professional standpoint is to sit down with every employee in the organization and talk with the people, not just on training, but what they've done, what they feel they are accomplishing in the workplace, what type of educational backgrounds they have, and try to make an assessment of what type of things they would like to do in the workplace in the future. What I find is that people have different needs, and one of the worst things you can do is force training, which you may believe needs to be done [but which] doesn't fit the need or the goal of the individual. Determining what training is appropriate is kind of a three-prong approach:
>
> 1. Sitting down with people and assessing them as far as educational background, their thoughts as far as direction, the type of things they want to do in the workplace, and what training they feel they need.
>
> 2. Working with and observing the individual. Sometimes we have to admit to ourselves that what we think we need is not actually what is appropriate. Personal observations of people's performance and activities in the workplace will help the leader to determine areas of strength and weakness and help to determine training needs.
>
> 3. Evaluating the overall organizational needs regarding what we need to accomplish and what we need from that individual. Sometimes an individual's needs don't always fit the organizational needs. You have to find ways to bridge those gaps. The perpetual question is "How will the organization benefit from the training that we are offering to an employee?" A big part of this is anticipating where the organization is going and how we need to prepare employees/staff to go there with us.

ATO #1: Technical Training

Technical training prepares people to discharge competently the duties they have been hired to perform:

- How to run the machine
- How to fill out appropriate support paperwork
- How to operate the phone system
- How to read test results
- How to load/unload the truck

These include other technical skills, including teaching the executive level how to replace paper in the copy machine! Technical training today has taken on profound new dimensions with the invasion of the computer and related advanced technologies.

For the most part, we do a good job of technical training in schools and in the workplace today. Workers are technically competent. Education in America is primarily technical preparation to do a job. As an example, we have heard many physicians make the statement, "I went to medical school to learn how to be a doctor, to diagnose and heal people. I never learned how to run an office, how to hire people, how to make the business decisions of running a medical practice." More of our schools are realizing that education must be broadened and not constrained strictly by concentrating in technical areas. Most organizations also do a good job of technical training. Of course, we could always be better, but Americans are technically proficient. Most people are technically capable of doing the job which they have been hired and trained to do.

Technical training may be a challenge for the performance-driven leader. At any given moment it's possible that employees/staff are more technically proficient than their leader. This is not meant to be critical but is strictly an observation. Think about it. Performance-driven leaders were technically proficient, that's why they were promoted to at least the first level of management within the organization. With that promotion comes assignment of other duties, and it's not uncommon for technical skills to wane. The performance-driven leader has many other responsibilities and it's hardly surprising that a little bit of rust may build up on the technical skills. The skills could be sharpened if the leader made a commitment to do so, and keeping these skills sharpened is a major component of the leader's ability to train others. Beyond just training new people in basic technical skills, it's very possible that performance-driven leaders may not be able to contribute to the technical development of their people. The leader's technical training influence tends to be at the two extremes — the initial training with a new employee or the very high-end, advanced technical training as new systems are introduced.

TECHNICAL TRAINING IS NOT AN ISSUE FOR MOST ORGANIZATIONS AND LEADERS IN AMERICA TODAY.

ATO #2: Interactive/People Skills

A huge potential trap for the performance-driven leader today is losing sight of people in the technical explosion in today's organization. Interactive/people skills are extremely important to success. In reality, what makes one organization more efficient than another is not its technical expertise, but the quality of the interaction of its people with each other and with its customer/client or patient base. Interactive/people skills include

♦ Communication
♦ Listening skills
♦ Conflict resolution
♦ Workplace confrontation
♦ Customer service
♦ How to deal with difficult customers
♦ Phone skills
♦ Problem solving
♦ Overcoming negativity
♦ Stress management, to name a few

Interactive/people skills are the least-trained skills in America today. We hold people accountable for possessing these skills, but we do a dismal job of teaching them. We believe that most people who are terminated from an organization are dismissed because of poor people skills. Think about it. Once people make it through their initial probationary period, they are technically competent to do their job. People are dismissed because they:

♦ Can't get along with others
♦ Can't be gotten along with
♦ Have poor communication skills
♦ Offend customers, clients, patients
♦ Are disruptive to leadership, workmates, and others

Interactive/people skills can be trained and this is an area of skill development in which the performance-driven leader can have a tremendous impact. Interactive/people skills are crucial to long-term performance, and there has been an adage for many years among people who do a lot of organizational hiring:

HIRE PEOPLE SKILLS;
TRAIN TECHNICAL SKILLS WHENEVER POSSIBLE.

One of the key issues of interactive/people skill training is that everyone within the department, team, or group must receive this training simultaneously. Many excellent models exist for this training, but the training is ineffective if only certain people have the knowledge and possess the skills. To train only some members of the group creates an uneven playing field and puts the untrained at a significant disadvantage.

Poor interactive/people skills are not limited to poorly performing employees. Oftentimes high performers demonstrate a lack of these skills and their behavior becomes so disruptive that disciplinary action becomes necessary. Kathy Foltner offers us such an example:

> I made a decision a long time ago that to help reduce fear that I was going to try not to fire people and while I have tried very hard to not have to go to that extreme, I have also realized that, at times, terminations are necessary. The last time I did it was with somebody who had worked with us for 6 years. He was an audiologist. He was technically very good, brought in more money than any other audiologist that I had on staff, but I also dealt with more patient complaints, more customer complaints all around, both internal and external. It got to the point where other employees were refusing to work with this person. I was hearing statements like, "I won't work with him." "If you put me with him I will leave." And it was obvious that this person demonstrated a lack of interactive/people skills, not the least of which was the ability to get along with others. His performance was not an issue. His interaction certainly was. I did everything that was possible to correct the situation, including arranging private consulting for him, to try to correct specific behaviors. All of this was at company expense.
>
> What I learned from this experience was that you can't change people who don't choose to be changed. And so I made the decision that it was time for him to leave. Even though this was a

high-performing employee, his behavior was so disruptive we could not afford to keep him within the organization. It was not an easy decision. In fact, when I sold the company, it came up because his name and the dollar generation was on some of our reports. The new owners asked me what happened to this one. And I said, "I had to ask him to leave." And they looked at me like I was out of my mind. And I said it was necessary because he cost this company more than he ever generated. I am really committed to creating a positive interactive environment because I know when you do it right, you'll be unstoppable. I knew that if I invested a lot of time, resources, and money on developing these skills and didn't get results, it would be my responsibility and someone could challenge my judgment and my position. But being able to positively turn the company around has added a lot more credence to this stuff. It's important to success.

ATO #3: Basic Business Skills Training

If we expect employees/staff to make good business decisions, we have to support them with basic business training, including teaching them how to

- ◆ Read a profit and loss statement (P&L)
- ◆ Determine gross profit percentages
- ◆ Understand corporate tax law
- ◆ Understand the relationships between expenses and profit and loss

Kathy Foltner offers the following examples:

Years ago when I still owned the company, we had several bad months back to back. We were $60,000 under where we should have been and money was getting tight. I had a staff meeting and said to the staff, "I'm going to give you some basic knowledge, some education on P&L's. Obviously we have revenues and we have expenses. When money is tight, there's only two things you can do. One, increase revenues, or, two, decrease expenses. We have a problem: we're down $60,000. So we need either to increase our revenues or decrease our expenses. How can we increase revenues?" Well, nobody could really come up with any significant ideas so then we began to address how we could cut expenses. They came up with a number of significant ideas, and we cut $60,000 worth of stuff. We never cut one salary, we never cut one employee, we never cut one benefit, but we were able to cut $60,000 out of that budget by raising their awareness, providing some training, and letting them have input into the decision-making process.

Kathy offered another example concerning remedial basic business skills training with an individual employee:

> One of our audiologists called me and she was being very straight and very honest and said, "Kathy, I don't get it. We have this budget to run our office with an awful lot of dollars in it, and when I back my compensation out, it looks to me like there's an awful lot of money left over. Where is all the money going?" My response was, "Well, let's take a look." So I presented her with the P&L and we started to consider each item. We've got $15,000 in rent, we've got $10,000 in marketing, we've got $18,000 in PCC, and we went through every item. She was able to see that the money that was budgeted was just enough to meet the expenses. This was a new office, and at the very beginning, it was only projected to break even. She just said, "Oh my god, I can't believe it. It seems like too much money." She was a smart person but she had never had an education in terms of what it takes to run an office. She realized that everything that I was saying was true. Utilities have to be paid. The PCC has to be paid. The rent has to be paid. And she began to see that these 10s and 15s and 3s and 5s began to add up. It's important to give your people a basic business knowledge if you want them to understand your business and make appropriate decisions.

ATO #4: Organizational Skills

These are the skills that allow us to work in an organized manner. They include

- ♦ Planning
- ♦ Prioritizing
- ♦ Goal setting
- ♦ Managing a desk (to avoid desk stress)
- ♦ Setting up a filing system

People are judged harshly for lacking highly developed organizational skills, but this is an area that has been neglected in training programs. We don't teach the skills, but we sure expect people to have them. Very few people have actually been exposed to organizational skill development, and workers/staff are rated lower on performance appraisals because they don't have these skills. Yet skills of organization are not difficult to teach. The issue is usually one of dedicating the time, and, again, the old adage applies, "We don't have time to teach it correctly, but we always have time to go back and redo the poor-quality work that results from poor skill development."

**A FACT OF ORGANIZATIONAL LIFE:
TECHNICAL SKILLS MAKE YOU GOOD. THE ADDITION OF
PEOPLE AND ORGANIZATIONAL SKILLS MAKE YOU GREAT.**

The performance-driven leader can have a significant impact on production, stress reduction, and increased job satisfaction by providing training and development in the skills of organization. We recommend:

- *Time Tactics of Very Successful People*, Eugene Graceman, New York: McGraw-Hill, 1994.
- *It's about Time*, Linda Sapadin and Jack McGuire, New York: Viking, 1996.

ATO #5: Remedial Educational Skills

These include:

- Reading skills
- Mathematical skills
- Business grammar skills

We make an expensive assumption when we assume that employees/staff bring high levels of these skills to the workplace. In the perfect world, remedial training wouldn't be necessary. In the real world it's a necessary element of both survivability and success.

With the changes in our welfare system laws, as more and more people enter the workplace and bring with them possibly deficient educational skills, our training efforts are going to have to make up the difference. A considerable number of people are going to be entering the workforce who may have the basic ability to perform a task, but will need to have the ability developed. Many organizations are offering educational support for employees to achieve their GED.

This information appeared in the *Wall Street Journal,* Tuesday, October 1, 1996: "Back to Basics: Business executives say about 37% of their workforces lack fundamental math and writing skills, according to a poll by Olsten Staffing Services, Melville, New York. But only about 15% of the companies provide math training, and 10% aid in reading."

If we want employees and staff to be able to read instruction manuals, we had better determine their reading competency level in the hiring process and help them to develop the skills necessary to do the job. If we can't hire the skills, we must be able to train them. If we want our people to be able to do mathematical equations, calibrations, etc., we need to provide training in basic math skills. If we want our people to communicate in writing, then it's incumbent upon us to offer basic grammar skills and business writing principles.

ATO #6: Fundamental Review of ATOs 1 through 5

Many leaders err in assuming that once training has been presented that it is forever learned and never has to be presented again. This couldn't be farther from the truth. All of our skills tend to erode over time, and the more we think we know about something, the more shortcuts we begin to take. In reality, as we said earlier, each one of us has forgotten more about our jobs than we will ever remember. So, often, the most meaningful training is the training that unlocks past learning. And many times, people will say to themselves, "I used to do that, but I've gotten away from it" or "I knew that, I had just forgotten about it." No one is ever so good or so professional or so effective that he or she cannot benefit from a basic review.

How should this fundamental review be structured? We don't recommend that every 6 months you make everyone go through new-person training. That's not what fundamental review is all about. However, dedicating a consistent portion of team, department, or group meetings to fundamental review has high payoff. Perhaps 20 minutes of each meeting can be spent having one of the employees/staff review the fundamentals of the tasks that are the core of the responsibilities of the group (this is one example where worker training worker can be very effective). The story has been told many times about Vince Lombardi, the legendary coach of the Green Bay Packers. When Lombardi's team didn't play well on Sunday or lost a game (which was very rare), he canceled the normal Monday day off. He required the team to come in for an extra day's practice, not to punish, but to review. The story goes that Lombardi would pull a football out of a bag, hold it up to his professional team, and state, "Gentlemen, this is a football." He would take them through basic drills just as if they were a junior high school football team coming out for the first football practice of their life, not to humiliate them or demean them, but to take them back to the fundamentals. When things aren't going well, that's not the time to teach sophisticated advanced techniques. That's when you work on fundamental blocking and tackling. Few organizations take appropriate advantage of basic review.

Kathy Foltner:

> I called our regional office in Illinois. It's 10:00 in the morning and I get flipped over into voice mail. That's not okay with me and it doesn't happen just once, not just twice, but repeatedly. I went to our operations manager and said this is not okay and listed all the reasons why. We're a professional office. Our 800 number is on our marketing stuff. We can't be using voice mail. I was concerned that the person answering the phone is using voice mail as a crutch. The phone people needed to have a basic review of their training. This is absolutely a training issue. I mean, the people needed to be trained in terms of how to deal with the phones. It's a very difficult situation. You've got somebody on the phone; the other phone is ringing. We needed to review with people how you get off the phone to get to the other call and get back, how to handle multiple phone lines that are ringing. This was not an opportunity to blame somebody; this was an opportunity to train, and the training was fundamental review of things that we have already learned and probably forgotten.

ATO #7: Life Skills Training

These are skills that employees/staff will take with them in other aspects of their lives. This training may include

- Personal financial training
- Budgeting
- Investing
- Consumer awareness
- First aid
- Self-esteem

♦ Nutrition
♦ Debt counseling

This training is designed to help our people increase the quality of their lives and of others who are around them. While it may not directly affect their performance on the surface, it certainly can increase commitment and job satisfaction. And when those two elements are high, performance and quality tend to rise as well.

Some organizations provide these training opportunities in the evening or on Saturday mornings and make them open not only to the employees/ staff, but to their family members as well. It helps to build a bridge between the employee and their support system and the organization. There are many groups and social service organizations who will provide this training at no charge (debt counseling agencies, Red Cross, banks, etc.). It may be that the organization has people with expertise in some of these areas (CPAs, legal counsel, etc.). Anytime we can increase the knowledge of our people, we raise their value to themselves and to the organization.

The Critical Issues of Learning

A big challenge facing the performance-driven leader is how to present training and information in a "package" that other people can absorb accurately. This is a lot harder than it sounds. The reason is this. As leaders, we tend to communicate and train commensurate with the way we learned. And at face value, that is not a bad strategy. The leader is a top performer, is part of the influential decision making of the organization, and has a demonstrated track record of success. If everyone performed as well as the performance-driven leader, the organization would be better off. This is not an appeal to ego; it's an appeal to common sense. Leaders tend to be the best performers and to struggle mightily to raise the performance level of those around them.

The key for the performance-driven leader is to realize that not everyone learns the same way. We all have three primary centers of learning and we have blended these together in a unique, individualized style of learning. Some people tend to blend all three styles while others tend to emphasize one or two. No two people tend to learn the same way.

The three centers of learning are

1. Visual — We learn by what we see.
2. Auditory — We learn by what we hear.
3. Kinesthetic — We learn by what we do.

In America, we have been strongly oriented toward visual learning. Our school systems, training techniques, and curricula have been designed to accommodate visual learning. People who learn visually have tended to do very well in our schools. They have advanced to higher education and to success in the workplace. The visual orientation that they bring with them to the workplace has resulted in

♦ Recreating training programs that mirror visual learning;
♦ Creating communication systems that reinforce visual learning (have you ever wondered why you spend so much time writing reports for the people above you?).

People at the top want the information in writing so that they can "see" it. An inordinate amount of time is spent in the American organization supporting reporting activity to put information into a visual form because it is the preferred style of the people in leadership positions.

Another major consideration in the presentation of training information is repetition. It is widely believed that adults must be exposed to information three to five times, repetitively, before they can actually own it or command it. One-time exposure to information makes us aware of its existence, but it takes repetitive exposures to allow us actually to use it effectively and to assimilate it into our inventory of knowledge and skill.

The obvious flaw in all of this visual learning is that not everyone learns visually. To accommodate learning styles other than visual, a training practice has existed for many years that encourages us to

♦ Tell them
♦ Show them
♦ Watch them

Obviously, when we use the model of "tell them," "show them," and "watch them," we are presenting the information a minimum of three times.

It's also appropriate for us to address the adult learning model. This information is certainly not new, and most performance-driven leaders will have been exposed to it at some point in their education or career. (Once again, we would state that we are never so good or so knowledgeable that we can't benefit from a basic fundamental review.) The adult learning model addresses the importance of repetition and tells us that if we want to communicate information, it must be done in a format that complements the learning process.

If you are going to train someone to do something, it's important that you tell them what you want them to do so they hear it. You show them what you want them to do so they visualize it. And you watch them do it so they have the opportunity to learn kinesthetically.

Following this model of tell them, show them, watch them ensures that the information will be put in three separate packages that accommodate all three centers of learning. You don't know whether the person you're training is a visual, auditory, or kinesthetic learner. And chances are each is a unique blend. There is no real reason to know. As long as the training accommodates all three styles, it will be effective.

Michele Murphy, a professional trainer and consultant, has developed the following four-step model to accommodate diverse learning styles and the adult learning model.

Step 1	I say	I do	You watch (tell them and show them)
Step 2	I say	You do	I watch (tell them, watch them)
Step 3	You say	I do	You watch (do they know it well enough to teach it?)
Step 4	You say	You do	You know (review and proof that an adequate skill level has been developed)

The S.E.T. Training Model (Shared Experience Training)

Performance-driven leaders incorporate these training techniques into the shared experience training model. This is an extremely effective, ten step format for presenting information, demonstrating task, providing immediate opportunity for reinforcement, and measuring comprehension and performance improvement.

1. Preview: Provide a general outline of the task(s) to be taught, emphasizing what it is, and why it is necessary.
2. Presentation: Explain the task in detail and present the process in its entirety. (Present not only their piece of the pie, help them understand the entire pie.)
3. Demonstrate: Actually show them your effective completion of the task. (Step-by-step, by-the-book.)
4. Transfer: Require them to do the task with your step-by-step narrative and visual guidance. (Tell them and show them while they follow your instructions. Note: Repeat this transfer step *three* successive times.)

5. Performance observation: Require them to complete the task in its entirety in your presence, without any guidance.
6. Reinforce, critique, and correct: Reinforce positively the things they do well, and critique and correct any areas of weakness. (Note: Repeat steps 5 and 6 three successive times.)
7. Measure their performance: Through observation and measurement, establish their current rate of performance. (This begins their benchmarking and provides a starting point for objectively determining performance growth.)
8. Establish goals for improvement: Clearly communicate the standards of performance and the timelines for achieving incremental growth. Involve the employee in the negotiation of realistic goals.
9. Establish review points: Determine a time-specific format for a review of their progress. (Essentially a repeat of steps 5, 6, and 7.)
10. Identify all resources available to them to assist in growth development and performance improvements.

Training Resources

The performance-driven leader has a myriad of training resources available. The challenge is not a shortage of training support but in choosing the resources that will be most helpful.

There are at least six "mother lodes" of training assets:

1. The training department
2. Outsourcing
3. Video- and audiotape libraries
4. The written word (manuals, books, articles, etc.)
5. Internally produced training materials
6. Professional affiliations/associations

The Training Department

Without question, the most valuable training resource available to the performance-driven leader is the training department. The training department is staffed with professionals who are skilled in

♦ Giving training presentations
♦ Assessing training needs
♦ Evaluating training results

- Researching relevant information
- Developing appropriate curricula

While we acknowledge there may be an antagonistic relationship between the Third Reich manager and the training department, today's successful leader will toil long and hard to develop strong alliances and relationships with the training department and to use this valuable resource to best advantage. Training professionals live and breathe training and have knowledge, resource, and networking capabilities far beyond the typical group leader or departmental manager.

As we have previously mentioned, in some organizations the performance-driven leader is the entire training department, and may not have access to this valuable asset. In that case, the entire burden of training responsibilities falls on the performance-driven leader. But, when the training department is available, successful collaboration will yield many payoffs!

Outsourcing

Outsourcing of training has many advantages:

- It provides professional training in areas where the performance-driven leader or the organization may lack expertise.
- It affords the opportunity to expand greatly the depth of the curriculum offered.
- It provides outside confirmation of internal practices, policies, and methods.
- It reduces overall training costs.

There are a significant number of specialized training organizations and highly qualified training consultants in the industry today. How do you find an effective vendor?

- *Word of mouth* — Find out from organizations similar to yours who they are using and what the results have been.
- *Professional recommendations* — Organizations such as the ASTD (American Society of Training and Development) can make recommendations.
- *Your professional affiliations* — The professional groups that you belong to (or should!) can make recommendations and will probably be "showcasing" prominent professional people at their trade association meetings, conventions, etc.

While there are many very competent professional organizations and consultants, we recommend

- Trinity Solutions, Peachtree City, GA (1-800-368-1201)
- Career Track Seminars, Boulder, CO (1-800-334-6780)
- Communication and Interactive Skills Training, Lani Arredondo (707-374-2807)

Another valuable source of training support can come from your local college or university. Contacting the various departments can yield a wealth of recommendations, whatever your training needs may be. These institutions can assist with testing, as well as with customized training, to help you achieve your goals.

Video- and Audiotape Libraries

With the explosion of technology, there is a wealth of training resources available in video- and audiotape, as well as on CD. In the past, training resources have been limited primarily to the written word. As we discussed earlier, not everyone learns effectively visually or by just reading a book. Today we have all kinds of material to appeal to the other centers of learning.

CD/Audiotape

Think of how much time average Americans, men and women, spend in their vehicles every year: commuting to work, weekends, vacations, etc. It has been estimated that we may spend an average of 500 to a 1000 hours in our vehicle every year. Most of us are concentrating to ensure safe driving while we listen to an entertainment tape or to the radio. This is a tremendous opportunity for people to "go to school in their cars." One of the biggest questions we face in training today is: When do we find the time to learn? CD and audiotapes can allow us to utilize travel time and increase our inventory of skills.

Repetitive learning requirements are readily accommodated by audiotapes. We can listen to them over and over again, selecting the sections that meet our needs and skipping over those that don't.

Videotape

Think of the workers in your environment who are 30 years of age and younger. They learned the very basics: the alphabet, how to count, how to read and spell the early words from video presentation (Sesame Street!). We have created generations of video learners and we teach it from the cradle. Doesn't it make sense to involve video presentation as a piece of your training pie? One third of public school teachers gave a top rating of "highly effective" to video teaching tools. Hands-on training material was rated highest by 55.2% of the teachers, while textbooks were rated most effective by 25.2% (*USA Today*, Wednesday, June 5, 1996).

Earlier in Chapter 10, we recommended sources for audio and visual training materials, and to these we would add your public library!

The Written Word: Manuals, Books, Articles

Your existing policy manuals, codes of conduct, written procedures, and training manuals contain very specific and valuable information to augment the training process. There is a wealth of quality books in any major bookstore in America to help performance-driven leaders develop not only their own skills, but also the skills of the people around them. These resources can be especially helpful in teaching some of the interactive/people skills.

There are a number of business publications that can also be helpful in keeping leaders and their people current on business trends and developments. Obviously, the *Wall Street Journal* and the higher-profile business magazines (*Business Week, Forbes, Fortune, The Economist,* etc.), as well as journals and publications specific to your industry, are all valuable tools. We have discussed the importance of performance-driven leaders sharing any and all relevant, current data with their people. An article from a magazine, photocopied and distributed, accomplishes a number of things:

- ♦ It emphasizes the leaders' commitment to keeping themselves current.
- ♦ It emphasizes the leaders' willingness to keep those around them current (raising the value of the people around them).
- ♦ It emphasizes that the leaders value the intellect of the people around them and perceive that this information would be of interest to them.

PERFORMANCE-DRIVEN LEADERS "FEED THE BRAINS" OF THE PEOPLE AROUND THEM.

THE PERFORMANCE-DRIVEN LEADER BECOMES THE BEACON OF LEARNING AND THE TRANSMITTER OF KNOWLEDGE.

Internally Produced Resources

With the technology that exists today, a myriad of internal training resources can be produced and distributed quickly and cost-effectively. In today's economic environment, speed in training response may be necessary for survival!

Videos

In-house videos can be created to show

- Role-plays of communication techniques, conflict resolution models, customer service opportunities, etc.
- The performance-driven leader performing a step-by-step explanatory session
- An expert or top-performing employee doing the task
- Safety guidelines and practices
- Equipment maintenance

These and many more opportunities exist for the use of in-house videos. Videos created for these purposes do not necessarily have to be of top professional quality. Some great training material has been developed with a borrowed handheld camcorder! (If it's good enough, copyright it!)

Videos can be used very effectively as introductory/organizational awareness training and initial workplace competency training in all phases. These are also valuable as follow-up training for review. The use of videos also can break up the monotony or boredom that unfortunately may accompany training.

Videotaping is also an excellent technique for critiquing an employee's performance. Put the employee on tape, review the tape jointly, and provide positive as well as "constructive" criticism on what you see. (It's tough to argue with a clear video replay.) Many high-performing professional athletes videotape their efforts for review and correction. This technique can be of great value in the workplace.

Audios

In-house audios are easily produced and can be a very effective training support tool, especially for the introduction and review of interactive/people skills.

Audio newsletters can be very helpful as reinforcements and review of previous training. Taping two or three high-performing employees in an informal conversation concerning the importance of training, the importance of doing the job by the book, the frustrations they may have experienced when they were new employees, and how their willingness to stick to the guidelines and use the training has paid high dividends to them can be very inspiring to a new employee as well as to an employee whose performance is subpar and with whom we are working to correct.

Developing in-house audios is also an excellent alternative, broad-based communication tool. Traditionally, we publish newsletters, write memos, and, with the advent of faxes and E-mail, we use those tools for both general and targeted communication. Audios can be an effective alternative. As we have discussed,

- Not everyone is a visual learner;
- Not everyone responds well to communication in writing only;
- Not everyone checks her E-mail or reads his memos promptly.

Putting important information in audio presentation form gives people the opportunity to slide a tape into the tape deck during their commute and be exposed to the information.

Additional Training Aids

- Charts
- Desktop instructions
- Checklists, posters
- Schematics
- Diagrams
- Illustrations, pocket-size guides

All of these and many more can be effective tools to use in following up and reinforcing training. Material that is presented in classroom or task demonstration can be put into various visual forms and used for review. These tools are very effective in such situations as

- ♦ When decisions are made on specific predetermined criteria
- ♦ When the task is not done consistently and intermittent review is necessary to maintain proficiency
- ♦ When accuracy is important and fluctuates from task to task (calibrating a piece of equipment, where the setting may be different each time the equipment is used)
- ♦ When the task is easily communicated in a simple step-by-step guide
- ♦ When review of the visual tool will help reinforce learning

These support materials should *not* be used

- ♦ When the task is repetitive and we can't stop to think about it everytime we do it
- ♦ When speed is a critical component of the task and reviewing information would slow the process to unacceptable levels

In these circumstances, the training support tools can become a "crutch" and can dramatically hinder performance. For example, when an employee must calibrate a piece of equipment and the calibrations change frequently. How to calibrate the machine must become "second nature" and a training aid would be a hindrance to performance. What setting to use to calibrate the equipment could readily be presented on a chart to enhance the performance.

Professional Affiliations/Associations

We strongly recommend that performance-driven leaders become involved in the associations that support their industry. These associations not only provide excellent opportunities for networking contacts and staying current on relevant information, they also offer opportunities for growth and development. Experts are available through these affiliations and associations to perhaps assist in on-site training or certainly to prepare performance-driven leaders to instruct their people. These professional affiliations/associations exist to raise the value of their members. Take advantage of them.

Vendor and Supplier Organizations

An often-overlooked opportunity for supplementing training exists with people with whom we currently do business. The local phone company can provide telephone skills training. The local utilities (gas, electricity, etc.) can provide safety and cost-containment programs. Suppliers have the capability of training you on their equipment, product, or service to boost proficiency and effectiveness. Governmental agencies can provide workshops and training on the awareness of applicable law, regulations, and compliance issues. The performance-driven leader takes advantage of all possible resource for training, growth, and development.

Leadership, change, communication, training, and all organizational behaviors are enhanced by appropriate recognition and reward. We now turn to a discussion of this essential activity of performance-driven leaders.

CHAPTER 12

RECOGNITION AND REWARDS

In rewarding the workforce, the performance-driven leader will use the entire range of rewards, both tangible and intangible, formal and informal. Compensation will be important. This includes wages, benefits, and incentives (performance pay). However, a creative reward system will also employ a wide range of nonmonetary rewards, including training and development (which we discussed extensively in Chapters 10 and 11), which helps employees to exchange present and future employability for the long-gone carrot of job security. Travel, merchandise, new and exciting work assignments, awards, plaques, pins, and the important technique of recognition are all a part of the reward system.

Compensation is always an issue. Some people claim that money is the only thing that matters. Others proclaim that money is a poor motivator and, in reality, has little impact. We think both of these extremes are dead wrong and their proponents need to "take a break" and "wake up and smell the coffee." Anybody who thinks that money doesn't matter is foolish. However, money is not the only consideration.

There is rarely enough money to motivate people. No matter how much someone makes, it's never enough. Look at the examples of athletes, who in some cases are making obscene amounts of money (millions and millions of dollars per year) to play a game, and, no matter how much they make, every year, every contract, they want more. Their desire for more money is insatiable! Money is very much like food. We have all had the occasion, usually around a holiday, to sit down to a carefully prepared, magnificent meal and to overindulge. At the end of the meal, we waddle to the nearest comfortable chair, proclaim in our discomfort that "I will never eat another bite of food again as long as I live." This vow remains in force only until the digestive process progresses. And either later that evening or, certainly, by the next morning we all begin to rummage through the cupboard or refrigerator looking for a bite of something. Money is the same way. We receive a raise (or provide raises for our people) and the impact is positive in the short term but it doesn't last. It's never enough. As we have already stated, the era of big raises and compensation is over in America. There are always exceptions to everything in life, but the years of the 10, 12, 15% (or higher) raises are *gone*. Organizations today are turning more to bonus plans or gain-sharing plans where everyone in the organization can participate in the organization's overall success. Traditionally, bonuses and gain sharing have been available to the executive and sales levels only, as they were perceived to be the "revenue generators" for the group.

Today's compensation packages should reflect a reasonable level of compensation, allowing employees an acceptable comfort level of being able to meet their ordinary expenses and to keep the "wolves away from the door." Compensation over and above that must be earned in accordance with contribution, performance, and overall success. It is not our intent to go into specific compensation program recommendations. However, the performance-driven leader will be a champion of a progressive compensation system and will commit to researching and preaching the appropriate changes. This will not be an easy task, and the easily daunted manager will give up and not fight the system. If we are to have long-term success and to maintain our competitive edge, we have to move toward progressive compensation systems.

Organizations no longer can afford to offer 10 to 12 to 15% raises even when they have a good year. The reason is quite simple. A raise given this year has to be covered and paid for every subsequent year. A 15% raise in a good year becomes an obstacle the next year when revenues may not be as great. Any new compensation increases are factored on that 15% of the previous year. Many organizations find that they can, in fact, offer bigger numbers of dollars to their people on a yearly basis in the form of a bonus or gain sharing than in the traditional percentage wage increase because of the hesitancy and cautious tentativeness of factoring in future impact. Obviously, the use of base compensation with gain sharing or bonus must be introduced into a high-trust environment. We are all aware of horror stories of executives extracting their millions in bonuses, while telling the frontline producers of the organization that there's no money for raises this year. While such unethical inequities continue to exist, they are diminishing.

In companies controlled by high-fear, low-trust Third Reich management there is *no* relationship between executive compensation and organization performance *at any level.*

When gain sharing and bonuses are distributed on a quarterly basis, it can add a dimension of consistency of performance because the rewards are shared frequently.

Recognition

Recognition is potentially the most powerful, but most underemployed form of rewarding employee behavior. Recognition can be both formal (organizational awards) and informal (spontaneous on-the-job praise); it can be flexible and readily available. Recognition can be especially powerful when delivered in the presence of peers or significant others (although public praising has its limitations, as we will soon discuss). A simple pat on the back can go a long way, particularly if witnessed by significant people in the employee's support system. Recognition must be credible, it must be valued by the employee, and it must come in response to a desired behavior that contributes to success.

As we discussed in our chapters on training, one of the first questions that has to be asked before we can train is "What is it we want to accomplish?" Similarly, one of the first questions we ask before we use recognition is "What is it that we want to accomplish?" Determine the behaviors that support our goals and structure recognition to reinforce them.

BEHAVIOR THAT IS RECOGNIZED AND REWARDED IS REPEATED.

Positive recognition, for example, can be eye-to-eye, immediately following exemplary behavior, or it can come in a timely, handwritten note, or even an E-mail message. "Well done, thy good and faithful servant" is one of the oldest published reports of recognition.

Another way we can recognize the importance of employees is to listen, really listen to their ideas and suggestions, not just by refraining from talking, but by really absorbing what they say. Obviously, this is difficult, especially in times of crisis or rapid-paced activity, yet these can be the times when it is most important. Some observers contend that nonmonetary rewards cost nothing. We do not believe this to be the case unless the time of our leaders and human resource staff members is considered worthless. At the very least, there is the lost opportunity cost associated with not being available to do something else (If you weren't providing recognition, what could you have been doing?). Further, the more successful recognition systems, both formal and informal, will require time, planning, training, and a commitment of resources, and we believe that the return on these investments will be high.

One of the painful truths of the American workplace is that no one receives the recognition that he or she deserves. One of the definitions of an American worker is

---

THE AMERICAN WORKER — OVERWORKED, UNDERPAID, UNDERRECOGNIZED.

Each and every one of you reading this book is not being given the appropriate recognition that you deserve, and the bottom line is that few people are able to maintain top performance in an environment of little or no recognition. When we achieve and recognition is not forthcoming, some of us will actually increase our productivity for a very short term, perhaps feeling that we just have not done quite enough to be appropriately recognized. When we increase our productivity and actually achieve even more and recognition is still not forthcoming, we will reduce our efforts downward commensurate with what we think the organization and our manager deserve.

Recognition is one of the most powerful and underutilized tools of the performance-driven leader.

Formal Recognition

The formal recognition systems in most organizations in America today are adequate. We formally recognize

- Length of service (usually at 5, 10, 15, 20 years, etc.)
- Perfect attendance

- Safety records
- Birthdays
- Anniversaries

Recognition at these levels is important and it's also very predictable. It tends to be considered as "nice" by those receiving this recognition but, in reality, has little impact on overall performance and job satisfaction.

We also have formal recognition programs for high levels of achievement:

- Employee of the year
- Rookie of the year
- "Most improved"
- Best idea of the year
- Best in customer service, etc.

These forms of recognition are designed to honor the "best in class" of all our employees and are designed to focus people on achieving organizational goals. These award levels are very important and tend to be highly motivating. However, there is a trap. Often, these types of awards become recognition levels of exclusion rather than inclusion. For example, consider idea of the year award. We have 100 employees who give us ideas to reduce cost, increase productivity, and increase efficiency. Typically, two thirds of these ideas cannot realistically be implemented, for various reasons. However, one third of the ideas tend to be realistic and can achieve the intended goal. Of these 33 ideas that contribute, we pick 1. So, 32 of the employees who contributed usable ideas are ticked off, and 99 of the employees who contributed any ideas at all are ticked off. And we honor 1.

This is an example of recognition programs of exclusion. One person is recognized to the detriment of others. An alternative: everyone who contributes an idea gets some form of recognition, or perhaps everyone who contributes a usable idea. When we honor the employee of the year, everyone else is walking around saying, "Why not me?" It is much more effective to expand the recognition program to recognize everyone who achieves a certain level of growth, productivity, cost reduction, whatever. Instead of picking one top employee, we might honor everyone who reached the level of a 10% productivity increase or better.

These exclusionary recognition systems can become very counterproductive when we repeatedly honor the same person, for the same thing. When it is predictable that John or Susan is going to win it again this year, many people in the organization begin to develop the attitude of "Why try?" A further dimension of this is what happens when John or Susan is finally dethroned? Many times, the perceived embarrassment of not winning the award that has been rightfully theirs for many years results in dethroned or embarrassed employees leaving the organization. This can have disastrous results to overall productivity.

THE PERFORMANCE-DRIVEN LEADER REALIZES THE IMPORTANCE OF CHANGING FORMAL RECOGNITION PROGRAMS TO AWARDS OF INCLUSION VS. EXCLUSION.

Informal Recognition Systems

Informal recognition systems are probably far and away the most motivating and are also the opportunities we make the *least* of. Informal recognition systems are best exemplified by the leader who looks an employee in the eye and says, "You're doing a good job and I really appreciate it." The Third Reich managers are incapable of this form of recognition. To their mentality, "If I'm not yelling at you or criticizing you, then you are doing a good job." We have probably all heard some variation of "Your recognition is in your pay envelope every week" or "You're getting paid to do the job. What more recognition do you want?"

There is some equivalent here to a child being raised by loving parents. Over the years, the child may begin to feel that he or she truly is not loved. The parents perceive that they love their child deeply, work hard to provide for the child's safety, well-being, education, and so on, working daily to maintain the child — clean clothes, good food, clean home, etc. However, these actions don't always speak for themselves. The child needs to be told and have verbally demonstrated that Mom and Dad do truly love the child. (This is a two-way street. Make no mistake. The child needs to return the recognition.)

The performance-driven leader will always frame recognition to be very sincere and very specific. Fewer things drive resentment higher than insincere, unspecific recognition. It leads people to believe that they are being handled, conned, and they are left infuriated that the deliverer of the recognition thinks they're stupid enough to be impressed by it. We experience this many times in a scenario such as this. One of the "big bosses" from the home office, thousands of miles away, flies in to "visit" one of the remote sites. Big bosses rarely put in an appearance at this site and are unknown to most everyone except top local management. The big boss, in an attempt to "identify with the little people" may line up at the time clock, shaking hands with everyone, telling them what a great job they are doing. Repetitiously we hear, "Oh, you're doing a great job; keep it up," over and over again. Employees are filled with resentment, thinking to themselves, "This guy doesn't even know who I am, has no idea what I do, or how well I do it. Who does he think he's kidding?" The proverbial slap on the back, telling people what a good job they're doing is probably a little better than a sharp stick in the eye, but from a recognition point of view accomplishes very little.

For example, instead of telling Nancy that she's "doing a great job," make it specific: "Nancy, the report that you turned in this morning was excellent. Not only did you present your ideas well, you also summarized your thoughts in a very concise and effective manner. I especially liked the point you made on...." This type of recognition

- Proves that the leader was paying attention
- Proves that the employee's work was deserving of positive comment
- Proves that the employee's efforts are not being taken for granted
- Proves that the employee truly makes a difference

**FOR THE PERFORMANCE-DRIVEN LEADER,
INFORMAL RECOGNITION IS VERY SINCERE AND SPECIFIC.**

Public Vs. Private Recognition

We have all heard the adage, "Criticize in private and praise in public." For many years, that has been a guide for American management. Unfortunately, most do the private criticisms, but few actually perform the public praising! Public praisings, such as mentioning individuals in newsletters, circulating positive comments received from customers, publishing reports showing top performance, etc., are very important and have their place. However, the performance-driven leader takes a harder look at public praising. While it has its advantages, it is also a mine field that can explode with negative consequences. When we praise publicly, two negative factors potentially come into play:

1. Nonrecognized employees witnessing the praising can become resentful. Perhaps similar past actions of theirs went unrecognized and
   a perception of unfairness is created. For example, we may loudly
   praise an employee for the employee's willingness to work late that
   night to help us get a specific task done, while, in reality, over the
   past few weeks, a number of employees have been willing to work
   late at various times to get an important task done, but the leader
   wasn't aware of that. Singling out one employee for praise when
   others may have done the same thing and gone unrecognized obviously drives resentment, anger, and hurt feelings. Anytime we publicly praise, we run that risk.
2. The publicly recognized employee can experience embarrassment,
   along with the pride of being recognized. One leader told us this
   story,

Very early in my managerial career, when I had read all of the
books, knew all of the buzzwords, was very full of myself, and
knew that I was supermanager, I had this experience. An employee did something over and above and deserved recognition.
Everything I had read said to praise publicly. I waited for an opportunity to do that, and the next morning I encountered the
employee in the lunchroom with a group of his peers. I walked up
to the table, looked him in the eye, and told him what a great job
he had done. I made the praising specific and said to those around
him, "You would have really been proud of this guy. He really,
really did good!" I smiled, left the cafeteria, emerged in self-con-
gratulations that, in fact, super-manager had struck again. And I
had done that job of public praising perfectly. A few hours later,
this same employee came to my office and asked to speak with
me. He even asked permission to close the door. I assumed he was
coming to return the favor, to tell me what a great boss I am, how
he's never worked for anyone as good as me, and I positioned
myself to receive the appropriate kiss on the ring. In fact, the
employee looked at me and said, "Don't ever do that to me again."
Taken aback, I asked what he was talking about. And he said, "In
the lunchroom a while ago, you came up and told me what a great
job I did. Make no mistake. I appreciate the kind words, but please
don't ever say that in front of those other people. For the past
couple of hours, I've had people blowing me kisses, rubbing their
noses, and some other gestures that I won't even describe. I don't

need this kind of pressure. If you have something nice to say, please say it, but say it to me one-to-one.

Think of the impact when the performance-driven leader calls an employee into the leader's office. Obviously, the employee is going to have some high level of anxiety, wondering what's wrong, anticipating that the boss is going to yell. The employee sits down, the leader looks the employee in the eye and says, "I want you to know that I appreciate the job that you do. You may not always be the top performer, but you are always here, working hard, doing the best you can. Sometimes the squeaky wheel gets the grease, but your wheel doesn't squeak. And sometimes I sense that I don't give you the attention and recognition that you deserve. In the heat of what we do, under the pressure that we all deal with, I don't always take the time to say thanks and to let you know that you make a real difference around here." If the Third Reich manager had that conversation with an employee, the employee would grab his or her heart, experience shortness of breath, and we would have to call 911. The performance-driven leader will have that conversation a number of times, appropriately, in an employee's career. People need to be recognized.

Another leader told us of a technique which she uses of calling employees at home in the early evening to just say thank you. She says:

> If an employee really does something over and above, I will acknowledge the person during the day and say thanks. Later that evening, right around dinner time, I hope, I will call and have a very quick conversation with the employee at home that says something like, "I'm very sorry to bother you at home, but I was thinking again of what it was you did today at work, and I just wanted to be sure that you knew how much I appreciated it. In the course of our business day, because of the pace and pressure, I don't always take the time to give you the thanks that you deserve. What you did was great. I hope I haven't disturbed your family. I did not mean to interrupt and I do not mean to make your job a 24-hour-a-day endeavor, but I just didn't want to let this opportunity to say thanks go by."
>
> Along with providing positive recognition this is also an excellent counterbalance to reducing the impact of the employee's occasional negativity which they may bring home once in a while, proclaiming how unfair the boss is, etc. When the employee starts venting, their spouse (or other significant people) may say, "Wait

a minute, Is that the same person that called you here a couple of weeks ago to tell you what a great job you were doing?" The reaction may have a neutralizing or buffering effect.

Recognition Models

In the past, the model of recognition has been: Perform, you get to keep your job. Do something really good, and I'll recognize you, maybe. In reality, probably not. But I will expect you to do it again!!!!!

For the performance-driven leader, the model may well be: I recognize you, you perform, I recognize you again. How can you front-end load recognition? Ken Blanchard, who wrote *The One Minute Manager* with Spencer Johnson and who has authored many very worthwhile books and tapes, has made a career out of the phrase, "Catch them doing something right." It doesn't take any talent to point out continually to people what they're doing wrong. That's easy. Catch them doing something well, and let them know it. Recognize them. Tell them they're doing a good job. Tell them what else needs to be done, and then recognize them when they do it.

Is it possible to overdo positive, sincere, specific recognition? Try!

Recognition from Above

Performance-driven leaders will also seek out appropriately timed opportunities to share with their superiors the performance of their employees, so that their boss can offer some recognition. Think of how motivating it is when the boss's boss comes up to an employee and says, "Boy, your boss told me how you handled that problem yesterday. She was really impressed and I wanted to let you know that I am too," or when an employee gets a handwritten note from the boss's boss, letting the employee know that the boss heard the employee did an unusually good job on a specific task. This is another example of how informal motivation can be the most meaningful tool performance-driven leaders have in their arsenal.

Performance and Satisfaction

As addressed in earlier chapters of this book, in an era when downsizing and other restructuring efforts are widespread and when fear-based management is common, managers will face a dual challenge: How to increase or sustain performance and how to restore employee satisfaction. There is ample evidence that concern with either satisfaction or performance to the neglect of the other can be a serious problem for the contemporary organization. Satisfaction as an important variable in the environment has been addressed for more than half a century, going back to such works as Kornhauser and Hoppoch's *Job Satisfaction,* published in 1935. Formal attention to performance as a workplace variable is even more venerated, going back at least to the beginning of the 20th century in the work of Frederick Taylor and other proponents of what became known as scientific management.

Performance is often expressed as productivity, and it is generally accepted that in an arena of intense global competition successful organizations must be able to increase productivity (performance) to survive. Although there is widespread disagreement about what *level* of worker satisfaction is essential, the general theme of the current literature is that producing quality products and services in an increasingly complex environment requires higher rather than lower levels of employee satisfaction. (Another example of the obsolescence of fear based management/motivation). At the very least, the organization must offer the opportunities for job satisfaction necessary to attract, motivate, and retain the *right* employees, that is, those whose performance can take us down the path to excellence. At any rate, today's manager will not be able to choose between being solely focused on performance or on satisfaction, but must achieve an appropriate balance at rather high levels of each.

**BOTH HIGH PERFORMANCE AND HIGH SATISFACTION
ARE DESIRABLE.**

Implications for Management

Although it is clear that both employee satisfaction and performance are the results of complex processes that may not have been completely understood, it is apparent that there are steps that management can take to influence both significantly. It is now fairly well established that rewards do influence satisfaction. For the leader who seeks to increase employee satisfaction, rewards are a valuable tool. Those whose only focus is to increase employee performance, while ignoring the issue of job satisfaction and the influence of rewards are short sighted at best.

Rewards based on current performance tend to significantly affect subsequent performance and employees who are rewarded for high, or increased levels of performance tend to experience higher levels of job satisfaction. While this sounds quite simple, it is not. Rewards are influenced by many variables including resource limitations, collective bargaining agreements and the cold reality of the organization's willingness to allow employees, at all levels to share in the fruits of their labors. Employees who do not experience an increase in rewards, whether this is due to poor performance of the organization's unwillingness to share, tend towards lower levels of satisfaction. This is further compounded by the prevailing attitude of entitlement to rewards (many employees expect to be rewarded because they feel they deserve it, whether they are performing or not). As discussed earlier, poor performance is not always the fault of the employee; however, the performance driven leader will do everything within their power to align rewards with performance.

Rewarding Team Performance

Most organizations report increasing reliance on teamwork and team performance to face the growing complex array of challenges being encountered on the road to excellence. Yet, the majority of these same organizations report that they have not revamped their reward systems, either formal or informal. We can expect employees to be confused if we preach teamwork (or ask for or demand it) and at the same time continue to reward individual achievement and internally competitive behavior. Competitive behavior, for example, should be addressed toward external competitors, not internal teammates. Most workers, being rational human beings, will tend to follow the reward structure.

In a culture that has historically focused on the individual, most companies will find it difficult to move to systems that effectively reward team or collaborative efforts. We are addressing, here, formally established teams. This suggests that as part of our plan for restructuring, we should identify and communicate exactly what are the critical and desired behaviors for the new organization. We should get employees actively involved in both identifying and communicating those new behaviors. Many of us have not been well prepared by education, training, or socialization to be effective team players. We are more likely to admire the superstar who makes the game winning basket than the less famous player who fed him the ball. We need training in team skills such as adaptability, collaboration, sensitivity to others, development of others, etc. And the entire range of job-related rewards, to include the compensation system, will likely have to be redesigned to support these new behaviors.

Motivating workers in the 21st century will require leadership, communication, training, development, and skilled use of both formal and informal, both monetary and nonmonetary rewards. These will be the necessary concomitants of success, and survival as well.

SUMMARY

Three things drive the dramatic, revolutionary changes facing the workplace today.

1. Explosive growth in technology
2. Globalization and externally changing markets
3. Growth, development, and maturation of people

Leaders who ignore the change in people and focus entirely on the technology and economics are burying their heads in the sand. To continue to manage in highly authoritarian, autocratic (Third Reich) styles is to ignore and deny this metamorphosis of the human element.

Fear-based management is obsolete. It has had its run; it is no longer effective.

Today's successful leaders must redefine and reinvent themselves and their relationships with the people around them. If success is determined by the people in an organization, leaders must abandon the eternal quest to flex their muscles and demonstrate their power by helping others develop their own authority and influence.

Performance-driven leadership demands that managers evolve from just guiding people through the existing policies, boundaries, and tasks of today, to leading them into the changes and challenges of tomorrow by:

- Practicing participative leadership
- Aligning authority with responsibility
- Reducing or removing fear, threat, and intimidation
- Planning and actively driving the change process
- Increasing the quality and scope of communication
- Developing people through training and enhanced experiences
- Recognizing people for their value and contributions

- ♦ Increasing job satisfaction and performance
- ♦ Motivating by providing gain, not by threat of punishment or loss

We hope this book has helped you to continue your journey of management evolution and creating in yourself a Performance-Driven Leader.

BIBLIOGRAPHY

Albrecht, Karl. *The Only Thing That Matters,* New York: Harper Business, 1992.

Allen, Timothy D., Deena M. Freeman, Richard C. Reizenstein, and Joseph O. Renta. "Just Another Transition? Examining Survivors' Attitudes over Time," *Academy of Management Journal,* 1995, pp. 78–82.

Allerton, Haidee. "Upsizing in a Downsizing World," *Training,* May 1996, p. 127.

"And Now, Upsizing," *Economist,* June 8, 1996, p. 72.

Arredondo, Lani. *How to Present Like a Pro: Getting People to See Things Your Way,* New York: McGraw-Hill, 1991.

Augello, William J. "The Downside Risk of Downsizing!" *Distribution,* May 1996, p. 62.

Barker, Joel A. *Paradigms,* New York: Harper Collins, 1992.

Barnett, David. "The Great Leader," *IPA Review,* 1995, pp. 21–25.

Barrier, Michael. "Improving Worker Performance," *Nation's Business,* September 1996, pp. 28–31.

Beagle, John and Trent Myers. "The Necessity of Downsizing," *Adhesives Age,* May 1996, p. 8.

Beam, Henry H. "Innovative Reward Systems for the Changing Workplace," *Academy of Management Executive,* August 1995, pp. 89–91.

Bennett, Linda. "Compensation Fads, Custom Pay Plans, and Team Pay." *Compensation,* March/April 1996, pp. 67–75.

Bennis, Warren G. "Managing the Dream: Leadership in the 21st Century," *Management Decision,* 1992, pp. 166–168.

Blanchard, Ken. "Creative Rewards," *Executive Excellence,* July 1993, p. 5.

Blanchard, Ken and Alan Randolph. "Empowerment Is Key to Growth," *Executive Excellence,* May 1996, p. 10.

Blanchard, Kenneth and Spencer Johnson. *The One Minute Manager,* New York: Berkeley Books, 1982.

Boyd, Malia. "Critics Railroad Employee Recognition Plan," *Incentive,* July 1994, p. 11.

Boyle, Daniel C. "Employee Motivation That Works," *HR Magazine,* October 1992, pp. 83–89.

Brecka, Jon. "Regeneration, Not Downsizing, Is the Key to Success," *Quality Progress,* April 1995, p. 18.

Brewer, Geoffrey. "Rewarding the Work Force," *Incentive,* May 1992, pp. 28–30.

Brooker, Lynda. "Fat and Mean: The Corporate Squeeze of Working Americans and the Myth of Managerial Downsizing," *Worldbusiness,* July/August 1996, p. 56.

Brookes, Donald V. "Today's Compensation Systems: Rewarding the Wrong Things," *Canadian Manager,* December 1994, pp. 10–11.

Brooks, Susan Sonnesyn. "Noncash Ways to Compensate Employees," *HR Magazine,* April 1994, pp. 38–43.

Brown, Carolyn M. "Finding an Upside to Downsizing," *Black Enterprise,* June 1996, pp. 44–46.

Brown, Tom. "The Human Side of Downsizing," *Management Review,* August 1996, p. 15.

Buhler, Patricia M. "The Keys to Shaping Behavior," *Supervision,* January 1992, pp. 18–20.

Byham, William C. with Jeff Cox. *Zapp! The Lightning of Empowerment,* New York: Harmony Books, 1988.

Campbell, Joseph. *The Hero With a Thousand Faces,* Princeton, NJ: Princeton University Press, 1949.

Carey, Robert. "Downsizing Becomes the Norm," *Incentive/Performance Supplement,* March 1995, p. 11.

Carnevale, Anthony Patrick. "Put Quality to Work: Train America's Workforce," *Training & Development Journal,* November 1990, pp. 31–49.

Carr, J. T. "Learning to Walk the Leadership Talk?" *Healthcare Executive,* March/April 1994, pp. 16–17.

Carter-Scott, Cherie. *The Corporate Negaholic,* New York: Ballantine Books, 1991.

Catoir, John T. *World Religions,* New York: Alba House, 1992.

Caudron, Shari. "Teach Downsizing Survivors How to Thrive," *Personnel Journal,* January 1996, pp. 38–41.

"CEO Selection: Crucial Qualities and Competencies," *Association Management,* August 1996, pp. 44–45.

Chapman, Thomas W. "Challenges of Leadership in an Era of Health Care Reform," *Frontiers of Health Services Management,* Winter 1993, pp. 3–26.

Chevan, Harry. "Loyalty Has Its Rewards," *Catalog Age,* November 1992, pp. 1, 46–47.

Choppin, Jon. "Total Quality Management — What Isn't It?" *Managing Service Quality,* 1995, pp. 47–49.

Ciccotello, Conrad S. and Steven G. Green. "Industry's Downsizing Lessons," *Government Executive,* July 1995, pp. 59–60.

Cichy, Ronald F. and Raymond S. Schmidgall. "Leadership Qualities of Financial Executives in the U.S. Lodging Industry," *Cornell Hotel,* April 1996, pp. 56–62.

Clark, Jim and Richard Koonce. "Engaging Organizational Survivors," *Training,* August 1995, pp. 22–30.

Click, Jennifer. "Downsizing Continues as Profits Climb," *HR Magazine,* July 1995, p. 14.

Corbin, Coralyn. *Conquering Corporate Co-Dependence: Life Skills for Making It within or without the Corporation,* Englewood Cliffs, NJ: Prentice Hall, 1993.

Covey, Stephen R. *The Seven Habits of Highly Effective People,* New York: Simon & Schuster, 1989.

Cox, Frank. "Well Done, Well Done!" *Journal for Quality,* September 1993, pp. 58–60.

Craig, Don. "How to Be Vulture Food. Not," *CMA Magazine,* July/August 1996, p. 3.

Crainer, Stuart. "Re-engineering the Carrot," *Management Today,* December 1995, pp. 66–68.

Curry, Lynne. "Rewards without a Sting in the Tail," *People Management,* April 18, 1996, pp. 40, 42.

Cusimano, Robert and Dana Davis. "Motivating Through the Best and Worst of Times," *Telemarketing Magazine,* June 1994, pp. 65–68.

Daniels, Aubrey C. "Making More Winners," *Executive Excellence,* November 1993, p. 9.

Dennis, Anita. "A Way to Build Future Leaders," *Journal of Accountancy,* May 1993, pp. 70–73.

Dinkmeyer, Don and Daniel Eckstein. *Leadership by Encouragement,* Delray Beach, FL: St. Lucie Press, 1996.

Doherty, Noeleen and Jim Horsted. "Helping Survivors to Stay on Board," *People Management,* January 12, 1995, pp. 26–31.

Dover, Rick. "The Challenges of Change," *Production,* February 1995, pp. 16–17.

"Downsizing Downpour Slows," *HR Focus,* February 1996, p. 11.

"Downsizing Downsized," *Institutional Investor,* December 1995, p. 28.

"Downsizing without Capsizing," *Management Accounting-London,* January 1996.

Drucker, Peter F. *Innovation and Entrepreneurship,* New York: Harper & Row, 1994.

Emmons, Natasha. "Corporate Spotlight: UPS," *Incentive,* August 1995, pp. 34–35.

Everitt, Skip. *Professional Supervision Skills,* Boulder, CO: Career Track Publications, audio and video, 1992.

"The Fallout of Downsizing?" *Supervision,* July 1995, p. 17.

"Flatten the Organization Not the People," *Management Services,* September 1995.

Frank, Norman. "The Reward and Recognition Process in Total Quality Management," *Quality Progress,* November 1995, pp. 138–139.

Frazee, Valerie. "When Downsizing Brings Your Employees Down," *Personnel Journal,* March 1996, pp. 126–127.

Gaines, Harry. "Employees Get Satisfaction, But Only When Properly Motivated," *Industrial Management,* September/October 1994, pp. 2–3.

Gebhart, Jane. "Focus: A Changing Workplace," *Sloan Management Review,* Winter 1995, p. 110.

Griessman, Eugene. *Time Tactics of Very Successful People,* New York: McGraw-Hill, 1994.

Graham, John R. "Twenty Trends Shaping the Way We Do Business and Earn a Living," *Supervision,* March 1995, pp. 6–8.

Grib, Gail and Susan O'Donnell. "Pay Plans That Reward Employee Achievement," *HR Magazine,* July 1995, pp. 49–50.

Griessman, B. Eugene. *Time Tactics of Very Successful People,* New York: McGraw-Hill, 1994.

Gross, Stephen E. and Jeffrey Blair. "Reinforcing Team Effectiveness through Pay," *Compensation,* September/October 1995, pp. 34–38.

Grossman, Robert J. "Damaged, Downsized Souls: How to Revitalize the Workplace," *HR Magazine,* May 1996, pp. 54–62.

Handy, Charles. *The Age of Unreason,* Boston, MA: Harvard Business School Press, 1989.

Harville, Donald L. "Motivation in Work Organizations," *Personnel Psychology,* Spring 1995, pp. 234–235.

Herbert, Evan. "Change Managers See More Pain, Downsizing," *Research-Technology Management,* May/June 1995, pp. 8–9.

Hopkins, Hampton. "A Challenge to Managers: Five Ways to Improve Employee Morale," *Executive Development,* 1995, pp. 26–28.

Howard, Malcolm. "Downsizing to Destruction," *Management Accounting-London,* July/August 1996, pp. 66–67.

Howell, Marion. *The Manager as Coach,* Boulder, CO: Career Track Publications, audio 1991, video 1993.

Joinson, Carla. "Reward Your Best Employees," *HR Magazine,* April 1996, pp. 49–55.

Juran, J. M. *Juran on Planning for Quality,* New York: The Free Press, 1988.

Katzenbach, Jon R. and Douglas K. Smith. *The Wisdom of Teams,* Harper Business, New York: 1993.

Kitaeff, Richard. "Managing in a Time of Shortage," *Marketing Research,* Fall/Winter 1995, p. 39.

Kowalewski, M. J., Jr. "Secrets of a Successful Employee Recognition System," *Quality Progress,* March 1996, pp. 108–110.

"Kudos to Employee Recognition Programs," *Risk Management,* April 1996, p. 13.

Laberis, Bill. "Loyalty Strikes Out," *ComputerWorld,* November 13, 1995, p. 36.

Lacey, Miriam Y. "Rewards Can Cost Nothing? Yes They Can ... Really!" *Journal for Quality,* June 1994, pp. 6–8.

"Leadership Qualities," *American Printer,* November 1995, p. 14.

"Lean, Mean and Better?" *Journal of Managerial Psychology,* 1995, pp. ii–iii.

Lear, Robert W. "Leading Questions," *Chief Executive,* June 1996, p. 10.

Lebediker, Jeremy. "The Supervisor As a Coach: 4 Essential Models for Setting Performance Expectations," Supervision, December 1995, pp. 14–16.

Levine, Hermine Zagat. "How to Recognize and Reward Employees" *Compensation,* May/June 1995, pp. 78–79.

Lindstrom, Robert L. "Training Hits the Road," *Sales Automation Supplement,* 2, June 1995, pp. 10–14.

Littlefield, David. "Wages Must Reward Skills and Innovation," *People Management,* February 8, 1996, p. 13.

Loeb, Marshall. "The Bad Boss Gets a New Life," *Fortune,* May 27, 1996, p. 192.

Love, Barbara. "Training Attracts Good Employees," *Folio,* May 1, 1993, p. 9.

Lupien, J. Jacques. "A New Approach to Training," *CMA Magazine,* June 1995, p. 11.

MacLachlan, Rob. *People Management,* November 16, 1995, pp. 13–15.

Marshall, Jeffrey. "Downsizing's Double-Edged Sword," *United States Banker,* February 1995, p. 8.

Martin, Roger. "Changing the Mind of the Corporation," *Harvard Business Review,* November/December 1993, pp. 81–94.

Maynard, Roberta. "Better Morale Typically Means Better Employees," *Nation's Business,* May 1994, p. 14.

McDonald, Tom. "The Art of Praise," *Successful Meetings,* April 1995, p. 28.

Menda, Kathleen. "An HR Pro Shares Downsizing Lessons Learned," *HR Magazine,* July 1996, p. 115.

Milas, Gene H. "How to Develop a Meaningful Employee Recognition Program," *Quality Progress,* May 1995, pp. 139–142.

"A Model for Downsizing," *Network World,* January 9, 1995, p. SS19.

Moore, Shirley, Marilee Kuhrik, Nancy Kuhrik, and Barry Katz. "Coping With Downsizing: Stress, Self-Esteem and Social Intimacy," *Nursing Management,* March 1996, pp. 28–30.

Mullin, Rick. "A Time to Grow: The Other Side of Reengineering," *Chemical Week,* June 7, 1995, pp. 27–33.

Murphy, Emmet C. *Leadership I.Q.,* New York, John Wiley & Sons, 1996.

Nelson, Bob. "Dump the Cash, Load on the Praise," *Personnel Journal,* July 1996, pp. 65–70.

Nelson, Bob. "Motivating Employees with Informal Rewards," *Management Accounting,* November 1995, pp. 30–34.

Nixon, Brian. "Employee Relations during Times of Change," *America's Community Banker,* July 1995, pp. 26–32.

Nolan, Paul. "Selling Recognition Programs Up, Down and All Around," *Training Supplement,* August/September 1991, pp. 10–11.

"Non-Financial Rewards Motivate and Drive Team Performance," *IIE Solutions,* March 1996, p. 6.

"Now (Surprise) The Trend in Business Is to Upsizing: What Will They Think of Next?" *Agency Sales Magazine,* June 1996, pp. 38–39.

Ohlheiser, James W. "Downsizing: A Guide for Facilities Managers," *IIE Solutions,* May 1995, pp. 45–48.

"Organizational Loyalty Is Not the Answer," *Managing Office Technology,* January 1996, pp. 30–33.

Owens, Wyatt E. "The Upside of Downsizing," *Life Association News,* March 1996, pp. 8, 31, 52, 100–104.

Pascarella, Perry. "Reward and Recognize to Get Results," *Transportation,* February 1993, p. 41.

Payne, Tom. "The Survivors," *Industrial Management,* May/June 1995, pp. 1–2.

Peters, Tom. *The Pursuit of WOW!* New York: Vintage Books, 1994.

Petreycik, Richard M. "Crucial Steps to More Effective Management," *Progressive Grocer,* June 1991, pp. 24–27.

Pickard, Jane. "Good HR Work Starts to Reap the Rewards," *People Management,* May 30, 1996, p. 17.

Pilinger, Evelyn C. "Attention!" *Managers Magazine,* December 1994, pp. 14–15.

Plishner, Emily S. "Helping Employees Do the Right Thing," *Chemical Week,* May 3, 1995, pp. 35–36.

Posner, Koules. *The Leadership Challenge,* San Francisco: Jossey Bass, 1995.

Prewitt, Milford. *Nation's Restaurant News,* February 12, 1996, p. 96.

Qubein, Nido, *How to Be a Great Communicator,* Chicago: Nightingale Conent. audio presentation, 1988.

Quinn, Judy. "Motivators of the Year," *Incentive,* January 1996, pp. 26–30.

"Reflections on the Downsizing Debate," *HR Focus,* July 1996, pp. 9–10.

"Rewards for Services Rendered," *Management Today,* January 1996, p. 80.

"A Rewards Program for the Masses," *Credit Card Management,* December 1995.

Rhode, Helga. *Dealing with Conflict and Confrontation,* Boulder, CO: Career Track Publications, audio and video, 1993.

Riggs, Joy. "Faster, Shorter, Cheaper Drives Training Today," *Personnel Journal/New Product News Supplement,* May 1996, pp. 1, 4.

Rodrigues, Carl A. "Developing Three-Dimensional Leaders," *Journal of Management Development,* 1993, pp. 4–11.

Rosen, Robert H. *Leading People,* New York: Viking, 1996.

Ryan, Kathleen D. and Daniel K. Oestreich. *Driving Fear out of the Workplace,* San Francisco: Jossey-Bass Publishers, 1991.

Sandelands, Eric. "The Role of Rewards on a Journey to Excellence," *Management Decision,* 1994, pp. 46–47.

Sapadin, Linda and Jack McGuire. *It's about Time,* New York: Viking, 1996.

Shandler, Donald. *Reengineering the Training Function,* Delray Beach, FL: St. Lucie Press, 1996.

Sheridan, John H. " 'Yes' to Team Incentives," *Industry Week,* March 4, 1996, pp. 63–64.

Sherman, Stratford. "How Tomorrow's Best Leaders Are Learning Their Stuff," *Fortune,* November 27, 1995, pp. 90–102.

Singh, Jai. "Downsizing Doesn't Translate into Dollars," *Info World,* May 22, 1995, p. 3.

Smith, Gregory P. *The New Leader: Bringing Creativity to the Workplace,* Delray Beach, FL: St. Lucie Press, 1997.

Solmo, Regan. "Just Rewards," *Successful Meetings,* March 1996, p. 7.

Sommer, Bobbe. *Psycho-Cybernetics 2000,* Englewood Cliffs, NJ: Prentice Hall, 1993.

"Speaking of Stress, ..." *HR Focus,* May 1996, p. 12.

Spiers, Joe. "The Profits Flowed," *Fortune,* April 29, 1996, pp. 260–261.

Stoyer, Ralph. "How I Learned to Let My Workers Lead," *Harvard Business Review,* November/December 1990.

Sulzer-Azaroff, Beth and Dwight Harshbarger. "Putting Fear to Flight," *Quality Progress,* December 1995, pp. 61–65.

Syedain, Hashi. "The Rewards of Recognition," *Management Today,* May 1995, pp. 72–74.

Tang, Thomas Li-Ping and Robert M. Fuller. "Corporate Downsizing: What Managers Can Do to Lessen the Negative Effects of Layoffs," *SAM Advanced Management Journal,* Autumn 1995, pp. 12–15.

"Team Reward: Part 1," *IRS Employment Review,* March 1996, pp. S2–S5.

"Team Rewards Introduced," *IRS Employment Review,* May 1996, pp. P11–P12.

"Training Investments Pay Off for Downsized Companies," *HR Focus,* February 1995, p. 20.

"Trends That Will Influence Workplace Learning and Performance in the Next Five Years," *Training and Development,* May 1994, pp. S29–S32.

Tully, Shawn. "So, Mr. Bossidy, We Know You Can Cut. Now Show Us How to Grow," *Fortune,* August 21, 1995, pp. 70–80.

"Two Cheers for Loyalty," *Economist,* January 6, 1996, p. 49.

Walton, Mary. *Deming Management at Work,* New York: Perigee Books, 1991.

Walton, Mary. *The Deming Management Method,* New York: Perigee Books, 1986.

Weidenbaum, Murray. "A New Social Contract for the American Workplace," *Challenge,* January/February 1995, pp. 51–55.

"What Makes a Good Team Compensation Plan?" *HR Magazine,* March 1995, p. 74.

Wigglesworth, David C. "A Guide to Motivating the Survivors," *HR Magazine,* February 1996, pp. 98–99.

Yehle, Lawrence C. "How to Succeed in Business without Laying off Employees," *Trustee,* February 1995, p. 21.

Young, Russell. "Intelligent Downsizing: Reducing Costs through the Use of a Service Agency," *Telemarketing,* April 1995, pp. 40–42.

Zenger, Todd R. "Why Do Employers Only Reward Extreme Performance? Examining the Relationships among Performance, Pay and Turnover," *Administrative Science Quarterly,* June 1992, pp. 198–219.

INDEX

A

Absenteeism, 42, 74
Achievement, measuring, 166
Activity
  high demand, 124
  illusion of, 29
Administrative Management, 41
Advertising department, 83
Anxiety, 59, 235
Areas for training opportunities (ATOs),
      204, 206
Assets, return on, 95
ATOs, see Areas for training
      opportunities
Attention, pursuit of, 78
Attitude problems, 35
Audios, in-house, 223
Audio tape libraries, 220
Authority
  figures, rebellion against, 78
  misalignment of, 8, 23
  ultimate-hiring, 116
Awareness training, 204

B

Background checks, 117
Bad news, 172
Bad storm, 143
Barriers, removal of, 199
Bedside manner, 144
Benefit packages, 91

Blaming, 31, 68, 76
Blind orders, 12
Board of directors, 15
Body language, 144
Bonuses, 33
Bottom-line issues, 42
Boundary clarification, 119
Brainstorm, 72
Breaks, scheduling of, 118
Brush fire problem, 127
Budgeting, 214
Business
  grammar skills, 212
  as usual, 191
Buzzwords, 103
By the book training, 190

C

Capital commitment, 82
Career growth, 55
Chamber of Commerce, 96
Change
  announcement of, 56
  experimental nature of, 53
  managing, 19, 41–62
    bottom-line issues, 42
    change process, 48–57
    change and stability, 45–46
    customer-centered issues, 44
    employee-centered issues, 43
    focus of change, 42–43
    introducing change, 54–56
    response to change, 56–57